DANCE EDUCATION AROUND THE WORLD

THE WORLD

Dance has the power to change the lives of young people. It is a force in shaping identity, affirming culture and exploring heritage in an increasingly borderless world. Creative and empowering pedagogies are driving curriculum development worldwide where the movement of peoples and cultures generates new challenges and possibilities for dance education in multiple contexts. In *Dance Education around the World: Perspectives on dance, young people and change*, writers across the globe come together to reflect, comment on and share their expertise and experiences. The settings are drawn from a spectrum of countries with contributions from Europe, the Americas, the Middle East, Asia, the Pacific and Africa giving insights into and fresh perspectives on contrasting ideas, philosophies and approaches to dance education from Egypt to Ghana, Brazil to Finland, Jamaica to the Netherlands, the UK, USA, Australia, New Zealand and more.

This volume offers chapters and case narratives on:

- Curriculum developments worldwide
- Empowering communities through dance
- Embodiment and creativity in dance teaching
- Exploring and assessing learning in dance as artistic practice
- Imagined futures for dance education

Reflection, evaluation, analysis and documentation are key to the evolving ecology of dance education and research involving individuals, communities and nations. *Dance Education around the World: Perspectives on dance, young people and change* provides a great resource for dance educators, practitioners and researchers, and pushes for the furtherance of dance education around the world.

Charlotte Svendler Nielsen is Assistant Professor and Head of educational studies at the Department of Nutrition, Exercise and Sports, research group Body, Learning and Identity, University of Copenhagen, Denmark.

Stephanie Burridge lectures at Lasalle College of the Arts and Singapore Management University, and is the series editor for *Routledge Celebrating Dance in Asia and the Pacific*.

DANCE EDUCATION AROUND THE WORLD

Perspectives on dance, young people and change

Edited by Charlotte Svendler Nielsen and Stephanie Burridge

Routledge
Taylor & Francis Group

LONDON AND NEW YORK

First published 2015
by Routledge
2 Park Square, Milton Park, Abingdon, Oxon OX14 4RN

and by Routledge
711 Third Avenue, New York, NY 10017

Routledge is an imprint of the Taylor & Francis Group, an informa business

British Library Cataloguing in Publication Data
A catalogue record for this book is available from the British Library

Library of Congress Cataloging in Publication Data
Dance education around the world : perspectives on dance, young people and change / edited by Charlotte Svendler Nielsen and Stephanie Burridge.
pages cm
Includes bibliographical references and index.
1. Dance—Study and teaching. 2. Dance—Cross-cultural studies.
I. Nielsen, Charlotte Svendler.
GV1589.D37 2015
793.307—dc23
20140387305

ISBN: 978-0-415-74360-0 (hbk)
ISBN: 978-0-415-74363-1 (pbk)
ISBN: 978-1-315-81357-8 (ebk)

Typeset in Bembo
by Swales & Willis Ltd, Exeter, Devon, UK

Jump for Joy
Photographer: Hu Hao-En

Circle of Life
Photographer: Lai Chih-Sheng from 'On-Works'

Photos from the Dance and the Child International (daCi) and World Dance Alliance (WDA) 2012 joint Global Summit *Dance, Young People and Change* hosted by the Taipei National University of the Arts (TNUA) School of Dance in Taiwan.

Printed and bound by CPI Group (UK) Ltd, Croydon, CR0 4YY

CONTENTS

Case narratives

CONTRIBUTORS

Eeva Anttila (Ed.Lic, Dr of Arts) has been involved in dance education since the 1980s, focusing on dance for children and youth and on contemporary dance pedagogy. Currently she is a professor in dance pedagogy at the University of the Arts Helsinki, Finland. Her dissertation (2003) focused on dialogical dance pedagogy, and her current research interests include somatic approaches to dance pedagogy, embodied knowledge and embodied learning. She has published widely in national and international journals and edited books. She is an active member in many organisations of dance and arts education.

Beatrice Ayi, a graduate of Ohio State University, is a lecturer at the Department of Dance Studies, University of Ghana. Her extensive roles, besides lecturing, include serving as a resource person for dance workshops such as those organised by Ghana Education Service for its Cultural Officers, and several summer programmes organised for international students. She also served as an assistant choreographer of the dance piece staged at the opening and closing ceremonies of the African Cup of Nations, which took place in Ghana in 2008. Currently, she is a doctoral candidate in the Department of Dance at Texas Woman's University, USA.

Ralph Buck (PhD) is Associate Professor and Head of Dance Studies, the University of Auckland, New Zealand. His leadership has been recognised with an Excellence Award in Equal Opportunities for Community Teaching, 2006; University of Auckland Sustained Excellence in Teaching Award, 2008; and Academic Leadership Award, 2010. His research and teaching have been presented in Korea, Sweden, Hong Kong, Brazil, Fiji, Australia and Finland. His work with the World Alliance for Arts Education and UNESCO draws attention to potential roles of dance as a dynamic agent for change within security, health and education concerns.

Stephanie Burridge (PhD) is the Co-chair of the World Dance Alliance Asia Pacific Research and Documentation network. A dance writer and critic, she lectures at LASALLE College of the Arts and Singapore Management University and is the Series Editor for Routledge *Celebrating Dance in Asia and the Pacific* books on Cambodia, India, Malaysia, Australia, Taiwan, the South Pacific and Singapore. She was Artistic Director of Canberra Dance Theatre (1978–2001) and was awarded the first Choreographic Fellowship at the Australian Choreographic Centre and an ACT Lifetime Achievement award.

Kerry Chappell (PhD) is a part-time lecturer at Exeter University's Graduate School of Education, UK, specialising in dance and arts education, creativity in education, and educational futures. She has co-developed the wise, humanising creativity idea, within secondary-level dance education, and more widely, e.g. interdisciplinary early years arts education (www.thecarouselproject.org. uk/our-impact/current-projects/round-round-you-turn-me) and blended arts/science education models (http://creatit-project.eu). She teaches on the secondary dance PGCE and MEd creative arts courses. She is also the Open University EU-funded C2Learn project (www.c2learn. eu) research fellow investigating wise, humanising creativity within digital learning. Her research is informed by her practice as a dance artist and previous aikido practice.

Lim Mei Chian is a Singaporean dance educator, dancer and choreographer and co-director and co-founder of two companies: John Mead Dance Company and Firefly Tales. Over the last twenty years she has performed and taught internationally in the United States, Italy, Germany, Cambodia and countries in the Middle East, amongst others. She graduated with a Masters in Dance and Dance Education from New York University, and is one of the first dance educators to initiate creative movement programmes as dance education in Singapore, which have been endorsed by the National Arts Council since 2001.

Sharon Friedman holds a BA (Hons) degree in history, an MMus (dance education) and a postgraduate diploma in education. Her teaching experience includes initiating, coordinating and teaching dance and movement programmes in a wide range of community projects in Cape Town, South Africa, and she has choreographed extensively in the contemporary dance medium as well as for opera and music theatre. She is co-author of *Teaching creative dance – a handbook* and editor and a co-author of *Post-apartheid dance – many bodies, many voices, many stories*. A senior lecturer at the University of Cape Town School of Dance until 2011, post retirement she works as a freelance dance education consultant and academic editor.

Robyne Garrett works at the University of South Australia, teaching in the areas of physical education, dance and sociology. Her research interests include gender and physical activity, dance and physical education teaching methodologies and alternative movement approaches. Her PhD thesis (2002) titled *How young women move* investigated the construction of gender in physical activity contexts for young women. The post-structural research employed a story-telling approach that resulted in 'physical stories' now used as a strategy for the development of critical reflection in teacher training courses. Current projects include aspirations for disadvantaged youth, well-being of university students and movement methodologies.

Kristen Jeppsen Groves, choreographer, dancer and educator, received an MFA from the Ohio State University and a BA in dance education from Brigham Young University, USA. As an emerging arts advocate, her research interests include cultural diplomacy, art exportation and art policy. She is founder and co-director of 'Artist, interrupted: a woman's art collective' and works as a choreographer and dance educator in North Carolina.

Veronica Jobbins (MA, FRSA) is Head of Learning and Participation (Dance) at Trinity Laban Conservatoire of Music and Dance, UK. She originally trained as a specialist dance teacher before teaching for 20 years in London secondary schools and further education colleges. She was instrumental in the formation of the UK National Dance Teachers' Association in 1988, of which she was Chairperson until 2008. She regularly writes for arts journals and presents at conferences internationally. She also serves on a number of dance, arts and education panels concerned with dance artist training, youth dance and dance in the curriculum.

Ann Kipling Brown (PhD) is professor emerita in dance education in the Arts Education Program in the Faculty of Education at the University of Regina, Canada. She works extensively with children, youth and adults and leads classes in technique, composition and notation. Her research and publications focus on dance pedagogy, the integration of notation in dance programmes, the application of technology in dance education and the role of dance in the child's and adult's lived world.

Susan R. Koff (EdD) is a clinical associate professor and director of the Dance Education Program in the Steinhardt School at New York University. She was previously at Teachers College, Columbia University, Louisiana State University in Baton Rouge, the University of Denver, Pennsylvania State University, and the Jerusalem Rubin Academy of Music and Dance in Israel. Her academic and service activities are in the area of dance education, within the United States and in an international arena. She currently serves as the secretary of the board for Dance and the Child International.

Cynthia Ling Lee (MFA) collides transnational, postcolonial and queer feminist-of-colour perspectives on South Asian contemporary performance. Her intercultural, interdisciplinary choreography and scholarship have been presented at venues such as the Asia Society (New York), Chandra-Mandapa: Spaces (Chennai), Congress on Research in Dance (Ann Arbor), Dance Theater Workshop (New York), Kuandu Arts Festival (Taipei), REDCAT (Los Angeles) and Taman Ismail Marzuki (Jakarta). She is Assistant Professor of dance at the University of North Carolina, Greensboro, a board member of the Network of Ensemble Theaters and a member of the Post *Natyam* Collective.

Catherine Limbertie is a PhD candidate in the Dance Department at York University, Toronto, and is a practicing teacher, dancer, folklorist and historian. This case narrative builds on her major research paper with which she earned an MA and York Graduate Student Award in 2010. Prior to entering the academy, she was executive director of the Community Folk Art Council of Toronto, an organisation formed by members of Toronto's many cultural communities to further the interests of maintaining multiple identities through dance.

Mary-Elizabeth Manley, Associate Professor at York University, has taught a broad range of courses in the Dance Department since 1974, including studio courses in modern technique, improvisation and composition, and lecture courses in pedagogy, education, dance science and community arts practice. Her research and publications typically focus on creative and modern dance pedagogy, dance education, and young people's choreography and performance. Published research appears in daCi conference proceedings, her editorial work in *The arts as meaning makers* and *daCi's first 30 years: rich returns*, and her writing in a forthcoming biography, *Roots and wings: Virginia Tanner's dance life and legacy*.

Rosemary Martin (PhD) is a lecturer in dance studies at the University of Auckland. She is a former dancer with the Royal New Zealand Ballet. She has also taught dance extensively within New Zealand and the Southern Mediterranean region. She has articles in the *Journal of Dance Education* and *Research in Dance Education*, and along with Associate Professor Nicholas Rowe and Associate Professor Ralph Buck is co-author of *Talking dance: contemporary histories from the southern Mediterranean* (2013).

Jeff Meiners works at the University of South Australia in arts education. He has taught extensively in schools, universities, as leader of a dance education team in London and with Ausdance. He works with the National Advocates for Arts Education, government and education departments, overseas projects and as movement director for children's theatre. He was Australia Council Dance Board Community Representative (2002–7), 2009 Australian Dance Award winner for Outstanding Services to Dance Education and dance writer for the new Australian curriculum's Arts Shape paper. His doctoral research titled *So we can dance* focuses on dance in the primary school curriculum.

Liz Melchior is a lecturer at Victoria University of Wellington, New Zealand, where she teaches dance in early childhood, primary and secondary teacher education programmes. An experienced classroom teacher and passionate advocate for dance in schools, she was a writer on the draft arts curriculum (1998), and a dance facilitator on a Ministry of Education contract, providing professional development and support for teachers implementing the dance curriculum in their classrooms (2000–05). A founding member of the New Zealand Dance Subject Association, she set up the Wellington Dance Education Network (Well Dance), which provides regular workshops for teachers in the region.

Marc Richard has taught at all levels of education and has worked as a private arts educational consultant and artist in education. He has taught in several faculties of education and currently teaches in the Musical Theatre Performance Program at Sheridan College, Toronto (Canada). He is the Canadian Representative for Dance and the Child International, the dance liaison for the Council of Ontario Dance and Drama Educators and has served as the dance consultant on the Ministry's arts webcast project. He is a graduate of the School of Toronto Dance Theatre and holds an MA in Dance and a PhD in Education from York University.

Marin Leggat Roper (MFA) has taught at Ohio Wesleyan University, Brigham Young University, Bingham High School (Salt Lake City, Utah, USA) and Asian International School (Colombo, Sri Lanka). In New York City, she founded M.E.L.D. Danceworks, committed to dissolving religious and cultural barriers through the art of dance. The U.S. State Department named her a cultural envoy to India in 2008. Other workshops and residencies have been taught at the Kali-Kalisu Arts Education Conference in India, at the Royal University of Fine Arts in Cambodia and at SUNY Purchase, New York.

Nicholas Rowe choreographed and performed with The Finnish National Ballet, Australian Ballet, Sydney Dance Company, Royal New Zealand Ballet, Nomad Dance Theatre and Modern Dance Turkey. From 2000–08 he resided in the Occupied Palestinian Territories working on dance projects with local artists and organisations. He holds a PhD from the University of Kent at Canterbury and is currently an associate professor in Dance Studies at the University of Auckland, New Zealand. His books include *Art, during siege* (2004), *Raising dust: a cultural history of dance in Palestine* (2010) and *Talking dance: contemporary histories from the southern Mediterranean* (2014).

Carolyn Russell-Smith is a dance educator, consultant and adjudicator for the Jamaica Festival of Arts annual competition. As the founder and artistic director of Khulcha Theatre School of Dance and the Khulcha Dance Company, she has been teaching dance for over thirty-five years, is the national (Jamaica) representative for Dance and the Child International, a member of the Jamaica Association of Dance and Drama Educators and has been one of the pioneer teachers of the Caribbean Examination Council's Theatre Arts (dance) examination for the past twelve years. She is a diploma graduate of the Jamaica School of Dance and also studied at the Laban Centre, Goldsmith College, London.

Adrienne Sansom (PhD) is a senior lecturer in the School of Curriculum and Pedagogy at the University of Auckland, New Zealand. She teaches dance/drama education and early years pedagogy. Her current research focuses on the body, embodied knowing and cultural identity primarily through the art forms of dance and drama. Recent publications include *Movement and Dance in Young Children's Lives: Crossing the Divide* and articles published in international journals: *Mindful Pedagogy in Dance: Honoring the Life of the Child, Daring to Dance: Making a Case for the Place of Dance in Children's and Teachers' Lives* and *Dance with Connections to Moving and Playing in the Early Years*.

Maria Speth studied theatrical and educational dance. She is a senior lecturer at the Fontys Academy for Dance Education, Tilburg, the Netherlands. She does extensive work with professionals in dance education and regular education and is involved in educational dance projects as well as projects for special education around the world. In her work with young people, she stresses the intertwining of dance and the other arts, in which the student is approached as a creative dancer. She is the author of *Dance spetters* I, II and III, handbooks and matching CDs about creative dancing for ages 4 to 18.

Susan W. Stinson (EdD) retired in 2013 as Emeritus Professor of Dance at the University of North Carolina Greensboro, USA. She has published her scholarly work in multiple journals and book chapters, and has taught and presented nationally and internationally. Her research has focused on both theoretical issues in dance education and how young people make meaning from their experiences in dance education. A founding member of Dance and the Child International, she has served as former international chair, conference co-chair and research officer, and has delivered keynote addresses at several conferences.

Charlotte Svendler Nielsen (PhD) is Assistant Professor and Head of Educational Studies at the Department of Nutrition, Exercise and Sports, research group Body, Learning and Identity, University of Copenhagen. She has contributed to books and scientific journals in Danish, English and Spanish and is co-founder and co-editor of *Nordic Journal of Dance – practice, education and research*. She is also co-editor of six books, the most recent being *DaCi's first 30 years: rich returns* (2012), an anthology holding one significant paper from each of Dance and the Child International's tri-annual conferences. She held an 1997–8 Erasmus scholarship in dance at the University of Brighton, UK, and a 1995–6 work scholarship at the Danish Dance Theatre.

JuanAnn Tai (Ann Hayward) (戴君安) is an associate professor in the Department of Dance at Tainan University of Technology in Taiwan, specialising in dance education, dance history and cross-cultural dance studies. She holds a PhD in dance studies from the University of Surrey, UK, an MA in dance and dance education from New York University, USA, and a BA in dance from Hunter College, the City University of New York. She is currently the chair of Dance and the Child International, Taiwan.

Isto Turpeinen (MA) is a dance researcher and pedagogue. His field of expertise is boys' dance education. He is currently completing doctoral studies at the Theatre Academy Helsinki,

Finland. He works as a graduate school research assistant at the Performing Arts Research Center. He is the chair of the Arts Cooperative Monkey Garden and the principal of the cooperative's Free Dance School. He was nominated as the chair of the Arts Council of the Uusimaa region and was awarded with the State Prize for Children's Culture in 2002.

Alba Pedreira Vieira (PhD) is Assistant Professor in the faculty of dance at the Federal University of Vicosa, Brazil, the author of book chapters and papers in Brazil and abroad, the organiser of the digital book *Education for the arts* (2010), and co-writer of the *Dance report and recommendations* by the 'Experts on Art Education in Latin America and the Caribbean – UNESCO'. Her work has been presented at several venues including National Dance Education Organization, Dance and the Child International and Congress on Research in Dance conferences, and published in several journals including *Dance Therapy*, *Dance Current Selected Research* and *Journal Scene*. At the university level, she teaches undergraduate courses in composition, dance history and somatics.

Liesbeth Wildschut graduated from the Fontys Dance Academy and from Utrecht University, the Netherlands. She lectures in dance history, theory, analysis and dramaturgy at Utrecht University. For her PhD she analysed the experiences of children watching a dance performance, focusing on kinaesthetic empathy, identification and interpretation. She explored the concept of kinaesthetic empathy further with empirical research. She is currently preparing a research project in collaboration with the Donders Institute for Brain, Cognition and Behaviour, Nijmegen, the Netherlands. She is co-editor of *Contemporary choreography* (Routledge, 2009) and Chair of the Dutch Society for Dance Research.

FOREWORD

Sir Ken Robinson

In Bradford, Yorkshire, young people who break the law may be sentenced to dance. The Academy is a rigorous training programme in contemporary dance, which is run within the criminal justice system by Dance United, a professional dance company. The participants have included young people with convictions for robbery, drug offences, burglary and assault. Conventional treatment of young offenders has high rates of recidivism. The aim of the Academy is not only to help them avoid re-offending, but also to discover their real potential to succeed. And it works. The mother of one regular offender was astonished at the change in her son. "It's like they cloned him," she said, "and made him good."

The professional staff of the justice system have been just as amazed by the programme. As one of them put it: "I've seen offenders working on building sites, offenders joining in team sports, and offenders doing behaviour and anger management courses. Contemporary dance, much to my surprise, is where I've seen them make the most progress over the shortest period of time." There is a deep irony in the success of the Academy. On the one hand, many young offenders did not do well in school; on the other, dance is usually at the bottom of the hierarchy in the curriculum. When these two are brought together in the right way, the results are often remarkable.

The Academy is one illustration of how often young people and dance itself are tragically underestimated in education. This book is full of many other examples. They come from all over the world, from Finland to South Africa, from Ghana to Taiwan, from New Zealand to America. They tell of the profound power of dance to enrich and transform people's lives: people of all ages and backgrounds, from many cultures and often in the harshest circumstances: in peace, in war, in abundance and in deprivation.

Revealing as they are in themselves, this book is more than a catalogue of examples. It is a book of analysis and reflection. Its intention is not simply to declare the power of dance but to fathom it. It is designed to deepen understanding of the many roles of dance in human life: in shaping cultural identity, in expressing our deepest feelings, in embodying relationships and in giving form to ideas that cannot be rendered so aptly in any other way. More than this, it interrogates the conditions that are needed, in education especially, for dance to fulfil these roles.

There are reasons why dance is so low on the food chain in many school systems. Some are to do with the origins of mass education in industrialism, which favoured disciplines that seemed most relevant to the economy. To the utilitarian, dance may seem pointless. Others are to do with the influence of universities on the academic culture of schools. The low status of dance is derived in part from the high status of conventional academic work, which associates intelligence mainly with verbal and mathematical reasoning. To the disembodied, dance may seem gratuitous. The chapters here explore the efficacy of dance education not only for self-realisation but also for the social and economic development of whole communities. They also explore how a deeper understanding of dance in all its forms will challenge dominant conceptions of intelligence, of achievement and consequently of education too.

In the 'developed' world, systems of mass education were initially shaped by the demands and character of the Industrial Revolution: these systems have been widely adopted in the emerging economies too. They are no longer fit for purpose. The world is changing faster than ever, driven in part by the transformative impact of digital technologies, by population growth and by the increasing strains on the Earth's natural resources and habitats. Around the globe, we face social, economic and cultural challenges that could elevate or consume us. To meet them, education has to be transformed too. Dance and the other arts have central roles in effecting this transformation.

Some of the chapters here look ahead to what this new settlement for dance education might look like and how we might get there. Making it happen will not be an easy task. Dance education embraces issues of curriculum, of pedagogy and of assessment. It has implications for the training and accreditation of teachers and of dancers too. It raises basic questions of social equity, of human rights and of political priorities in the re-shaping of public education. It's a task that has to be engaged. For those who take it on, the chapters here are a rich repository of evidence, insight and inspiration.

Dance education is not a new field. There is a long tradition of expert practitioners and dedicated advocates of dance education that dates back well before the emergence of mass schooling and far into antiquity. There is a considerable body of contemporary research and scholarship on the power of dance to transform the lives of people everywhere. Some of these studies are referenced in these pages. They add up to a compelling case to bring dance into the mainstream of education for all young people, wherever they are. If that were to happen, far fewer of them might feel swept aside by the lifeless current of standardisation that now swirls through education around the world.

I said there is an irony in the success of the Academy. Actually, there are two. The young people on the programme are literally in custody for their offences. For most of them, though, their training in dance proves to be a liberation. By connecting more deeply with themselves and with the people around them, they learn that they can live life differently. That should be the promise of all education and it's one of the differences that an effective dance education can make. Understanding why and how that is so is the urgent theme of this book.

April 2014, Los Angeles

Sir Ken Robinson, PhD is an international authority on creativity and innovation in education and business. Videos of his famous talks to the prestigious TED Conference are the most viewed in the history of the organisation and have been seen by an estimated 300 million people in

Sir Ken Robinson

over 150 countries. He works with governments and education systems in Europe, Asia and the USA, international agencies, Fortune 500 companies and some of the world's leading cultural organisations. Called one of the world's elite thinkers by *Fast Company Magazine*, he has received numerous awards for his groundbreaking work. He was included in the Thinkers50 list of the world's leading business thinkers and was named one of Time/Fortune/CNN's Principal Voices. His book, *The element: how finding your passion changes everything*, is a *New York Times* best seller and has been translated into 23 languages. A 10th-anniversary edition of his classic work on creativity, *Out of our minds: learning to be creative*, was published in 2011. His latest book, *Finding your element: how to discover your talents and passions and transform your life*, is also a *New York Times* best seller. In 2003 he received a knighthood from Queen Elizabeth II for his services to the arts.

ACKNOWLEDGEMENTS

This book is supported by Dance and the Child International (daCi) and the World Dance Alliance (WDA).

DaCi is a non-profit-making association, founded in 1978, dedicated to the growth and development of dance for children and young people on an international basis.

The WDA serves as a primary voice for dance and dancers throughout the world, and encourages the exchange of ideas and the awareness of dance in all its forms.

We are indebted to the support of the organisers of the 2012 Global Dance Summit *Dance, Young People and Change*. DaCi and the WDA, with hosts Taipei National University of the Arts School of Dance, brought together people from across the world to reflect on key issues and point to future directions for dance in young people's lives – this volume continues the conversations and advocacy for dance proposed at the Taiwan meeting.

The editors would like to acknowledge the outstanding contributions that the authors have made to this book, which is a vibrant account of dance education across continents and countries. We are grateful to Sir Ken Robinson for his thoughts and insights in the Foreword and his inspiring advocacy for arts education throughout the world. Finally, the editors would like to thank Routledge for their foresight in commissioning this volume and their understanding of the complexity of assembling such a rich and diverse collection of authors for the anthology.

INTRODUCTION

Charlotte Svendler Nielsen and Stephanie Burridge

Dance has the power to change the lives of young people. It is a force in shaping identity, affirming culture and exploring heritage in an increasingly borderless world. Creative and empowering pedagogies are driving curriculum development worldwide where the movement of peoples and cultures generates new challenges and possibilities for dance education in multiple contexts. In this volume, writers across the globe come together to reflect, comment on and share their expertise and experiences. The settings are drawn from a spectrum of countries with contributions from Europe, the Americas, the Middle East, Asia, the Pacific and Africa giving insights into and fresh perspectives on contrasting ideas, philosophies and approaches to dance education from Egypt to Ghana, Brazil to Finland, Jamaica to the Netherlands, the UK, USA, Australia, New Zealand and more.

Dance and the Child International and the World Dance Alliance, with hosts Taipei National University of the Arts School of Dance, welcomed delegates of all ages to the 2012 joint Global Dance Summit *Dance, Young People and Change* in Taiwan. The major 2012 Summit brought together people from across the world to reflect on key issues and point to future directions for dance in young people's lives. The conference included young people, educators, choreographers, researchers, policy makers and others from around the world who shared their knowledge, experiences and thoughts considering the role of dance in young people's lives. It provided critical discussions and reflections on approaches to dance learning, teaching and curriculum for young people, and offered opportunities to critique the relevance of dance for young people within education and community situations. This volume continues these conversations and debates and opens new directions to questions such as: what do we mean by dance? How is the term 'education' applied across diverse cultures, education systems and government policy documents? What kinds of change through dance are possible with regards to the cultural and geographic locations of dance programmes?

The book is divided into five key areas but there are many points of interconnection. The sections are: curriculum developments worldwide; empowering communities through dance; embodiment and creativity in dance teaching; exploring and assessing learning in dance as artistic practice; and imagined futures for dance education. Each section holds a number of chapters and case narratives. The chapter authors are inspired by and base their work on different theoretical perspectives approaching issues of dance education through extensive research. Case narrative examples are situated within diverse social and cultural, philosophical and sociological frameworks and often represent a specific geographical perspective. They cover dance education involving different genres, age groups, approaches to pedagogy, and the artistic and creative processes. Some relate to specific projects and activities while others take a broader perspective; however, a common thread to all the contributions of the book is that they explore change processes that come about in the lives of young people through dance.

At first glance our selection of authors may not seem to accomplish an endeavour to cover the whole world on an equal basis. We do have a majority of native English-speaking and Western authors; but when reading their contributions, we hope that readers will view a broader perspective on cultures and education than what is mainstream in their own specific countries. Many of the discussions are 'global' in nature, taking up exactly this issue with a critical view of the Western world's hegemonic perspective in worldwide discussions and developments of dance education. In the current times of globalisation it is easier to share, discuss and collaborate in research, practice and advocacy endeavours. Cultural differences are reflected in the writings of the authors, showing how emphasis is placed on different pedagogical approaches while they present views of how and why dance is important in their specific environments.

Reflection, evaluation, analysis and documentation are key to the evolving ecology of dance education and research involving individuals, communities and nations. Exploring interaction and connectivity via non-linear processes for twenty-first-century dance education is crucial in provoking creative learning, conversations and partnerships. How we do research and how we communicate our findings in the area of arts education is moving into a future where embodied knowledge and performative and practice-based approaches are becoming more accepted and acknowledged as new ways of finding 'evidence' for what can be learned in and experienced through dance. There is a growing awareness of the need to explore such processes in new ways as they cannot fully be grasped by the traditional qualitative interview, by surveys or 'objective' approaches to observation. Many examples of these initiatives are discussed in the various chapters of this volume. These insightful writings reflect on key issues and point to future directions for supporting the crucial role of dance education in young people's lives.

Charlotte Svendler Nielsen

Stephanie Burridge

PART I

Curriculum developments worldwide

PHOTO 1.0 Students of the Fontys Academy of Dance Education, the Netherlands.
Photographer: Noortje van Gestel

1.1

APPLIED DANCE CURRICULUM

A global perspective

Susan R. Koff

Introduction

Curriculum is a framework for establishing the structure of courses or experiences that a student should have from one point to an end point in an educational setting. That end point is defined by what the student should be, or what the designers wish the student to be. When arts education entered the curriculum discussion, it was on the heels of curriculum theorists who emphasise the importance of focusing on the aims of education which are often ignored when the curriculum discussions go directly to the outcomes or end points of current standards (Noddings, 2009). Current curricular theorists move the discussion into the postmodern era and encourage curriculum developers to examine traditional practices (Barrett, 2007).

In this realm, curriculum discussions also include an analysis of who is excluded from the discussion. According to William Pinar, curriculum theory is the "scholarly effort to understand the curriculum" (2012: 1) and the "curriculum is that complicated conversation between teachers and students over the past and its meaning for the present as well as what both portend for the future" (2012: 2). When considering curriculum in arts education, Elliot Eisner (1994) opened the discussion to forms of representation and argued that public schooling treats forms of representation with very narrow definitions, thus narrowing the curriculum.

Dance in the curriculum has been an ongoing discussion among dance educators worldwide for more than 35 years. Since the first discussions, it has faced challenges throughout the world for reasons that are both specific and global. The place of dance and arts education in general in the curriculum is constantly being threatened due to increasing focus in schools on math, science and literacy, as well as world financial concerns.

Within arts education, dance education has a history in the traditional curriculum as a part of physical education. When dance education in the USA moved to be its own discipline within education, it did so with the advocacy strength of the combined arts; dance, art, music and theatre (Hilsendager, 2013). Art and music have a longer tradition as part of the school curriculum, but even they have struggles (Manley-Delacruz, 1990). Dance education advocates saw strength in joining forces with the other arts, rather than independent advocacy.

Some of the struggles experienced by arts education in schools are that it is considered outside the core or essential curriculum. To be an accepted part of the core, some curriculum designers have tried to make the arts look like traditional, or core, subjects. The curriculum took on these formal models. As some curriculum theorists moved to postmodern paradigms within the curriculum (Giroux *et al.*, 1981), some disagreement can be seen within each arts discipline (Manley-Delacruz, 1990) about whether it should adhere to traditional standards, or attempt to represent a different curriculum theory.

My own experience with arts education, and specifically dance education curriculum, is that the discussion mostly resides in the "what shall we teach?" domain, and rarely covers "who shall decide?" (Blumenfeld-Jones and Liang, 2007: 246). This is adhering to the traditional curriculum. The question of educational value is rarely discussed. As I summarise this curriculum event and the outcomes of focused discussions, I will analyse it in terms of curriculum theory. I will then be able to demonstrate why, though focused and quite serious in intent, curriculum discussions and documents that have been created are placing the discipline of dance in a position of severe disadvantage.

The curriculum event

At the 2012 meeting with international dance educators, our discussions considered the following questions:

- What are the latest developments in curriculum around the world that are shaping the meaning of dance education?
- If dance is not happening – what are the obstacles?
- Can countries learn from each other?
- Is there a difference between dance in advanced countries and dance in developing countries?
- Is this ongoing discussion based in theory and, if so, what are the theories?
- What kind of benchmarks would be helpful to get a high-quality standard for dance education, particularly in schools?
- Is it useful to establish a diverse and well-balanced dance concept for general education that is internationally recognised? What role can dance artists play in developing and implementing dance in the curriculum?

New questions arose during the discussions, particularly a need to specify what we mean by dance, the role of the teachers and a careful look at the values being carried through curriculum development. Topic areas and themes are discussed in the following categories and include shared experiences, reportage, debates and questions arising from the diverse international platforms that currently exist and are planned. Overall, common strands that appear across many countries include creating, performing, responding, connecting/relating, body cognition and research.

Around the world: curriculum discussions with case examples

The questions introduced here are framed within curriculum discussions from several countries as outlined in the abstract. Each noted the current state of dance education in their individual countries and then shared the progress and roadblocks to curriculum development.

In 2000, dance was included in the New Zealand curriculum with the expectation that all students would have opportunities to learn dance as part of their schooling. By the end of 2008, dance was the fastest-growing curriculum subject and professional development was closely linked to the university level. After a change of government, professional development in the arts in New Zealand was withdrawn in favour of numeracy and literacy, and dance was no longer viewed as a priority in many schools. It was emphasised that specialist teachers exist only at the secondary level. The focus in primary schools is to integrate dance as opposed to dance as a discrete subject, which seems to be the philosophical thrust of this curriculum. A complex question arose about whether dance is a means, an end or both.

Meanwhile, Australia is currently moving towards the implementation of a national curriculum developed by the Australian Curriculum, Assessment and Reporting Authority, with dance included in the arts' learning area. An interesting aspect of directions in the development of a dance curriculum in Australia was that more generalist teachers will be encouraged to include dance in their teaching, anticipating the possibility of increasing the number of students participating in dance and being prepared for lifelong dance opportunities.

In Estonia, dance is in the process of making its way into schools of general education. The Estonian Dance Education Union developed and introduced a dance curriculum that was included in the curriculum of general physical education. Dance as one part of this mandatory subject focuses on three main areas of dance: creative dance, Estonian and other folk dances, and standard/Latin dances. In addition, an elective module focuses on technique, creative dance, composition and analysing dance. One challenge is that the physical education teachers are generally not prepared to teach dance. Teacher education is being examined to see why this is so.

In many Indian schools, dance is part of extra-curricular or even co-curricular activity, but dance has always been given more importance as a product rather than a process. It has generally been neither a tool for communication and connection between mind and body nor an area that has potential for developing a connection between images and experiences in life.

The development of the Croatian dance curriculum is new and its fields and expected achievements have been influenced by certain parts of curricula from Scotland, New Zealand and Saskatchewan (Canada).

The current situation in Germany is the presence of dance artists as the primary teachers in public schools; it is now part of physical education and music everywhere in Germany with a quality framework that was created by the Education Ministry, which includes a holistic approach.

Canada, which has a long tradition of dance in schools beginning in physical education in the 1950s, now considers dance an art form and includes creating, performing and cultural appreciation in the curriculum; however, there are currently not many institutions that train dance educators, which is a challenge. Mostly dance is included in generalist teacher education.

Dance and other arts standards were rewritten in the USA as the National Coalition of Core Arts Standards – dance, music, theatre, media arts and visual arts – in 2013. The new vision includes body cognition and new research. The standards are voluntary, as has been the history of standards in the USA, and are based on the following: twenty-first-century skills, international standards literature, college-level arts standards, new technology and Bloom's taxonomy (revised), "Backwards by design" and "Cornerstone assessments." The framework will include creating, performing, responding and connecting/relating. Because these revisions are so clearly based on research and theory, they raise the question of how many dance standards incorporate these components.

The Taiwan curriculum and the place of dance within it has a focus on the fact that all learning must be connected to life experience. Like New Zealand, performing arts (dance and drama) is a learning area.

In Slovenia, a new curriculum is currently being written. At present, dance is well integrated in the preschool curriculum, and in the primary curriculum dance is part of physical education and music, with most of the focus on production rather than creative processes and exploration.

In Portugal dance is located in physical education in secondary schools, and in primary schools, the generalist teacher covers some ballroom dance and traditional dance; teachers seem to not cover creative movement and no one is actually checking to see what is being taught.

Jamaica has a unique problem whereby dance is recognised as a cultural activity, but there is a prevalent attitude that it does not need to be taught since it is so widely practised. Within schools dance is included in physical education, taught by general teachers and is also an extra-curricular activity. Generally dance is more about product than process, leaving opportunities open to only skilled dancers.

Finland has different challenges. Dance is well developed in the private sector, which, quite unique to Finland, has a very strong connection with the school system and the Ministry of Education, but it is not in schools on its own. It is more traditionally included in physical education.

To conclude this overview, there was a presentation of the concept of the International Baccalaureate, which is not situated within any country. In 2014, the aim was to include a dance degree following a pilot programme in many schools. It will be examined at a standard and higher level. The actual curriculum is connected to the theory of knowledge sector – a basic tenet of this international degree.

Summary of curriculum discussions

Having listened to the common and unique aspects of dance education and curriculum development across a range of countries, it is useful to find commonalities in the goals and objectives of dance education around the world. What are common, international concerns and what become unique contexts within which aspects of dance education vary, diverge and respect the diversity of specific cultural heritages, as well as other differences? The following areas have been established to explore these questions in depth, again with input from educators across borders. First I will present a summary of discussions of educational goals and frameworks, considering dance education in relation to general education and possible differences across locations. The role of teachers was discussed, which also includes how teachers are prepared. Discussions of the concept of voice included who has a voice in preparing the curriculum. Finally, this section will conclude with a summary of the discussion of advocacy and how we can most clearly and articulately advocate for curriculum in dance.

Educational goals

Educational goals are complex and cannot be universal, but need to be discussed in local entities. Within an existing formal education system, a structural approach that theorises the diverse educational values of dance (beyond just a leisure activity) can be very useful. The dominant Laban-derived model provides this. The Laban model allows for the art aspect to be emphasised. In response, the following issue arises: a regional discussion might be how the current discipline/content-driven categories in formal education systems best provide a possibility for a way of knowing, such as dance, to be integrated.

Regional identity should determine how dance is valued and how it is then taught. When formulating these sensitive discussions, there can be questions about who determines regional and national identity and in some instances this can be as oppressive as global/ imperial hegemony.

Dance instils self-discipline and focus to achieve a personal best, as well as encouraging communication, creativity and collaboration. Dance is both inclusive of all in the community, as well as a location for personal excellence.

Role of teachers

Depending on the location, the teachers are sometimes generalists, sometimes specialists and sometimes a combination of the two. As these are local issues, there is not one type of teacher that is better. Standards and outcome documents often direct the role of the teacher. In every instance the teacher needs to be an advocate who pushes from within. The preparation should be for teaching dance in the classroom. The teacher should be prepared with postgraduate education, be prepared to take risks and be aware of the possibility and potential of dance to make learning enjoyable and meaningful for the students.

Teaching and preparation of teachers

Who teaches dance in schools at primary, secondary and tertiary level? This is different even within the same country, and can be dance specialist teachers, physical education teachers, general teachers and artists. Motivation to teach can be very different, but it is not possible to generalise – it has mainly to do with personal interest in dance. An explanation for the difficulty many teachers encounter with dance and a reason why they choose not to teach it is if they did not meet dance when they were in school themselves. Some countries have good experiences with models where artists and teachers teach together. Regardless of the setting, there is a strong need for in-service courses at different levels.

Voice

When a curriculum is developed and implemented, many voices need to be present. Teachers' voices should be incorporated – all teachers should be involved in various stages. This includes teachers from public education, private schools of dance and communities. In addition, the voices of parents, government and national organisations, researchers, experts and students within the discipline should be heard.

Advocacy

To have dance as an accepted curriculum, advocacy is important. This goes beyond voice but begins from that point. Service organisations are best positioned to provide and create the organised efforts for advocacy. There also needs to be access to information and developed materials for effective advocacy. Organisations can develop a model for the management of knowledge data with evidence that might be useful for advocacy, such as the curricula in different countries, theses and dissertations, research and practice methodologies used, and philosophies supporting/

leading dance in the education systems; from these many materials, organisations can then create and disseminate press releases that support dance curriculum development across the world.

Information needs to be continually collected and disseminated. A survey for the Ministries of Education and Culture in each country as well as established standards/recommendations for dance artists working in schools will be helpful. It would also be most effective to have one platform to share information, for example through developing an international network that focuses on dance curriculum, and to develop a quality framework with guidance and recommendations for dance curricula.

Challenges and steps ahead

We have learned that many countries have a dance curriculum in some form, and some (for example, countries from Africa) worry that they are losing their own culture with the current Western political emphasis on literacy and numeracy. Research has not been a major part of the curriculum discussions and developments so far, so research across borders to create knowledge of dance within the curriculum could be fruitful for further developments worldwide. Similarly, training dance artists in schools can easily disempower teachers and produce negative results. In both these instances, can collaboration with the teachers be a focus rather than coming as the "dance expert"?

When looking at the whole world it is essential to consider cultural and religious differences that offer unique possibilities and also challenges. For example, in Muslim countries like Malaysia and Indonesia there is a question whether Western dance styles such as contemporary or ballet should be practised at all other than within a religious framework. Dance educators need training to work within contextual frames in schools and communities to assess the appropriateness and needs of each unique situation.

Unpacking the responses

Through the focused dance curriculum discussions, we learned of the developments and obstacles in formal dance curricula around the world and that countries are learning from each other. However, when they do, they emulate the knowledge from the other, and have not necessarily taken a critical look at what dance means within their own country.

There was also a difference between dance in advanced countries and dance in developing countries, and issues that differ between East–West and North–South. But this is not being acknowledged in developing countries as they emulate advanced countries in developing Western paradigms in dance curricula. This only enforces the idea that curriculum is inherently political (Pinar and Bowers, 1992) and could ultimately result in devaluing indigenous dance. Inserting curriculum theories into these considerations would help to refocus these discussions.

The original question about benchmarks points to the lack of theory framing the discussion and leads directly to outcomes in the course of bypassing theory. Ultimately, an internationally recognised concept, if formulated in the mode of these curriculum conversations, would ignore the value of dance and human expression as identified in diverse cultures and will not be productive for the continuation of the intrinsic values of dance.

The concept of curriculum theory and curriculum history is absent in curriculum changes that have occurred in many places today. Many curricula instead begin with actions that reflect all the initiatives that have led to the creation of the curricula that have been presented: actions that centre around the question of what students need to know and are able to do. These driving questions have become the centre of dance curricula throughout the world, regardless of culture. This driving force derives from the Western (and mostly USA)-led discussions of gaining legitimacy for dance within public education, as its own discipline aligned with the arts. Two issues are evident when reviewing these dance curriculum discussions:

1. When considering the curriculum, countries are following a Western paradigm, regardless of the nature of the individual country; and
2. Decisions are based on questions of what people do in dance, and not what this means to them as humans.

Nel Noddings posits that we have been driven to the discussion of outcomes and standards through financial and political forces that see education as a necessity for personal and governmental financial stability and growth, rather than discussing education to support "the pursuit of happiness" (2009: 425). Curriculum discussions in the literature often point to the shift of the discussion from a question of value to what we should teach (Blumenfeld-Jones and Liang, 2007; Stinson, 2007).

Though there were some statements of dance in multiple settings, most of the discussions were about dance in formal settings. For instance, a Jamaican representative mentioned the place of dance in life activities, and the disconnect with dance in formal schooling in Jamaica. The discussions in the future need to bring in the value of dance in life, and not only outcomes of dance in formal settings.

From a cultural perspective, dance can be seen to be as old as civilisation. However, from an academic perspective, dance is relatively young (Hagood and Kahlich, 2007). Perhaps we can shift the discussion from following curricular models, regardless of the culture, back to a discussion of the value of dance in our lives.

Rounding off the discussion: towards the future

Discussions of the similarities and differences in the provision of dance in formal settings, in multiple locations in the world, provided a clearer picture of dance in this increasingly globalised and connected world. However, dance in formal settings, regardless of the culture, has followed not only a Western paradigm but has also followed the other arts and the Western-dominated established structure of formal education. Scholar in dance education Susan Stinson noted in the discussions that there are always multiple forces that guide curricula; governments are involved and usually there are short timelines for creating new documents.

In creating new standards and curricula, we always ask, "What do students need to know and be able to do in dance?" Starting with existing documents, we too often end up replicating what has been because that is what we know. We should ask instead, "What might be?" and "Since time is a limited resource, what matters most?" Stinson reminded us to step back and consider, "What does it mean to be human?" and "How should we live together?" By considering these questions, and concurrently considering the provision of dance in formal, non-formal and informal settings, we can discuss dance as its own discipline and not as trying to emulate some other form of education, be it arts or something else.

As long as dance models itself in the shape of traditional (and Western) forms of education, we will forever be advocates of a discipline that is not quite sure what it is, rather than a discipline that is about human expression. Returning to our roots, defining dance as human expression, and then discussing how human expression is an essential and defining aspect of being human can influence the developments of curricula broadly. When we do this, we will be clear about what is the scholarship of dance in its own form, rather than emulating the scholarship models of other forms of education, which would lead to curriculum forms of other disciplines (Pinar, 2012). We will be creating, instead, curriculum models that are true to dance and true to each culture in which it is situated, rather than a political dictate from a Western paradigm (Pinar and Bowers, 1992).

Acknowledgements

The entire conference curriculum event would not have been possible without the preparation and assistance of Charlotte Svendler Nielsen. I also want to thank Liz Melchior, New Zealand; Anu Sööt, Estonia; Urmimala Sarkar Munsi, India; Cornelia Baumgart and Dörte Wolter, Germany; Ivančica Janković, Croatia; Marc Richard, Canada; Yi-Jung Wu, Taiwan; Vesna Geršak, Slovenia; Elisabete Monteiro, Portugal; Nicholeen Degrasse-Johnson, Jamaica; Fanny Gurevitsch, Finland; and Ann Kipling Brown, representing the International Baccalaureate, without whom the original curriculum discussion would not have been possible.

References

Barrett, J.R. (2007). Currents of change in the music curriculum. In L. Bresler (Ed.), *International handbook of research in arts education* (pp. 147–62). Dordrecht, The Netherlands: Springer.

Blumenfeld-Jones, D. and Liang, S. (2007). Dance curriculum research. In L. Bresler (Ed.), *International handbook of research in arts education* (pp. 245–60). Dordrecht, The Netherlands: Springer.

Eisner, E.W. (1994). *Cognition and curriculum reconsidered* (2nd ed.). New York: Teachers College Press.

Giroux, H.A., Penna, A.N. and Pinar, W.F. (1981). *Curriculum and instruction: alternatives in education.* Berkeley, CA: McCutchan.

Hagood, T.K. and L.C. Kahlich (Eds.). (2007). *Perspectives on contemporary dance history: revisiting Impulse 1950–1970.* Amherst, NY: Cambria Press.

Hilsendager, S. (2013). Impulse 1953. In T.K. Hagood and L.C. Kahlich (Eds.), *Perspectives on contemporary dance history: revisiting Impulse 1950–1970* (pp. 53–84). Amherst, NY: Cambria Press.

Manley-Delacruz, E. (1990). Revisiting curriculum conceptions: a thematic perspective. *Visual Arts Research*, 16(2), 10–25.

Noddings, N. (2009). The aims of education. In D.J. Flinders and S.J. Thornton (Eds.), *The curriculum studies reader* (3rd ed.) (pp. 425–38). New York: Routledge.

Pinar, W.F. (2012). Studies in curriculum theory series: what is curriculum theory? (2nd ed.). Florence, KY: Taylor and Francis.

Pinar, W.F. and Bowers, C.A. (1992). Politics of curriculum: origins, controversies, and significance of critical perspectives. *Review of Research in Education*, 18, 163–90.

Stinson, S.W. (2007). Making sense of curriculum research in arts education. In L. Bresler (Ed.), *International handbook of research in arts education* (pp. 143–46). Dordrecht, The Netherlands: Springer.

1.2

AN AUSTRALIAN DANCE CURRICULUM FOR SOCIAL JUSTICE

Potentials and possibilities

Jeff Meiners and Robyne Garrett

Dance, transformation and school curriculum

This chapter focuses on the pursuit of an inclusive primary school dance curriculum for all young people in Australia where a new curriculum stimulated agreement for a foundational entitlement in each of the arts, including dance. Dance has in many schools been noted for its transformative potential to motivate and encourage the participation of marginalised young people who struggle to engage with longstanding traditional curricula. Projects demonstrate that participation in dance may counter the production of inequalities driven by poverty, racism and cultural and physical difference, and educators have noted positive impacts on students.

> Students who had been self-conscious and hesitant were overcoming their nerves and were 'coming out of their shells'. Students with 'attitude' were learning the importance both of self-discipline and of listening closely. . . . Leaders were emerging. . . . Students in wheelchairs were able to express themselves just as effectively as the others. . . . These young people of all physical sizes, shapes and abilities were metamorphosing into dancers!
>
> *(Hunter, 2011: 53)*

The outcomes of such projects suggest that dance could strengthen mainstream curriculum renewal to transform young people's lives for a genuine Australian education revolution in the pursuit of social justice. However, within the insidious cultures of neo-liberal consumerist and capitalist democracy where individual rights are championed, it appears that those with particular social and financial assets gain access to dance. As a result of their background, some young people receive opportunities and encouragement, enculturating them into certain dance curricula and pedagogies that dominate. We are also conscious that body practices and pedagogies around dance can be shaped by social constructs including class, gender, ability and race, and that not all young people in schools benefit equally or realise their potential through dance. With this chapter we explore critically how dance in the curriculum may contribute to "building a democratic, equitable and just society – a society that is prosperous, cohesive and culturally diverse, and that values Australia's Indigenous cultures as a key part of the nation's history, present and future" (Ministerial Council on Education, Employment, Training and Youth Affairs, 2008: 4).

We are interested in which curriculum and related pedagogical discourses appear as a result of the implicit and explicit meanings located in the new dance curriculum and consider the socially just enactment potential implied by the content. How might a new curriculum offer access to meaningful dance content and practices that embrace diversity and the right of young people to dance?

In particular, the changing sociopolitical climate of Australia has led to urgency for improving the lives of Indigenous peoples. A focus on Indigenous culture has gained prominence with considerable interest in Indigenous dance, "the only form of dance, old and new, that Australia can claim as its own" (Sykes, 2012: 1). Australia's Indigenous cultures are diverse across the continent and include mainland Aboriginal peoples identifying with languages and numerous countries of origin within the land established prior to colonisation, as well as Torres Strait Islanders who are the Indigenous people of the Torres Strait Islands, part of Queensland. As the original inhabitants, diversity across Australia's Indigenous population has at times been made invisible by colonial Anglo, Irish and European influences. With European settlement, government policies (until 1969) forced the removal of Aboriginal children from their families and communities (the 'stolen generations'), resulting in social devastation, loss, grief and mistrust (NSW Department of Community Services, 2009).

Immigration policies for a 'White Australia' (Commonwealth of Australia, 2009) similarly led to perspectives related to race and ethnicity in schooling that included the dominance of particular movement and dance practices. Consequently, in the context of Australia, the pursuit of an accessible and more socially just dance curriculum presents complex challenges as well as the possible inclusion of Indigenous dance.

Social justice

The contested concept of social justice in relation to production, consumption and the redistribution of wealth may be traced to late twentieth-century notions of both human or civil rights and of disadvantage within economic and political currents. Children enter schooling from different structural positions and socialisation experiences where they embody distinctive cultural dispositions. Such variation means that some children lack the ability to engage with the hegemony of the school curriculum. We remain uneasy about a prescribed curriculum in dance for all students that may maintain the status quo and division between groups.

Although equal opportunity policies are often in place, opportunities are sometimes not equal in practice and inequity continues to be replicated through schooling. Students who do not fit in with the values of a school and curriculum that make no connection to their own fields of knowledge are often categorised as 'disadvantaged', and we seek to unsettle such deficit views of students. Attention to dance curriculum content and enactment highlights hegemonic practices along with continuing contestations. Some teachers may hope for a curriculum with opportunities for elite dance training. Others strive for a more inclusive and socially just curriculum that offers possibilities for all students to find ways to dance as active and informed citizens, and where all may have opportunities if they wish to pursue a career in dance. This stance embraces students' life experience as an asset rather than a 'disadvantage'. Here we explore how to create a more socially just dance curriculum that embraces an understanding and valuing of the real lives of diverse young people and what they bring to their schools.

Understanding the dance curriculum in Australia

As researchers engaged in curriculum development it is important for us to understand how we have arrived at what we know to be dance in the Australian curriculum. This is foundational to grasping the field's potential and possibilities within current developments. In our research we identify and reflect critically on earlier beliefs and practices that have come to underpin what we see and understand as dance within the context of education as we trace how developments in dance more widely have impacted on the construction of the new Australian dance curriculum.

Dance is a complex human activity that takes place within social, historical and cultural contexts. We draw on our reinterpretation of historical accounts which include various types of dance identified in specific contexts, and consider the ambiguity of disparate factors shaping common-sense ideas. This process involves *re-viewing* (as in looking again more critically) familiar literature circulating from the dance education field at particular times and locations to consider the constructed truths about dance and why certain practices and discourses have become synonymous with dance education in Australia. Discourses for scrutiny include those concerned with assumptions about the meaning of dance, the dancing body and the enactment of dance in the curriculum. Discussion includes students as curriculum subjects, constructed and disciplined through dance pedagogies and in relation to a range of diversities.

Our genealogical investigation aims to illuminate processes and activities that allow particular accounts of dance to achieve legitimacy. For example, while the curriculum may present the impression of a balanced and broad study, what counts as dance at present times in Australian schools tends to be dominated by Western-led dance practices such as ballet and contemporary dance styles. These practices determine understandings about student learning, bodies, styles of dance and teachers' work. Pedagogical practices are then often equated with one-directional knowledge transmission from teachers to students of highly stylised techniques, technical correction of the body and particular movements that privilege particular types of dance and people, and may exclude others.

The following sections present a concise genealogical account of dance education influences on the Australian curriculum followed by a consideration of prominent discourses. We then locate dance in the Australian school curriculum and consider possibilities for a more socially just dance offering for diverse young people.

Influences on dance education in Australia

In tracing dance education from the nineteenth century to the present, we aim to understand how the discipline has been constructed in Australia. As in other countries, widespread social and economic events of industrialisation, political forces, mass schooling and world wars impacted on Australia and provide compelling contexts for researching dance in Australian schools. Particularly important was the early absence of Indigenous dance:

> Although numerous depictions of Aboriginal dancing made by artists on the 18th and 19th century expeditions to Australia exist, performing artists and dancers in the colonies took much longer to develop an interest in the Aboriginal version of their art form.
>
> *(Burridge, 2012: 40)*

Asian dance in the school curriculum also lacked presence because of the effects of immigration policies favouring Europeans. Rather, overseas models from Anglo, American and European influences have been crucial to past and current dance education in Australian schools. Australian dance educators were influenced by modern dance pioneers in America and by German expressionist dance (Ausdrückstanz) over a century ago. Later, postmodern dance also influenced Australian dance education, focusing on everyday movement, improvisational processes and other concepts that supported a democratic approach to dance education in schools.

Diaghilev's Ballets Russes also left a legacy of dance teachers in Australia where ballet has remained a dominant force with the foundation of the Australian Ballet and Australian Association for Dance Education, now Ausdance, during the 1970s. With an earlier lack of attention to Australia's Indigenous heritage and location within the Asia-Pacific, Indigenous dance training at tertiary level was introduced with the establishment in 1976 of the National Aboriginal and Islander Skills Development Association Dance College (NAISDA Dance College, 2014), founded by African-American dancer/choreographer Carole Johnson. NAISDA is advised by traditional cultural owners[1] and classes are led by Indigenous and Western trained choreographers and educators. This supported the presence of Indigenous arts in the States and Territories 1990s school curricula.

These early, modern and postmodern trends are reflected in former and recent ambitions for a school dance curriculum. Led by dance, arts and physical educators influenced by overseas developments, dance became located across school curriculum areas. These trends emerged with competing pedagogies of elite training for those with cultural and economic capital juxtaposed against an education in dance for all.

The discourses of dance education

Divergent orientations to dance learning emanating from early influences led to varying and contested global discourses of dance education – there are commonalities such as the use of Laban's models, physical education and arts advocacy, and debates around pedagogical approaches. Such strands are central to understanding dance in the Australian curriculum. Various terms emerging from North American and British literatures were used to describe dance within education in Australia. Emphasis on dance as physical training shifted to dance as art and an orientation to the free, expressive and educational nature of dance for individual learning. Reflecting scholarly interests in children's dance, Janet Adshead's central organising principles of dance – making, performing and appreciating – were particularly influential (Carter and O'Shea, 2010). Used by Robert Osmotherly (1991) in Australia, they formed the basis for the earlier curriculum (Australian Education Council, 1994).

So too educators have given varying emphases to technical skills, movement principles, expression, and creative and aesthetic dimensions of movement, highlighting ongoing dialogue about 'dance training' and 'dance education'. Australian dance curriculum documents have encompassed approaches which aligned with British author Jacqueline Smith-Autard's theoretical framework for 'The Art of Dance in Primary Schools' with an equal emphasis on process and product (1994: 55–63).

In the latter part of the twentieth century, dance education discourses were influenced by consideration of dance as a social phenomenon learned through social interaction within a cultural context. Recently, dance educators have drawn on research evidence connecting the field of neuroscience with dance (McKechnie, 2007). Such advances informed statements shaping dance in the school curriculum (Australian Curriculum, Assessment and Reporting Authority (ACARA), 2014). These developments are indicative of genealogical synergy between current curriculum concerns in Australia and early, modern and postmodern dance practitioners' interests in arguing significance for dance learning.

Locating dance in the Australian school curriculum

Determinations about dance in the curriculum are also important for tracing influences upon primary school dance. Despite limited research in the area of curriculum design, dance as a learning experience in schools owes much to physical education leaders throughout earlier decades of the twentieth century with more recent curriculum trends leading to dance in some parts of the world, including Australia, as an entitlement for all children.

Within physical education, a global trend has generally seen the utilitarian purpose of dance for health and well-being where dance has been positioned alongside debates about fitness, sport and bodily movement practices aimed at competition. Concern for dance as an offering for school students within a more socially just curriculum is shown in various policy documents from English-speaking parts of the world, and holds potential for Australian curriculum developments. As neo-liberal governments globally created national curricula (Maisuria, 2005), lobbying coalitions of arts educators sought equity for the arts, including dance, as an essential part of curricula for young people. More recently, dance has been located within generic 'arts' national curricula in certain countries. This shift in the curriculum location of dance in the USA aligned with similar developments in the UK and Australia.

However, the question of the place of dance in the curriculum is probably one with multiple answers. Dance may sit comfortably across more learning areas as a means to achieve different outcomes, illustrated by Britain's House of Commons Culture, Media and Sport Committee:

> Most people agree that dance is an art form – in terms of composition and appreciation as well as performance. However, the dance world seems to be undecided as to whether dance should, in any way, be defined as a physical activity . . . and/or as a participatory social activity.
>
> *(2004: 21)*

The Australia Dance Plan 2012 set aspirational goals: "By 2012 we will have the benefits of dance clearly stated and understood at every level of education. Dance will have parity with other art forms in the curriculum, from early childhood through to tertiary level" (Australia Council for the Arts and Ausdance National, 2008: 14).

A new Australian dance curriculum

The new online Australian dance curriculum is intended to provide a foundational entitlement for all students aged 5–12 to study dance sequentially and with increasing complexity from the first year until the end of primary school (ACARA, 2014). This presents a significant opportunity to explore the potential of dance in the curriculum but contradictions arise regarding what is valued in the new offering. Educational change in Australia occurred in the context of government policies influenced by economic liberalisation and a new "generalised human capital theory" (Taylor *et al.*, 1997). A continuing trend from nineteenth-century curricula driven by industrialisation towards homogeneity in a twenty-first-century national curriculum means that achievement standards are set against principles of entitlement, individual needs and equity of access for all in a culturally diverse Australia: "The curriculum should be based on the assumptions that all students can learn and that every student matters" (National Curriculum Board, 2009: 8).

Meeting the diverse needs of all learners is therefore a key issue for twenty-first-century dance educators. However, resistance to providing access to dance for everyone is apparent in a range of limited conceptions of dance, curriculum and pedagogies. Neo-liberal trends inherent in Australian culture that privilege students with cultural capital may be enacted through the curriculum. Attention is required to matters of power, control and freedom implicit in dance pedagogies. As pedagogical polarities, practices emphasising technical skill development, direction and discipline led by a teacher contrast with approaches offering learner autonomy with creative opportunities and freedom to make choices and decisions.

Debates about dance education continue as dance truths are constructed in accordance with established dominant values about dance training and the purpose of dance. Powerful practices such as elite opportunities for those selected as talented in dance performance usually support those with inherited cultural and economic capital who have been able to access private dance classes. Such students have often been enculturated into prevailing dance teaching methods and developed specific understandings and technical skills in dance outside the school environment.

Dance pedagogies from the traditions of the powerful commercial studio sector or professional training methods in wider Australian society are pervasive. By focusing on the acquisition and practising of performance skills, attention is drawn to technical ability. These pedagogies establish a culture of hierarchy, privilege and competition within the social structure of dance classes in and beyond schools. They are juxtaposed against educational approaches considered more appropriate for facilitating participation by all young people with diverse needs and interests. This hierarchy plays out in the physical reality of dance classrooms where those who know, understand and embody long-inscribed movement skills and techniques lead with pedagogies of inclusion or exclusion.

Participants in dance classrooms are acutely aware of the existence of such hierarchies; practices that exclude divide those who do not embody the dance rules of engagement from those who do. Marginalised students feel alienated and may choose to compete or withdraw in the complex contest for teacher approval or peer acceptance. We seek to disrupt such common-sense dominant readings of desirable dance by problematising these dance pedagogies which divide students in Australian schools and beyond. We wish to encourage fresh critical perspectives on how to teach dance in the primary school dance curriculum. How might teachers support shifts in thinking about dance education that enable all students to participate?

An approach to dance curriculum that offers a balance between learning technical skills for performance as well as student-centred, creative processes is reflected in the new Australian dance curriculum: "Learning in Dance involves students exploring elements, skills and processes through the integrated practices of choreography, performance and appreciation."[2] We call for a critical approach that seeks congruency between the written text and its enactment.

Possibilities for diverse learners and social justice in the new dance curriculum

Australia's diversity includes urban Aboriginal people who were displaced by colonisation, those living in regional and remote communities using native languages and cultural traditions, as well as those with colonial or migrant heritages. Recent census data showed that while more than 300 different languages are spoken in Australian households, 76.8 per cent of Australians speak only English at home. Recent migrants to Australia include those from the UK, India and China and beyond, with rising numbers of Australian children living in poverty well documented. To effectively engage all school students, Australia requires a socially just curriculum that meets the needs of culturally and linguistically diverse young people. Recognising, valuing and celebrating the individuality of diverse learners in classrooms have been important themes for social justice in recent decades, as emphasised in curriculum documents across Australia and elsewhere. Diversity manifests in individuals in various ways and positions held towards constructs of class, gender, bodies, ability, race and ethnicity may reinforce or challenge notions of difference, suitable bodies, ability and what is of value in dance. The new Australian curriculum is intended for all young females and males, with a range of body types, abilities and cultural backgrounds.

Income and wealth are not evenly divided in a modern consumer democracy such as Australia and social stratification, class divisions, their definitions and mobility across these structures continue as issues. Access to learning dance where payment is required is not easily available to those categorised as lower class such as the poor and marginalised Aboriginal or migrant populations. Studio schools operating as businesses within the commercial sector provide access to those with economic and cultural capital who are able to choose and pay to learn particular types of dance. Lessons generally focus on specialised genres and styles such as ballet, tap, modern or flamenco, and more recently hip hop. The new curriculum may point to a more socially just offering in dance beyond catering for those who can afford it – but if dance is to be offered as a curriculum entitlement for all young people, the question arises: which kinds of dance should be taught in schools?

Consideration of gender diversity is also central to enactment success for the dance curriculum. As a key social issue, gender equity highlights disparities in power and opportunity for males and females and long-established gender positions about dancing females and males continue. Advertisers present 'ideal' images of perfect young people with desirable bodies. In Western and Asian cultures, dance generally privileges youthful, slender, lean and toned bodies for both females and males. A particular type of youthful body is objectified, epitomised in dance with young female bodies (and more recently male bodies) scrutinised in terms of size, shape, flexibility and technical skill. This affects students' sense of self, values they attach to dance and the way dance is taught. Such attitudes and opinions can infiltrate schooling systems at school culture and classroom levels. Based on our research, we call for an inclusiveness that offers opportunities for a range of both girls' and boys' bodies, including those with bodies different to persuasive media representations. For an equitable curriculum offering, attention must be given to ensure that opportunities are provided for all to demonstrate their abilities rather than being viewed as having particular deficits (Meiners and Garrett, 2013). We therefore ask a further question: which bodies are able to dance?

While social constructs such as race and ethnicity may be seen as convenient for categorising those who share language, culture, history or origin, labelling or stereotyping can also be limiting. Racism and discrimination remain problematic in Australia (Markus, 2014), the results of colonialism particularly with regard to Indigenous and migrant groups outside a white-dominant norm. An important question for educators is thus: which groups are privileged by the dance content as a consequence of the new curriculum?

Curriculum reform offers potential to include approaches that lead to more learner-centred and culturally responsive dance content. We align ourselves with attempts to resolve concerns regarding the imposition of a "dominant western paradigm for teaching dance" (Shapiro, 1998: 5) and tension between teaching western high art and local culture (Stinson, 2007). Dance curriculum content that stems solely from the western tradition and excludes other dance forms may be regarded as problematic as it may have little cultural relevance or meaning to learners (Dils, 2007). A statement in the new curriculum suggests students should "begin with their experiences of dance from their immediate lives and community and identify the reasons why people dance."[3] The curriculum therefore appears to acknowledge the life experiences of young people and may offer opportunities to reduce alienation from hegemonic content and practices.

Opportunities for young people to learn about cultural diversity in and through dance are also present in the new curriculum. Dance is suggested as one way to explore identities, differences and similarities between cultures, to develop intercultural understanding, new perspectives on diversity beyond the known, and empathy, open-mindedness and appreciation of disparate cultures. This signifies a cultural shift towards a curriculum that emphasises valuing differing viewpoints and various types of dance.

Recent Australian curriculum documents included Indigenous arts for their contribution "to students' understanding of Australian society" (New South Wales Board of Studies, 2000: 9). Australia's Dance Plan 2012 presented a statement that reflects a shift in Australian awareness regarding the foundational significance of Indigenous culture:

> In Australia we are fortunate to be driven by two streams of consciousness in our pursuit of excellence in the performing arts. One is the respect, understanding and promotion of its ancient cultures. This lies at our foundation, giving resonance and spirit to the creative force. And second is the fundamental belief that dance is a characteristic ingredient in the social, political and artistic bloodline of our country.
>
> *(Australia Council for the Arts and Ausdance National, 2008: 1)*

In the 2007–13 Labor government policy, the new curriculum also gives emphasis to all young Australians learning about these ancient and continuing cultures. The "Aboriginal and Torres Strait Islander histories and cultures' cross curriculum priority suggests that working with histories and belief systems, students explore 'relationships between People, Culture and Country/Place'."[4] An example is provided whereby students experience the dances of contemporary and past Aboriginal and Torres Strait Islander artists and communities.

Here, opportunities to involve Aboriginal and Torres Strait Islanders in sharing dances with children may lead to understanding diverse Indigenous cultures and reconciliation between Indigenous and non-Indigenous Australians. Thus dance in the curriculum may work towards building better relationships between Indigenous and non-Indigenous Australians. Guidance is provided to teachers to ensure sensitive and respectful community consultation and endorsement protocols are considered.[5]

Another cross-curriculum priority supporting diversity encourages students' investigation of the role of the arts in the rich cultural diversity of Asia. Thus dance may contribute to students' understanding of diversity as "the dances and influences of Aboriginal and Torres Strait Islander Peoples, and those of the Asia region" are introduced from the first year of school.[6]

Will such curriculum initiatives be realised? At the time of writing, the prevailing Coalition government's curriculum review is underway with some critique of the Indigenous and Asian content, indicative of politicians' interests. Successful enactment will be dependent on continuing government support and opportunities for teachers to gain professional development in these areas.

Conclusion

Our discussion about diversity in this chapter is considered in the context of a developing genealogy and in pursuit of an inclusive dance curriculum for all young Australians. The new Australian dance curriculum reflects ACARA's (2014) aspirations for excellence and equity in education. 'Excellence' and 'equity' suggest high standards and a more just society for those less advantaged and experiencing inequality, but these goals may lead to conflicting ideologies of privilege and inclusion.

We therefore challenge adherences to hegemonic dance practices and pursue the development of socially just pedagogies that disrupt common-sense and dominant readings of desirable bodies and desirable dance. We seek critical pedagogies that position thinking about a socially just education to encourage diversity and cultural change by promoting access to a dance offering that includes all body types, shapes, sizes and abilities. This thinking begins with the pursuit of a re-narration of disenfranchised students' experiences as positive and different to the dominant narrative. Such an approach requires dance educators to critically reflect on how we might draw upon the new curriculum offering to improve teaching practices for students by asking questions such as:

- What does dance mean to these students and what are their interests in dance?
- What powerful funds of knowledge do these students bring from their life experience?
- Whose dance is being privileged and how might students gain a sense of ownership by making their own dances?
- How can I work with students' experiences and interests in the spirit of co-learning in dance?
- How can I develop strategies to work with diverse students with various bodies and abilities in a dance class through performing, creating and appreciating dance?

Critical reflection makes considerable and worthwhile professional demands upon educators to undertake intellectual and emotional labour as we move out of comfort zones to problematise longstanding habits, take risks and try new approaches for teaching dance. Change from the known is challenging as students may also have expectations of familiar practices. A process might include teachers mindfully observing, describing and reflecting upon customary practices, and negotiating with students to inform decisions about trialling fresh approaches in spaces that encourage more inclusive outcomes for all learners.

The new online curriculum offers possibilities to connect teachers across Australia by sharing classroom-based action research, engaging in curriculum review and effecting change informed by critical reflection on our visions for dance, young people and a better world. In particular, working with defined content and learning experiences for performing, choreographing and appreciating dance may provide a useful focus for critical investigation of more socially just approaches that consider matters of power and difference in the realisation of a genuinely transformative and empowering Australian dance curriculum.

Notes

1 This refers to appreciation and respect for the cultural protocols and beliefs of Australia's Indigenous people.
2 ACARA, 2014: www.australiancurriculum.edu.au/thearts/learning-in-dance.
3 Ibid.
4 Ibid.
5 The Australia Council for the Arts also provides protocol guidance for working with Indigenous arts: www.australiacouncil.gov.au/__data/assets/pdf_file/0016/32353/Performing_arts_protocol_guide.pdf.
6 ACARA, 2014: www.australiancurriculum.edu.au/thearts/cross-curriculum-priorities.

References

Australia Council for the Arts and Ausdance National (2008). *Dance Plan 2012*, Australian Government, Australia Council for the Arts and Ausdance National. Retrieved from http://2014.australiacouncil.gov.au/resources/artforms/dance [Accessed 5 December 2014].

Australian Curriculum, Assessment and Reporting Authority (ACARA) (2014). The arts. Retrieved from www.acara.edu.au/curriculum/learning_areas/arts.html [Accessed 5 December 2014].

Australian Education Council (AEC) (1994). *A statement on the arts for Australian schools*. Melbourne, Victoria: Curriculum Corporation.

Burridge, S. (2012). Connecting through dance and story. In Burridge, S. and Dyson, J. (Eds.), *Shaping the landscape: celebrating dance in Australia*. New Delhi: Routledge.

Carter, A. and O'Shea, J. (Eds.) (2010). *The Routledge dance studies reader*. Oxon and New York: Routledge.

Commonwealth of Australia (2009). *Fact Sheet 8 – Abolition of the 'White Australia' policy*. Retrieved from www.immi.gov.au/media/fact-sheets/08abolition.htm [Accessed 5 December 2014].

Dils, A. (2007). Social history and dance as education. In L. Bresler (Ed.), *International journal of research in arts education part 2* (pp. 103–12), Dordrecht: Springer.

House of Commons Culture, Media and Sport Committee (2004). *Arts development: dance, sixth report of session 2003–04*, by authority of the House of Commons, London: The Stationery Office Limited. Retrieved from www.publications.parliament.uk/pa/cm200304/cmselect/cmcumeds/587/587.pdf [Accessed 5 December 2014].

Hunter, M.A. (2011). Australia Council community partnerships artist in residence program evaluation 2009–2010. Sydney: Australia Council for the Arts.

Maisuria, A. (2005). The turbulent times of creativity in the national curriculum. *Policy futures in education*, 3(2), 141–52. Retrieved from: www.wwwords.co.uk/pdf/validate.asp?j=pfie&vol=3&issue=2&year=2005&article=3_Maisuria_PFIE_3_2_web [Accessed 5 December 2014].

Markus, A. (2014). Mapping social cohesion: the Scanlon foundation surveys recent arrivals report 2013. Victoria: Scanlon Foundation, Australian Multicultural Foundation, Monash University, Australian Government Department of Social Services. Retrieved from http://scanlonfoundation.org.au/wp-content/uploads/2014/07/mapping-social-cohesion-national-report-2013.pdf [Accessed 5 December 2014].

McKechnie, S. (2007). Thinking bodies, dancing minds. *Brolga: An Australian Journal about Dance*, 27, 38–46.

Meiners, J. and Garrett, R. (2013). Unsettling dance and 'disadvantage' in the curriculum. In S.W. Stinson, C. Svendler Nielsen and S-Y. Liu (Eds.), *Dance, young people and change: proceedings of the daCi and WDA Global Dance Summit*. Retrieved from http://ausdance.org.au [Accessed 5 December 2014].

Ministerial Council on Education, Employment, Training and Youth Affairs (MCEETYA) (2008). *Melbourne declaration on educational goals for young Australians.* Retrieved from www.curriculum. edu.au/verve/_resources/national_declaration_on_the_educational_goals_for_young_australians. pdf [Accessed 23 December 2014].

NAISDA Dance College (2014). www.naisda.com.au [Accessed 5 December 2014].

National Curriculum Board (2009). *The shape of the Australian curriculum.* Retrieved from www.acara. edu.au/verve/_resources/The_Shape_of_the_Australian_Curriculum_May_2009_file.pdf [Accessed 5 December 2014].

New South Wales Board of Studies (2000). *Creative arts K-6 syllabus.* Sydney: New South Wales Board of Studies.

New South Wales Department of Community Services (2009). Working with Aboriginal people and communities: a practice resource. Aboriginal Services Branch in consultation with the Aboriginal Reference Group. Ashfield, NSW: NSW Department of Community Services.

Osmotherly, R. (1991). *Dance education in Australian schools.* A position paper prepared by the Australian Association for Dance Education. Queensland: Department of Education.

Reconciliation Australia (2011). *The apology to the stolen generations: apology factsheet.* Kingston, ACT. Retrieved from www.reconciliation.org.au/wp-content/uploads/2013/12/Apology-fact-sheet.pdf [Accessed 5 December 2014].

Shapiro, S.B. (1998). *Dance power and difference: critical and feminist perspectives on dance education.* Champaign, IL: Human Kinetics.

Smith-Autard, J.M. (1994). *The art of dance in education.* London: A & C Black.

Stinson, S.W. (2007). Prelude: making sense of curriculum research in arts education. In L. Bresler (Ed.), *International handbook of research in arts education part 2* (pp. 143–6), Dordrecht: Springer.

Sykes, J. (2012). Shaping the landscape. In Burridge, S. and Dyson, J. (Eds.), *Shaping the landscape: celebrating dance in Australia.* New Delhi: Routledge.

Taylor, S., Fazal, R., Lingard, B. and Henry, M. (1997). *Educational policy and the politics of change.* London, New York: Routledge.

1.3

RECIPROCAL ENGAGEMENT IN DANCE

Empowering encounters in New Zealand early childhood settings

Adrienne Sansom

Introduction

> *Kia whakatōmuri te haere whakamua.*
> My past is my present is my future.
> I walk backwards into the future with my eyes fixed on my past.
>
> *(Māori Whakatauki)*

In an early childhood centre in suburban Auckland, a group of young children and their teachers begin another day in the hustle and bustle of the multitude of events that occupy their lives in the centre. The children are all two years of age and defined as being part of the toddler group – one step up from the babies – but not yet part of the three to five-year-old group of children. The centre is busy, as usual, with the arrival of parents and children – all being greeted by the teachers. Some parents and teachers become engaged in conversations; other teachers interact with the children as they part company from their parents and begin to settle into the various activities that proliferate the early childhood setting. Suddenly, music begins to fill the air – it isn't necessarily familiar music to everyone in the centre, but for one young boy there is an almost immediate reaction. The young boy spontaneously starts to dance, as if he and the music resonate with each other – or have found each other like long-lost friends. One of the teachers notices the young boy's dancing and from this kernel of an incident, a whole new phenomenon begins to evolve that is eventually to become a life-changing event, not only for the child, but also for other children and the teacher.

The above scenario is an interpretive account of the beginning of a particular event at an early childhood centre. This scenario helps set the scene for the ensuing learning stories that form the basis of this chapter. The learning stories allow for an interpretive analysis of the text where theory and narratives intersect to produce a type of praxis that addresses ways the teacher/ child relationship can be examined (Steinberg, 2012). The context for these learning stories is a toddler group (two-year-olds) at an early childhood centre in Auckland, New Zealand. The centre supports a large multi-cultural population.

As a lecturer in dance education, in an early childhood teacher degree programme, I am particularly interested in how teachers perceive dance and whether these perceptions assist or hinder the existence of dance in the early childhood curriculum. I am also interested in notions of power and the ways in which power relationships can be navigated within the teaching and learning space. For these reasons, research into teachers' stories about their experiences and viewpoints of dance, as well as their beliefs about pedagogy, offer the opportunity to understand how dance can potentially contribute to creating an empowering teaching and learning experience for both the child and the teacher. As a consequence, dance can act as a transformative agent in children's and teachers' lives.

As an entry point into this area of investigation, I have drawn on one teacher's perspective about dance with young children as conveyed through a series of learning stories. These learning stories arose as a result of the teacher, as illustrated in the above scenario, noticing the young child's dancing and documenting the experiences over a period of time. In these learning stories, which are used as a form of narrative assessment for learning in early childhood settings (Carr, 2001; Lee *et al.*, 2013), the teacher's narratives provide insight not only into what the children are doing, but also, in this case, what the teacher herself is reflecting upon regarding her own pedagogy. The teacher's reflexive accounts echo the concept of *currere* (Pinar, 1975, 1994, 2004), which, as the following section describes, acts as a conceptual framework for this investigation.

Currere as a conceptual framework

The overall reason for choosing *currere* as the conceptual framework is to work towards uncovering what has been constructed regarding dance in teachers' own lives from a historical, social, cultural and political standpoint. This enables an examination of the way these constructions have influenced the presence (or absence) of dance as an area of teaching and learning in their pedagogy and, as a consequence, in the lives of young children.

Currere, drawn from "the Latin root of the word, curriculum" (Kincheloe, 1998: 129), the gerund form meaning 'to run' (Sellers, 2013), is a process of regressive and progressive recollection and retrospective reflection, which implies a form of looking into the past (Villaverde and Pinar, 1999). As Pinar explains: one "re-enters the past to thereby enlarge – and transform – one's memory. In doing so, one regresses: one returns to the past, to capture it as it was, and as it hovers over the present" (2004: 36). The progressive step looks towards the future, the not yet, to imagine what could be. Both the past and the future inhabit the present. The purpose is to bring that past and future into the present to effect change – the analytical and synthetical phase – when one consciously "re-enters the lived present" (Pinar, 2004: 37). Change, especially for the emergence of agency in teachers' and young children's lives, creates a space for a re-visioned pedagogy within early childhood settings. As educators Stephanie Springgay and Debra Freedman point out:

> *Currere* . . . provides students and teachers with an embodied understanding of the interrelations between knowledge, life experiences, and social reconstruction. *Currere*, like its counterpart, self-reflexivity, "is an intensified engagement with daily life" (Pinar, 2004: 37), in which conceptions of self-knowledge are always understood in relation to others.
>
> *(2007: xxi)*

By employing *currere* as a conceptual framework, the intent is to view all phenomena through a critical lens to examine one's own story or lived experiences (Van Manen, 1990) as well as other people's stories. People's stories tell us about their histories, and, thus, the events that shaped their lives. These stories may be especially pertinent when it comes to examining the existence (or non-existence) of certain things that become evident in the everyday practices in which people are involved. As Marg Sellers elucidates:

> The autobiographical approach foregrounds the significance of understanding matters of personal educational experiences and that these living–learning experiences matter. *Currere* breathes life back into traditional views of curriculum, by considering curriculum as living and lived experience with/in which learners–teachers are embodied.
>
> *(2013: 31–32)*

Our lives as teachers, therefore, become integral to what effectively occurs in the teaching and learning space and invite examination.

When addressing who we are as teachers from a historical perspective, there is the possibility to interrogate the sociocultural and political contexts that inform what we do, especially in those areas that are seen as marginal components of the curriculum or that have been limited or absent in our own lives. Dance can be viewed as one of those areas that is either eschewed or stigmatised because of long-held historical attitudes that have seeped their way into everyday practice and life (Shapiro, 2008). As stated by Pinar: "When we listen to the past we become attuned to the future. Then we can understand the present, which we *can* reconstruct" (2004: 257–258) (emphasis in the original). Concomitantly, *currere*, as Joe Norris (2008: 233) notes, "conceptualizes one's history as a composite of learning experiences and thus makes it an informal curriculum," thereby influencing what occurs in the teaching and learning space.

Currere can act as a method to transfigure the world in which we live. As Pinar remarks: "The point here is not only 'to promote learning', but also to make the curriculum vivid and immediate, a form through which individuals might refashion themselves and the worlds they inhabit and envision" (2006: 139). *Currere* provides an avenue to reflect critically on what has been to envision what might be (Greene, 1988). *Currere*, therefore, opens up possibilities of reconceiving curriculum and how it is enacted by honouring and validating the experiences children and teachers both bring to the curriculum. In a sense, *currere* can become an embodied curriculum created by everyone involved in the process of learning and teaching, which links to John Dewey's (1934/2005) belief of learning as experience and the principles established in the foundations of New Zealand's early childhood curriculum, *Te Whāriki* (Ministry of Education (MoE), 1996) as expanded upon further in the following section.

The New Zealand early childhood curriculum *Te Whāriki*

New Zealand's early childhood curriculum, *Te Whāriki* (MoE, 1996), provides the setting or potential for agentic acts of transformation that encompass the spiritual, historical, sociocultural and political dimensions of being human. *Te Whāriki* was conceptualised as a bi-cultural curriculum where Māori (the Indigenous people of New Zealand) and Pākehā (European settlers who came to live in New Zealand) worked together to create an early childhood curriculum that was holistic and empowering. The curriculum is underpinned by the principles of holistic development (kotahitanga), empowerment (whakamana), family and community (whānau tangata) and relationships (ngā hononga). The sociocultural aspect of *Te Whāriki* resonates with the principle of relationships (ngā hononga), where children learn through "reciprocal and responsive relationships with people, places, and things" (MoE, 1996: 9), which means beyond just simply being in social or environmental domains. As emphasised in the curriculum, reciprocity and responsiveness are realised through "belonging, participation and community" in a "relationship between the individual and the collective or environment" (Lee *et al.*, 2013: 44).

These principles intersect with the strands of well-being (mana atua), belonging (mana whenua), contribution (mana tangata), communication (mana reo) and exploration (mana aotūroa). The principles and strands, together with the goals evident under each strand, complete the weaving of the mat (whāriki), which signifies a place where all can stand together (Te One, 2003). This mat or whāriki encapsulates the diversity of early childhood education in New Zealand and creates a structure for different philosophies, programmes and environments to exist within the framework of *Te Whāriki* (MoE, 1996).

A strong component of early childhood teacher education in New Zealand is an emphasis on critical reflection, especially pertaining to the principles of holistic development and empowerment. While being core principles in the early childhood curriculum *Te Whāriki*, these principles are also evident in the foundations of the Treaty of Waitangi (Tiriti o Waitangi), which reflect not only the bi-cultural aspirations of the early childhood curriculum, but also the larger sociocultural and political aspects for all people of New Zealand. Although it is particularly important for Māori to be affirmed as people who are empowered, it is equally important for all citizens of New Zealand to understand the significance of the principle of empowerment or agency (whakamana) and self-governance or self-determination (tino rangatiratanga) for both Māori and non-Māori alike (Ritchie and Rau, 2010). The acknowledgement of both whakamana and tino rangatiratanga is especially significant if the country is to aspire to become a bi-cultural and subsequently multi-cultural nation.

The act of critical reflection for teachers is part of the transformative process. Ultimately, the specific intention here is to highlight the empowering and transformative nature of dance in young children's lives. When teachers are engaged in critical reflection about their own lives, it influences what they do in their engagement with young children. It is perhaps equally important to note that research with young children is beginning to show that they are competent with analysing pedagogy and understanding their own agency within the teaching and learning environment. As stated by Julia Oliveira-Formosinho and Sara Araújo (2006: 30), children's recognition of their own knowledge and conscientiousness "can be a stimulating input for transformative pedagogy." When learning is thought of as an empowering process, the prospective for dance education is promising, not only at an early age, but life-long.

For the purposes of setting out to demonstrate how both an empowering and transformative pedagogy might materialise, I commence with an extract from the first of the documented learning stories that act as the core focus for this chapter. This learning story, which, as referred to earlier, is one teacher's perspective on a dancing experience, acts as an initial springboard for my inquiry into early childhood teachers' perceptions about dance. The learning story is written by the teacher (Sally) as a narrative to the child (Sid) acknowledging the interest and learning the child has exhibited as interpreted by the teacher.[1]

The beginning – learning story one: our dancing journey

Sid's passion: dancing!

> One day after talking to your mum, Fae [another teacher] discovered how much you love one particular song from India. Fae thought it would be a good idea to bring a copy of the CD for you to keep in the centre. I agreed too, because, indeed, it was an amazing coincidence that you both liked the same singer and songs!
>
> So, that was how our dancing journey started. I could not imagine where you were going to take us with this.

The beginning of this learning story is followed by another narrative chronicling how the entire experience came about and what resulted in the ongoing journey. The learning story not only pertains to the teacher's view of the child's experience, but also records her own reflective account of the effect this experience had on her learning as a person and as a teacher. It is noticeable in the following story how the overall experience became a transformative event for the child and for the teacher. The learning story also reveals the teacher's thoughts and feelings about her own practice and thus acts as a reflection of her pedagogy.

The initial provocation – learning story two: what dancing did to make us change

The day we started playing Indian disco music

> Today was a big surprise for Sid. After his mum had gone, suddenly without warning, music started playing and Sid reacted with all of his senses. Obviously he was very familiar with the song. But I was not!!!
>
> Sid started dancing. He seemed to know the song well. The music was playing very loud but the rest of us could not relate to it. It simply did not have the same meaning for us as it had for Sid. After the song had finished, Sid wanted to play it again and again.
>
> Other children were arriving with their parents. I found myself thinking "How is this going to make us look? What would parents think? How would they feel about this music? What is educational in all of this?"
>
> And then, whilst all of these questions were zooming through my head, I looked at Sid dancing and thoroughly enjoying himself. He looked completely immersed in his dance. His dancing involved moving the whole body while standing, then rolling on the floor doing some special twists, and then getting up and moving his arms in and out, up and down. It was so fascinating!!!
>
> But in a split second I found the answers to my questions. Suddenly, all the dilemmas seemed so clear and simple. After all, Te Whāriki talks about understanding an individual within the group. It is about the motivation to learn alone and with others based on their individual interests with us as their early childhood educators being there to support them all the way in this process. It is about accepting and understanding the individual for who he/she really is.
>
> From this moment I knew we would be supporting Sid's interest to dance and there would be no problem justifying this educationally, as it was clearly part of our curriculum. This song and dance had become a toddler group hymn of complete acceptance and understanding of 'the other'. For me it also represents a move away from the rhetoric of

sociocultural curriculum to what learning, teaching and leading in a democratic society really means.

Sid – you helped me to become more comfortable with myself too. As I started learning how to dance with you I started getting rid of some of the many fears that are buried deeply in me.

(learning story, written by Sally, March 2008)

In the above account, there is evidence of a teacher's profoundly meaningful and critical reflection, which reveals that those things buried within, when given the opportunity, can come to the forefront to open up new possibilities and ways of being. The teacher's reflection gives rise to some questions, which act as catalysts for further investigation. These questions concern issues of culture, societal attitudes (fear), power and relationships. For example, some of the questions that come to the fore are:

a. How does it feel when the music introduced for dance is unfamiliar?
b. What does it mean if the music and dance arise from another culture that is foreign to the teacher and other families in the centre but familiar to the child?
c. How does this impact the teacher or teaching?
d. How might this affect the other children?
e. What does it mean if the teacher is also from yet another culture, an outsider, but in spite of being an outsider she is also an insider – one who possesses power as a teacher in the centre?
f. What is meant by the teacher's comment about "getting rid of some of the many fears that are buried deeply in me"? Where do these fears come from and what are these fears?
g. Are these fears just related to dance, or are they aligned with other experiences?

Pedagogically, these are important questions to ask and prompt further inquiry, especially when working towards creating an empowering curriculum in dance.

The learning story or narrative recording the event provides a rich opportunity to analyse many facets pertaining to both the teacher's perception of the situation and the interpretation of the child's/children's experience. The aforementioned questions resonate with the belief Pinar (1975, 1994, 2004) presents in his work about ways to re-conceptualise the curriculum through the process of critical reflection using the notion of *currere*. Through an analysis of her own thinking, and addressing things that are "buried deeply in me," the teacher is able to confront some of those aspects that may hinder her participation in areas such as dance. Because of this analysis, the teacher experienced liberating and, as a consequence, transformational ways to engage with the children in their dance. A re-conceptualisation such as this mirrors the underpinning principles of holistic development (kotahitanga), empowerment (whakamana), family and community (whānau tangata), and relationships (ngā hononga), which, as described earlier, are evident in the primary aims of New Zealand's early childhood curriculum *Te Whāriki* (MoE, 1996).

The teacher's narratives continue to provide evidence of further reflection and show acknowledgement of the empowering nature of the child's actions, while recognising the importance of relationships with home and family and understanding others' cultures. In the following narrative, it is clear that the teachers are equally involved in the learning process initiated and led by the child. From a Māori perspective, this approach reflects 'ako', the Māori concept of reciprocal learning between the child and teacher (Pere, 1994), and illustrates a re-positioning of the teacher (as one who has become the learner) and the agency of the child (who is in the position of teaching).

Learning story three: it all started one day when we discovered . . .

Sid the dancer and choreographer

> Sid has been with us for a long time, but we did not know anything about his passion.
>
> What came first? I think it was you slowly introducing your dancing moves to your teachers and your friends. Victor was there with you all the time.
>
> We are all trying very hard to learn Sid's moves. As time will show these moves will become very famous, copied and remembered by many children. Our dancing would also change and be modified as each child contributed to it through their own personal style. It looks as though everybody made their own contribution to the dancing initiated by Sid.
>
> What kind of a dancing leader would you be if you don't have your dancing followers? Everyone was willing to join in and take part. It turned out that the favourite move was when we placed both our hands on the floor at the same time as lifting up one leg. Then we repeat the same move but with the other leg. Sid would find a way to extend this even further.
>
> *(learning story, written by Sally, July 2008)*

The learning story expands to include another young child in the toddler group as Victor emerged as a contributor to the group dance choreography.

> Victor, together with many other children, had got the 'dancing bug' in the toddler group. We did not know that our dancing fever had just started.
>
> It was a very busy day on our dance floor today. Victor had decided to introduce his own new move. Every now and then he would call "Look, look!" Then he would do his move. His face was lit up with pride, and so were ours. This made us conscious of how much children are aware of their own achievements and just how important it is to them if adults support them along the way.
>
> *(learning story, written by Sally, July 2008)*

Recognition of the children's agency is clearly evident in the above script, as is the importance of supporting young children's achievements. As noted in the following narrative, the teacher's astute observation of the children's developing dance skills led to new discoveries about the children's personalities. The expressive language used to describe the dance movements demonstrates the attentiveness given by the teacher to these special moments of accomplishment and creation.

> Similarly to Sid, Victor loved this special Indian disco song. Initially, whenever we started playing the song, there would be an instant reaction from both of them. The evidence was there in their immediate engagement in the dancing. Victor learned Sid's initial moves very quickly. I also noticed how much Victor wanted to make his own contribution. Working towards his own goal helped his teachers to discover another side of him. This was the Victor that was not shy and quiet, but very aware of himself. Victor was willing to share this with everyone else. His attempts to create a new movement were successful. Victor's move consisted of a little jump then spreading his legs wide, followed by turning his hand in circles in front of his body. Trying to make a difference inventing new dance moves was his contribution to our programme planning. He was able to verbally share this with all of us. We were extremely proud of his efforts and achievements and we certainly let him know this.
>
> *(learning story, written by Sally, August 2008)*

A teacher's reflection: embracing our embodied stories

Now, as time passed by, the more I reflect the more I understand how significant this dancing journey has been for me personally and professionally. Interestingly, I do not see it as a journey about dancing, but about people – groups as well as individuals.

So, Sid, it looks as though your learning and my learning and the learning of our group were connected in so many ways. I liked it this way and I think you did too.

It appears from the teacher's accounts that a revelation has occurred as a form of epiphany, which led to further self-actualising experiences because of a new-found understanding of pedagogy and relationships. In a sense, the principles and aims of *Te Whāriki* came to life and validated the teacher's belief in the true meaning of reciprocal relationships, which, as referred to earlier, are realised through "belonging, participation and community" in a "relationship between the individual and the collective or environment" (Lee *et al.*, 2013: 44).

Conclusion

As evidenced in the above discussion, Pinar's use of *currere* provides an analytical mode for understanding the educational experience (Kincheloe, 1998) through connecting with both students' and teachers' lived experiences. This approach necessitates a shift in knowledge production and "new ways of teaching, learning, and relating" (Villaverde and Pinar, 1999: 248).

Ingrained in the learning stories are references to culture, autobiographical experiences, evidence of future possibilities and an emphasis on relationships. At a deeper level, there is a glimmer of history and the past events that have shaped life experiences and influenced the attitudes, values and beliefs that are brought to any given situation. As Pinar further explains: "As the method of *currere* aspires to support temporality in the character structure of the individual, curriculum theory insists that the education of the public is necessarily and profoundly historical . . . historicity infuses all subjects" (2004: 253).

In relation to the New Zealand early childhood curriculum, *currere* echoes the concepts of empowerment or agency (whakamana) and self-determination (tino rangatiratanga) as a living, breathing curriculum of humanity (Pinar, 2004), which signifies the rights of children by honouring their dignity, identity, cultural heritage and citizenship rooted in historical, cultural and social contexts.

The teacher's recognition of the children's discovery of their own dance and the awesomeness this experience offered enabled the teacher to enter the unknown as a place of wonderment and new learning. Not only did the teacher find her own dance, she also discovered the importance of making connections – knowing the children, developing relationships, becoming immersed in group dynamics and learning from each other. Ultimately, the teacher recognised the emergence of democracy as applied pedagogical practice.

I also believe that "we need to take young children seriously and openly receive their curricula performativity as expressions of their understandings" (Sellers, 2013: 41). This is exactly what unfolded in the above scenarios where the teacher(s) became open to the children's creative expression and received a curriculum of dance authentically created by the children. These moments replicated genuine instances of reciprocity between children and adults unrestricted by possible constraints that may be imposed by adults. Indeed, this truly was an authentic embodied experience where there was still room for uncertainty alongside the possibility of transformation for both the children and the teachers.

Glossary of Māori terms

ako	reciprocal learning
kotahitanga	holistic development
mana aotūroa	exploration
mana atua	well-being
mana reo	communication
mana tangata	contribution
mana whenua	belonging
Māori	Indigenous people of New Zealand
ngā hononga	relationships
Pākehā	European settlers
tino rangatiratanga	self-governance or self-determination
Tiriti o Waitangi	Treaty of Waitangi
whakamana	empowerment
whānau tangata	family and community
whāriki	mat

Note

1 Pseudonyms have been used to protect the identities of the participants evident in the narratives.

References

Carr, M. (2001). *Assessment in early childhood settings: learning stories.* London: Paul Chapman.
Dewey, J. (1934/2005). *Art as experience.* New York: Penguin.
Greene, M. (1988). *The dialectic of freedom.* New York: Teachers College Press.
Kincheloe, J. (1998). Pinar's *currere* and identity in hyperreality: Grounding the post-formal notion of intrapersonal intelligence. In W. Pinar (Ed.), *Curriculum: toward new identities* (pp. 129–42). New York: Garland.
Lee, W., Carr, M., Soutar, B. and Mitchell, L. (2013). *Understanding the te whāriki approach: early years education in practice.* New York: Routledge.
Māori Whakatauki, retrieved from http://natswb.wikispaces.com/Whakatauki [Accessed 6 December 2014].
Ministry of Education (1996). *Te whāriki: he whāriki mātauranga mō ngā mokopuna o Aotearoa: early childhood curriculum.* Wellington, New Zealand: Learning Media.
Norris, J. (2008). Duoethnography. In L.M. Given (Ed.), *The Sage encyclopedia of qualitative research methods* (pp. 234–7). Thousand Oaks, CA: Sage.
Oliveira-Formosinho, J. and Araújo, S. (2006). Listening to children as a way to reconstruct knowledge about children: some methodological interpretations. *European Early Childhood Education Research Journal,* (14)1, 21–31.
Pere, R. (1994). *Ako: concepts and learning in the Māori tradition.* Wellington, New Zealand: Te Kōhanga Reo National Trust Board.
Pinar, W. (1975). *Currere:* toward reconceptualization. In W. Pinar (Ed.), *Curriculum theorizing: the reconceptualists* (pp. 396–414). Berkeley, CA: McCutchan.
Pinar, W. (1994) *Autobiography, politics and sexuality: essays in curriculum theory 1972–1992.* New York: Peter Lang.
Pinar, W. (2004). *What is curriculum theory?* Mahwah, NJ: Lawrence Erlbaum.

Pinar, W. (2006). *The synoptic text today and other essays: curriculum development after the reconceptualization.* New York: Peter Lang.

Ritchie, J. and Rau, C. (2010). Kia mau ki te wairuatanga: countercolonial narratives of early childhood education in Aotearoa. In G.S. Cannella and L.D. Soto (Eds.), *Childhoods: a handbook* (pp. 355–73). New York: Peter Lang.

Sellers, M. (2013). *Young children becoming curriculum: deleuze, te whāriki, and curricular understandings.* New York: Routledge.

Shapiro, S. (2008). Dance in a world of change: a vision for global aesthetics and universal ethics. In S. B. Shapiro (Ed.), *Dance in a world of change: reflections on globalization and cultural difference* (pp. 253–74). Champaign, IL: Human Kinetics.

Springgay, S. and Freedman, D. (2007). Introduction: on touching and a bodied curriculum. In S. Springgay and D. Freedman (Eds.), *Curriculum and the cultural body* (pp. xvii–xxvii). New York: Peter Lang.

Steinberg, S. (2012). Critical cultural studies research: bricolage in action. In S.R. Steinberg and G.S. Cannella (Eds.), *Critical qualitative research reader* (pp. 182–97). New York: Peter Lang.

Te One, S. (2003). The context for te whāriki: contemporary issues of influence. In J. Nuttall (Ed.), *Weaving te whāriki: Aotearoa New Zealand's early childhood curriculum document in theory and practice* (pp. 17–49). Wellington, New Zealand: NZCER Press.

Van Manen, M. (1990). *Researching lived experience: human science for an action sensitive pedagogy.* Albany, NY: State University of New York Press.

Villaverde, L. and Pinar, W. (1999). Postformal research: a dialogue on intelligence. In J. Kincheloe, S. Steinberg and L. Villaverde (Eds.), *Rethinking intelligence: confronting psychological assumptions about teaching and learning* (pp. 247–56). New York: Routledge.

1.4

FROM CONCEPT TO CLASSROOM

Challenges facing the implementation of the dance curriculum in the Western Cape of South Africa

Sharon Friedman

The arts in South Africa, having emerged from, and been shaped by, a history of colonialism and apartheid, were subject to reinvention and reimagining after 1994 in a manner that attempted to adjust to the acknowledgement that the poly-culturalism of South African society should be celebrated. In the schools' curriculum, a dance studies programme at all levels of schooling was created that allowed for the study of a range of dance traditions that should enhance understanding and appreciation of this diversity. Indeed, the implementation of the curriculum has demonstrated that it is the very multiplicity of cultures, dance genres and fusion of styles that have emerged that are exciting in South Africa.

However, 20 years of democracy have not led to solutions in politics or education but to ongoing transitions in many aspects of South African life and the dance curriculum has been part of the transition in education. The current (from 2011) Curriculum Assessment Policy Statement (CAPS) stipulates carefully scaffolded syllabi that allow for a progression of skills for all age groups. The curriculum is written with the three most popular dance forms in South Africa in mind, namely African dance, classical ballet and contemporary dance (although other styles including Flamenco and some urban dance are included), and improvisation and choreography modules take into account the styles referred to above and the emerging fusion of these styles.

The decision to build the curriculum around those specific styles is not without areas of debate. Issues of identity are reflected in the questions that surround the teaching of dance in public schools in South Africa. The question 'whose dance?' is centred around an ongoing debate as to the relative merits of the teaching of a multiplicity of dance genres in South African schools. The question is also political. Even if we accept a notion of an international dance language best served by a variety of contemporary dance techniques to build strength, flexibility and mobility, dance needs to be sensitive to the national and cultural issues that are part of education in South Africa where the challenge is:

> To build a South African culture and concomitant artistic endeavour, from a disparate heap of differently-valued ways of life and forms of expression and remember the exceptional nature of our endeavour: we do not have a host population attempting to accommodate immigrants – our immigrants are already here, our indigenous population

is looking for its place in the sun where the immigrants kept them until very recently in the shadows and the shade.

(Maree, 2004: 89)

Dance education in the South African education curriculum is taken seriously. However, regardless of the strength of the written curriculum, at some point this has to come off the paper and onto the floor – from concept to classroom, so to speak. Indications are that the implementation of these ideals and transformative dance teaching is hampered by the context of dance education in South Africa and in particular in the Western Cape, where dance programmes in both junior and high schools are numerous and well developed.

Educating South African dance teachers: the challenges

As a senior lecturer at the University of Cape Town School of Dance until 2011, training dance teachers for the state schools was one of my areas of focus. From 2007, having spent many years observing student practice teaching in schools, I revised the programme to include the study of critical pedagogy and a weekly full day of practice teaching in the schools for third-year students to attempt to prepare them for teaching in the state schools in particular.

A recurring problem in the schools remains finding sufficient time within a generalist timetable to provide not only practical classes of appropriate duration that reflect the diverse cultural interests, but also to accommodate both the practical and theoretical components of the dance syllabi in a challenging teaching context. Western Cape policy has been to locate as many dance programmes as possible in areas regarded as previously disadvantaged.[1] Many of these schools are affected by current social and political strife, which includes increasing gang activity, drugs, HIV/AIDS, teen pregnancy and both student-on-student and student-on-teacher violence.[2]

In many of the schools it is a constant struggle to remain motivated and attempt to fight for the material conditions necessary for the practice of the teaching, let alone achieve the noble tenets of the curriculum and teacher education. Younger teachers in particular, with some few notable exceptions, despite all the attempts to prepare them and imbue them with the ideals of best practice dance teaching (and supporting them with mentors and workshops provided by the Education Department), tend to give up or resort to uncreative and military style instruction to retain control.

Responding to the challenges

That said, while many dance teachers are not coping for all the reasons discussed, there are teachers, old and young, who have turned the lives of students from disadvantaged homes around. I have been in schools where students return to the dance room/studio at all the break times to practise and choreograph; where little ones cannot wait to get into their gear and move; where a culture of creativity and expression is slowly being formed. For every school where one despairs and teachers wail, there is one where dance is happening and alive and well, where children are dancing and dancing with joy. According to Senior Education Specialist Nicola Schorn, the changes wrought by dance education are extraordinary and headmasters have noted that not only do the dance students shine with energy and enthusiasm, but absenteeism is lower on days when dance is on the programme (personal communication, August 2013).

As to what is being achieved in the name of 'dance', certainly students emerge with a dance literacy that provides a level of bodily and movement skill and an increased sensitivity to movement and its meaning. Yet indications are that those moving onto training towards a vocation in professional dance performance or related careers are those who have received additional training outside the school environment. This in itself is not necessarily an indictment of the school curriculum where students with potential are being identified and even more importantly for South Africa, dance audiences are being built.

In conclusion

In the schools, as in the work of professional choreographers, there is a continuing attempt to move towards developing a unique South African cultural expression. As we journey into the twenty-first century, attempting to offer our school learners both an education and training in dance as an art form, which in the South African context is perceived as poly-cultural, and attempting to find a South African identity, we are left with more questions than answers. The gap between theory and praxis that emerges in the classroom because of social discord is peculiar neither to South Africa nor to other developing countries. If dance education is to continue to provide all that it purports to do in the many, many journal articles and conference papers that have been presented at conferences over the years, then it is time serious attention is given to research that explores ways in which the gap between concept and classroom may be bridged, as similar social and political ills beset many school environments globally.

Notes

1 In South Africa, this refers to the previously disenfranchised population groups in South Africa, i.e. blacks, coloureds and Indians.
2 The South African Human Rights Commission report, which was released in 2008, suggests virtually impossible teaching environments for many young teachers, and gave equal space to the violence that teachers experience every day, noting that teachers were presenting with severe symptoms of post-traumatic stress, which resulted in them experiencing negative feelings about their employment. This report is a clear indication of prevailing concern and is surely not confined to the South African classroom.

References

Maree, L. (2004). Culture in the South African classroom: culture in the arts curriculum: culture in dance. *Proceedings of Confluences 4: dance education shaping change* (pp. 89–95). Cape Town: UCT School of Dance.
University of Pretoria (2008) *Report of the public hearing on school-based violence.* Retrieved from http://edulibpretoria.files.wordpress.com/2008/03/sbvreportintro1.pdf [Accessed 6 December 2014].

1.5

DANCE IN THE NEW ZEALAND CLASSROOM

Making connections

Liz Melchior

Introduction and background

The New Zealand curriculum describes dance education as a way of knowing, enabling students to engage in ways that integrate thinking, feeling and moving. The curriculum promotes a vision of young people as "lifelong learners who are confident and creative, connected, and actively involved" (Ministry of Education, 2007: 4). These statements provide a persuasive rationale for dance to be an integral part of teaching and learning in the primary classroom. However, although dance is well established in the arts learning area, the expectation that all children will have quality dance experiences as part of their education is still to be realised.

A change of government in 2008 resulted in funding cuts for arts education and money being poured into the development and implementation of national standards for reading, writing and mathematics. This put a great deal of pressure on schools, often pushing dance further into the margins. It is widely acknowledged that dance education offers children many ways to see and interpret the world and to develop new understandings of self and others. At a time when educators around the globe are concerned about lack of connectedness and empathy among young people, this narrowing of the curriculum seems such a shortsighted response.

A way of knowing

Dance is defined in the curriculum as "expressive movement that has intent, purpose, and form" (Ministry of Education, 2007: 20). A concept of dance literacy promotes students as participants in learning experiences that focus on dance as a way of knowing and as an evolving body of knowledge. Students develop the ability to communicate and interpret meaning through four interrelated strands, or key areas of learning: understanding in context; developing practical knowledge; developing ideas; and communicating and interpreting. Teachers' pedagogical knowledge is of prime importance in interpreting the curriculum and enabling their students to see the purpose of the learning in relation to their world of understanding.

Through active engagement and participation in dance, students develop embodied knowledge (connecting body and mind). As they make connections with their own and others' ideas, stories and cultural identities, they develop positive relationships with each other and with dance.

According to New Zealand educational scholars and researchers Professor Russell Bishop and Mere Berryman, the way to improve student engagement in learning is by creating contexts where students' contributions are voiced and valued. Positive interactions with their teachers and peers encourage students to "bring who they are and how they make sense of the world" (2006: 5) into the classroom. I believe this is highly relevant for dance and the way it is taught in the classroom. Effective teachers provide an interactive environment where the roles of teacher and learner can be interchangeable, where children are challenged and supported in their learning and also given space for freedom and discovery. When they are encouraged to explore movement concepts through structured improvisation, creative problem solving, sharing, responding and reflecting, students take ownership of their learning and shared meanings are constructed. Recognising that children learn in different ways and relating movement concepts to their experiences acknowledge and celebrate diversity.

Making connections – a view into one New Zealand teacher's practice

Teachers who know their students well and know how they learn can make connections within and across the curriculum to find relevant and meaningful contexts for learning dance. One such teacher is Kirsten, who teachers a junior class (5–7-year-olds) in a New Zealand primary school. With no prior experience in teaching dance, Kirsten participated in teacher professional development in dance education (2005–07). Since then I have maintained regular contact with Kirsten, who continues to teach dance as an integral part of her classroom programme (Melchior, 2011).

Kirsten initially developed confidence to teach dance as creative movement by using her pedagogical knowledge and identifying her strengths in language literacies. She explains how she adapted teaching strategies she used for written language as a model for teaching dance:

> I make links to literacy. We read big books [large picture books for early readers] and we find the action words in the story. Dance action words are now in the language the children use in class. Dance is great for language development – so many descriptive words go with dancing and it's such rich language, and there's the instructional language too, *'Hear it, do it, remember it'*. When dancing children revisit movement, ideas and vocabulary and basic words are reinforced, adding more layers and challenges each time.

Kirsten knows what she is teaching, how she is teaching and why it is important. Making meaningful connections to other learning does not compromise learning in dance. Kirsten gives her students plenty of opportunity to explore the dance elements and encourages them to extend their personal movement vocabularies. She sets creative problem-solving tasks that involve them working in groups; sharing ideas, feelings and experiences. As active participants in the creative process, children need to cooperate and negotiate with others, express and justify their opinions and make individual and collective decisions: all essential qualities for lifelong learning as well as dance. Kirsten noticed that students with special learning needs who find socialising difficult develop confidence and social skills through participating in dance:

There are some children with extreme behaviours in this class. They were unwilling to participate [in dance] at first as they don't like working with others, but now they all join in most of the time. One child, for instance, has auditory processing problems; she has difficulty socialising in a group as she finds it hard to make decisions, but she loves to dance. She made up a movement so I put her in a group and the other children copied her movement. For the first time she was like any other kid in the class.

For Kirsten and her students, dance has opened up a whole new world of possibilities and ways of learning. As she says: "Dance is an important part of how we learn and how we express our learning." She describes one of these contexts illustrated through Photo 1.5.1:

We're doing *'Me in my environment'*, bringing in a Māori perspective, using Māori movement words for the elements [the guardians of nature] and learning Māori movement patterns that the children can use to create their own dances about the environment. They have such creative ideas; they blow me away!

PHOTO 1.5.1 Sascha, Phoebe and Summer.
Photographer: Krista Huber

As well as teaching dance in ways that enhance knowledge and understanding of other learning, Kirsten uses dance to teach language structures and mathematics concepts. She is convinced that making dance an integral part of her classroom programme has benefitted all her students, sometimes in unexpected ways. Describing them as a diverse group, with different cultural backgrounds, interests and learning needs, she elaborates: "Dance enables the children to shine who wouldn't otherwise . . . children who have difficulty with formal learning in class." According to Kirsten, participation in dance helps her students develop confidence and self-esteem, as they make positive connections with each other and with their learning.

The children in Kirsten's class know that dance is important and valued as part of their learning, as it is made visible on the walls of the classroom. Displays of dance words, captioned photos of creative dance processes, and children's written descriptions of their dance learning can also be seen by parents, caregivers and other members of the school community.

Conclusion

With decreased government funding for teacher professional development in dance and increased pressure on teachers to raise student achievement in numeracy and language litera-cies, it is hardly surprising if dance is overlooked, in spite of strong evidence that mathematics and language concepts can be taught effectively through dance. Most primary teachers want to provide the best education they can for their students and look for ways to motivate and actively engage them in their learning. The challenge remains to convince education policy makers that the New Zealand curriculum vision statements can be realised through creative dance and that learning to move can also be 'moving to learn'.

References

Bishop, R. and Berryman, M. (2006). *Culture speaks: cultural relationships and classroom learning.* Wellington, New Zealand: Huia Publishers.

Melchior, E. (2011). Culturally responsive dance pedagogy in the primary classroom. *Research in Dance Education*, 12(2), 119–35.

Ministry of Education (2007). *The New Zealand curriculum for English medium teaching and learning in years 1–13.* Wellington, New Zealand: Learning Media.

1.6

CREATIVE DANCE EDUCATION IN A SINGAPORE PRIMARY SCHOOL

Lim Mei Chian

Creative dance in an Asian context

Since 1989, the Singapore government has made a remarkable effort to promote the local creative arts industry to inculcate the appreciation of arts as a mainstream cultural pursuit in Singapore's society. Various government agencies, such as the National Arts Council and the Ministry of Education, have been instrumental in introducing the creative arts to mainstream education, so that children become exposed to aesthetically orientated subjects to develop their creativity and explore their interests. While this is a positive development, the effort to promote aesthetic education in schools is not without challenges.

In creative dance education, where the individual voice is to be encouraged, the close-knit social fabric of the Asian cultures that populate Singapore and the focus on the importance of the group over the self pose a challenge. This is especially so with older students, who tend to be more afraid to stand out in a group as they become increasingly conscious of their social environment. The difficulty of inculcating creativity and a critical voice in students within an Asian social context in this regard becomes apparent. In spite of this difficulty, teaching for creativity often remains a great success in the lower primary grades since students at that age are still self-motivated and individualistic.

The following case study illustrates a positive framework for an Integrated Dance Education Programme as exemplified by the one at Shuqun Primary School in Singapore.

A model framework in a Singapore school

> Our pupils have become more aware of themselves, their body and the spaces around them. They were given many opportunities to explore diverse kinds of movement, shapes and to work in different contexts. . . . The integrative dance programme is a truly enriching and worthwhile experience and our pupils have enjoyed themselves very much.
>
> *(Wang Ee Ling, Head of Performing Arts, Shuqun Primary School, 2005)*

The John Mead Dance Company (JMDC) began the Integrated Dance Education Programme at Shuqun Primary School in Singapore in 2005. This occurred when the school was exploring alternative teaching methods for its students to provide a well-rounded education, especially for the lower primary-aged children. Later, in 2010, Firefly Tales, the dance education arm of JMDC, assumed the direction of the programme.

In the first few years of the implementation of this programme, my co-director Mr. John Mead and I conducted teachers' workshops to align classroom teachers with the principles and concepts of creative dance education so that they could support their students in their learning. Different platforms were also set up to enable the students to display their skills and creativity. There were parent 'sit-ins' and informal showings at each level. The programme received a substantial amount of positive feedback from the teachers and parents.

During the course of study the students attend an hour-long weekly lesson in creative movement. Throughout the module, each student is assessed in the areas of dance skills, improvisation, conceptual understanding and social skills. Individual progress, as opposed to a pre-set collective standard, is used as the basis of assessment. This evaluation, together with pieces of artwork and reflective writing, are then collated into a portfolio as 'take-aways' for the children's parents.

Teaching for awareness

Throughout a creative movement lesson I pay close attention to class discipline, which plays a crucially important role in the craft of dance education. The discipline is derived from observing the rules and boundaries inherent in the structure of a class, so that children can make intelligent choices and learn through guided and progressive instruction. The fun comes from the discovery of new ideas through invested exploration, so that a disciplined class is not at odds with the possibility of having a good time.

I emphasise the need for each child to find self-control, learn spatial awareness, practise respect for others, value discovered individual differences, adhere to boundaries and follow a given creative structure. The class environment is one of 'focused fun' and 'committed effort', as captured in Photo 1.6.1.

As the children explored the space around them, sculpting and moulding it with jumping body shapes, they seemed caught in a moment of focus and joy. This is an example of how children's self-control can be optimised by drawing their awareness to the space around them. While some of the children are working creatively by moulding the space with their body parts, others are required to observe attentively and to comment on their peers' creative work; for example, by naming the movement elements their classmates have used in their improvisation, or the things they would change if they were to do the activity themselves. This kind of peer observation and feedback develops skills in dance appreciation and communication, and teaches children to respect and value individual differences.

Another example of an activity that the children enjoy is 'sculptor and statue', where they work in pairs to take turns moulding one another into interesting shapes. Amidst the fun of manipulating their partner's body parts, they learn to develop an eye for beauty – as if their partner is a piece of clay and they have to find their own best way to craft it into a masterpiece of artwork.

PHOTO 1.6.1 Integrated Dance Education Programme (2005).
Photographer: John Mead

The aims of the programme within the Singapore context

One of the objectives of the programme at Shuqun Primary School is to develop a structure whereby a student's interest in dance can be sustained throughout his/her primary education and beyond. With that goal, the programme has been successful in providing a sound foundation in movement training for students in the primary one and two levels, while exciting those who are interested in more formal training in dance to opt into the various dance co-curricular activities (CCAs) (contemporary, Malay and Indian dance), available in the school from primary three onward (see Figure 1.6.1).

Another broad aim of the programme is to provide talented students with a platform to experience dance as a performing art.

As an example of this objective, students from the school have at times been given opportunities to perform directly with the JMDC in their professional concerts. In 2006 the company chose a primary two student to perform in its main stage performance of *Moment*, alongside thirteen professional dancers. Subsequently, in 2008, four primary three and four

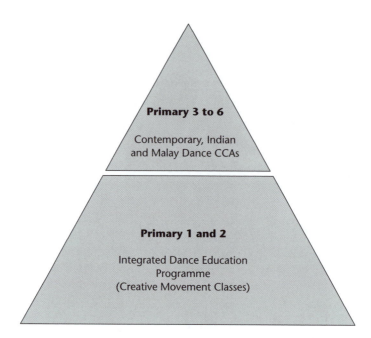

FIGURE 1.6.1 Structure of the dance education programme at Shuqun Primary School.

students were also given the opportunity to perform in *Icons* which featured seventeen company dancers. These professional performance platforms concretise dance as an artistic practice for all the children that participate.

Conclusion

Shuqun Primary School's creative dance programme has been an inspiring success. Individual initiatives such as this, along with productive government programmes that aim to integrate creative arts instruction into mainstream education, have led to a growing awareness in Singapore of the importance of dance as an integral component of a complete education. However, the quality of dance education in many local schools has continued to be inconsistent. While many schools do adopt enrichment programmes in dance, the aesthetic and educational values of some of these still operate below their potential. This problem indicates a need for a more widespread development of critical pedagogic values and knowledge of arts practitioners who conduct projects in local schools.

A coherently planned, systematic and developmentally appropriate creative dance programme can foster creativity, divergent thinking and integrated learning. The value of a single, individual human being and the importance of his inquiring mind are fundamental not only to dance education but also to education in general. It is for this ultimate value of nurturing individuals who are intellectually sophisticated and aesthetically cultivated that creative dance education plays a crucial role within the larger framework of holistic education in Singapore.

Acknowledgement

This case narrative is an adaption from my chapter that appeared in Burridge, S. and Carino, C. (Eds.) (2014) *Evolving synergies: celebrating dance in Singapore*, New Delhi: Routledge.

Reference

Wang, E. L. (2005). *NAC-AISS post-program report* (p. 18). Jurong West, Singapore: Shuqun Primary School, Performing Arts Department.

PART II
Empowering communities through dance

PHOTO 2.0 Children dancing in Brazil.
Photographer: Alba Pedreira Vieira

2.1

EXPLORING THE RIGHTS OF THE FIRST NATIONS CHILD THROUGH THE ARTS

Our dreams matter too

Mary-Elizabeth Manley

Introduction

Exploring the rights of the First Nations child through the arts: our dreams matter too was a collaborative research/creation project jointly designed by Chief Executive Officer Cindy Blackstock of the First Nations Child and Family Caring Society of Canada (FNCFCSC) and the author, Mary-Elizabeth Manley, associate professor in the Dance Department at York University. While embracing all of UNESCO's recommendations reported in its 2006 *Road map for arts education*, this two-year research/creation project contributed chiefly to the directive of "building creative capacities and cultural awareness for the 21st century" (UNESCO, 2006: 12). The project primarily explored links between arts education, rights education and indigenous pedagogy as they relate to the social abilities, active citizenship and empowerment of First Nations children. Furthermore, this project sought to advance knowledge and understanding of First Nations children's views on their rights relative to the UN Declaration of the Rights of the Child (UNESCO, 2006: 12). The research also examined how, by the direct endorsement and teaching of "children's rights to children," guidelines "for healthy personal development and respect for the civil and political forces that underpin stable societies" might be promoted (Save the Children, 2006: 12).

Background

In the winter of 2011, as a guest speaker in the Children's Studies Program on the York University campus, Dr. Cindy Blackstock shocked students and faculty when she revealed the deplorable conditions on most First Nations reserves. Poor housing, substandard education facilities, inequitable child welfare allowances, insufficient health care, neglect of First Nations culture and language heritage; these top the list of issues facing most native communities. As director of the FNCFCSC, Blackstock has tackled all these challenges by having clearly established the Society's goal of ensuring that "First Nations children and their families have equitable opportunities to grow up safely at home, be healthy, achieve their dreams, celebrate their languages and culture and be proud of who they are" (www.fncaringsociety.com, 2013).

Entirely inspired by Blackstock's passion for her work with the FNCFCSC, and with much empathy for the plight of Canada's First Nations, I began to question how, as a non-aboriginal dance educator and artist, I might be able to facilitate change through arts education with First Nations children. In May 2011, while meeting with Cindy, I proposed that a social justice dance/theatre work focusing on the UN Rights of the Child, as applied to First Nations children, be created for the 2012 Dance and the Child International/World Dance Alliance Global Summit in Taipei (as I soon discovered, the proposed performance date was quite unrealistic). Blackstock immediately linked my idea to the story of Shannen Koostachin, a champion for children's rights from the First Nations Cree community of Attawapiskat on the shores of James Bay in Northern Ontario. As a child advocate for equity in culturally based education on reserves, Shannen (with her elementary school classmates) successfully lobbied the government for a new school to be built in the tiny Cree community. Throughout Shannen's quest to have suitable schools and a culturally sensitive curriculum for First Nations children, the FNCFCSC was there to support her efforts. The story drew much attention from the press and in 2009, Cindy nominated the 14-year-old Shannen for the International Children's Peace Prize. Sadly, in 2010 Shannen passed away in a car accident while attending high school in the Northern Ontario town of New Liskeard.

While following Shannen Koostachin's lead of addressing the social justice issue of the right to equitable and culturally appropriate education for First Nations children, this research/creation project had a broader scope; the principal aim was to develop guidelines for teaching the ten basic principles of the UN Rights of the Child through a culturally appropriate First Nations arts curriculum. And secondly, the project, with associated exploratory arts education and creation residencies, sought to give definition to the whats, hows and whys of the transformative experiences that arts education can provide to First Nations young people as they learn about children's rights. The experiential research vehicles used were dance, drama, storytelling, music and visual arts.

Indigenous knowledge literature

UNESCO's *Road map for arts education*, produced following the World Conference on Arts Education in March 2006 in Lisbon, Portugal, is an exceptionally comprehensive treatise that shares a vision for building a creative and culturally responsive society through arts education. The Lisbon conference was a direct result of the 'International appeal for the promotion of arts education and creativity at school', approved by the 30th session of UNESCO's General Conference in 1999. The 'Road map' document calls on teachers, artists, administrators, community members, researchers and other constituents to explore "the role of Arts Education in meeting the need for creativity and cultural awareness in the 21st century" (UNESCO, 2006: 3).

While acknowledging the larger and overarching UNESCO appeal, the recommendation to explore "the links between Arts Education and identity, active citizenship, and empowerment" with First Nations children has had a significant influence on the development of this study (UNESCO, 2006: 13). Various other reports such as *Nurturing the learning spirit of First Nation students* (Haldane *et al.*, 2012), *Founded in culture: strategies to promote early learning among First Nations children in Ontario* (Best Start Resource Centre, 2010) and *Indigenous knowledge and pedagogy in First Nations education: a literature review with recommendations* (Battiste, 2002) indicate that First Nations culture is inherently connected to identity, active citizenship and empowerment. While the reports do not directly refer to arts education, the activities themselves – the arts of singing, storytelling, dancing and drumming – are often listed as important to incorporate in educational settings.

In general, research addressing the teaching of rights education through arts education with First Nations children is scarce. However, Battiste (2002) provides a thorough exploration of the educational issues facing all levels of First Nations society, from young learners to teachers, parents and government policy makers. While arts education is not specifically mentioned in this paper, Battiste's deep understanding of indigenous knowledge and her ability to explain it allow us to link this project's objectives to certain of her recommendations. One goal of this study – to create an educational/pedagogical model and educator/artist curriculum resource package for introducing rights education through arts education in First Nations elementary classrooms – clearly dovetails with Battiste's line of thought. Calling for the development of fresh theories and innovative practices, she envisions the construction of "new models for decolonizing and revitalizing the education of First Nations students" (Battiste, 2002: 36).

"Fostering growth of First Nations arts in partnerships" (Battiste, 2002: 37) is another of Battiste's recommendations that is reflected in the project's structure. Resonating with the Roots Research and Creation Collective (RRCC) and FNCFCSC partnership, similarities have also arisen in the multiple partnerships that have emerged between and among the community members of Attawapiskat and the educator/artists; such partnerships have allowed for greater transference and mobilisation of knowledge. The web of connections, links, associations, collaborations and partnerships inherent in the structure of this project has laid the groundwork for a rich and exciting exchange of ideas. Two topical reports, *Nurturing the learning spirit of First Nation students: the report of the national panel on First Nation elementary and secondary education for students on reserve* (Haldane et al., 2012) and *Our dreams matter too: First Nations children's rights, lives, and education* (Auger et al., 2011), are seminal support documents relating to the main research goal of this project. Each text speaks to aboriginal children's rights, culture, language and identity, a quality education, and innovative programmes to support their strengths in and knowledge of indigenous arts and culture.

In the FNCFCSC document prepared and submitted by Blackstock (2011) as an 'alternate' report to the UN Committee on the Rights of the Child for Canada's 3rd and 4th periodic reviews, significant inequities are revealed through the voices of children. The poignant letters and short essays of both aboriginal and non-aboriginal youngsters speak to the inequalities regularly experienced in First Nations schools and communities across Canada. Clearly evidenced in their writings is the utter lack of support and understanding that exists for these children's education, health care, culture, language and recreation, especially when living on reserves (First Nations, 2011). With its chief goal of exploring the links between arts education, rights education, identity, active citizenship and empowerment for First Nations children, this research/creation project has built on the notions presented in these key reports and associated literature.

Research design

While the research/creation project began as a partnership between Cindy Blackstock and I, and our respective organisations (FNCFCSC and RRCC), after much of the initial planning was completed late in 2011, as mentor/facilitator to RRCC, I then took on the project's direction/coordination. Initially, Cindy and I collaborated on the project's design, which exhibits a multiparty, multilayered, experiential, indigenous knowledge approach. We also worked in partnership on details of the project's timeline, segments and fundraising, which have given the research and creation phases structure and purpose. In the spirit of the wise African saying, "It takes the whole village to educate the child," this study was fashioned after the "whole village" approach (James and Hartwig, 2011: 3).

As such, the study ensured that multiple aboriginal perspectives were represented by engaging First Nations educator/artists, teachers, elders, children, parents, administrators and community volunteers in the arts education and creation residencies. While the study embraced both urban and reserve First Nations cultures (a pilot project was conducted with aboriginal children at the Scarborough Family Life Centre in Toronto in January 2013), the main contributors to the project were the RRCC educator/artists along with the administrators, teachers, and children at J.R. Nakogee Elementary School, a few parents, and other residents of the on-reserve community of Attawapiskat, Ontario.

All contributors to the project have engaged in the research and creation processes through a "Participatory Action Research" (PAR) model (Kemmis and McTaggart, 2005: 560). By applying a PAR approach in this study, members of the First Nations community of Attawapiskat with off-reserve educator/artists became part of the research team and contributors to the research process and its outcomes. The roles, responsibilities and contributions of members of the research team are clearly set out: as the principal investigator, I guided the educator/artists who acted as the project leaders, and formed a collaborative inquiry team. This group subsequently engaged a collection of education/community members in the project. At intervals during the project, I reported on the initial outcomes of the research. Best practices for presenting rights education have resulted from reflection on and critical analysis of the arts education workshops directed by the RRCC educator/artists; workshop leaders, children, teachers and school administrators all contributed to assessing students' learning about children's rights through arts education.

By means of a PAR model, the knowledge flows from the participants, is transformed to reveal the essence of this knowledge and is then shared with the participants and others. All members who were engaged in the project contributed to its outcomes through various consultative research methods; participants were invited to share their ideas and responses through focus groups, interviews, reflective journaling, drawings, stories, dances and music. Educator/artists reflected on their experiences of working with the children in the classroom and/or after-school programmes. Teachers, administrators, parents and community workers also contributed their observations on the arts workshops and art making in which the First Nations children participated.

Research methodology

The workshop leaders (RRCC educator/artists), teachers, administrators and the project director/coordinator were all involved to varying degrees with the process of collecting qualitative data. Following an ethnographic/creation research methodology, data and responses were gathered through: journals, arts projects, group discussions, questionnaires and informal interviews. Information was also collected through observations of and responses by the children, their teachers, educator/artists and community members, recorded during the arts education and creation residencies. Further material was sought through interviews conducted with school and community participants on the rights of the aboriginal child, and through the artist/educators' photographs and video recordings.

Following the fourth arts education residency, the research process entered the stage of applying content analysis to the qualitative data. Typically, content analysis entails such tasks as searching for conceptual themes or patterns of meaning, writing data summaries, clustering data to form relationships, condensing information to the most significant meanings and writing stories (Miles and Huberman, 1984: 429). The results of the content analysis of material generated in the educator/artist workshops during the four arts education residencies informed the creation phase of the project. Following two creation residencies, the performance work, *Our dreams matter too: guardians of the Muskeg*, was presented in September 2014 at the new Kattawapiskat Elementary School in Attawapiskat. An educational/pedagogical model and educator/artist curriculum resource package for teaching rights education through arts education will be written and published for use in First Nations elementary classrooms. Finally, a documentary film will be released featuring scenes of the research/creation processes, the culminating performance of *Our dreams matter too* and interviews with participants who shared their thoughts based on their involvement in the project.

Project structure

Drawing on the power of the arts (dance, visual arts, drama, storytelling and music), in January 2013 a pilot project was conducted in a two-week series of after-school workshops at the Scarborough Family Life Centre in Toronto, Ontario. In May 2013, phase I of the research/creation project began in Attawapiskat, a First Nations Cree community located on the western shore of James Bay in Northern Ontario. Over a one-year period, four two-week arts education residencies were conducted in Attawapiskat at J.R. Nakogee Elementary School. First Nations and Métis educator/artists, James Adams, Jackie Hookimaw-Witt, Starr Muranko and German-Canadian Norbert Witt engaged close to one hundred children from grades three, four and five in arts education workshops during each two-week residency.

Designed primarily by the project director and the educator/artists, input and assistance was provided by the school's administrators, teachers, staff and invited artists. Two classes of each grade were often combined for daily one-hour arts sessions over the two-week period. During the workshop classes, students were guided in an exploration of children's rights through dance, visual arts, drama, storytelling and music activities. Through these experiences, the young First Nations students were encouraged to express and shape their ideas concerning identity, active citizenship and empowerment that concern them. Practical learning experiences incorporating course content from Cree/English languages, creative writing, civics, physical education, science, health and wellness were included by integrating the workshop explorations into the curriculum content. As the workshops occurred during school time for two hours a day, the plan provided an equal opportunity for children to participate despite limitations regarding after-school obligations (many children play on hockey teams while others are often responsible for the after-school care of their younger siblings).

In phase II, the creation stage of the project, community arts practice methodologies as well as creative processes known to indigenous artists and elders were applied in the construction of the performance work, *Our dreams matter too: guardians of the Muskeg*. All material generated during the various arts education residencies (written, oral, visual, physical and photo/video ideas) provided background support in the production's creation. This dance/theatre piece was constructed using a Cree story, *The Guardians of the Muskeg*, gifted to Dr. Jacqueline Hookimaw-Witt by Attawapiskat Elder, Emily Toomakatik. Art forms that resonate with First Nations children – especially dancing, drumming, storytelling and visual art – were key in the process of creating the performance.

Research/creation outcomes and knowledge mobilisation

Our dreams matter too: guardians of the Muskeg

Presented on stage in Attawapiskat's new Kattawapiskat Elementary School gymnasium, *Our dreams matter too: guardians of the Muskeg* was performed for the inaugural assembly with the elementary school children, teachers, TAs, administrators, staff, several parents and community members in attendance. The children's presentation exemplified how the arts ably provided meaningful and empowering avenues through which these First Nations young people could express both their respect for ancestral wisdom and their cultural and personal identity. In a world that continues to devalue the cultures and languages of indigenous peoples, it was encouraging to see the ownership taken by the young people and community members in the creation of *Our dreams matter too: guardians of the Muskeg*. Through the experience of performing the work, the young people renewed their respect for and belief in ancestral wisdom, while appreciating the remarkable leadership shown by Shannen Koostachin and her classmates in advocating for children's rights, especially regarding education.

Indigenous knowledge educational model and educator/artist curriculum resource package

This research/creation project contributes greatly to our knowledge of First Nations arts education in general, and First Nations arts education pedagogy in particular. By investigating through the lens of indigenous knowledge, the project has revealed how rights education taught through arts education may be incorporated into First Nations elementary school curricula. As Battiste states: "Indigenous knowledge is systemic, covering both what can be observed and what can be thought. It comprises the rural and the urban, the settled and the nomadic, original inhabitants and migrants" (2002: 7). Through exploring by means of indigenous knowledge, such inquiry has furthered our understanding of the unique and valuable approaches to First Nations arts education. Also, by identifying those arts practices that clearly resonate with First Nations children, fresh and inevitably unusual routes to educating in and through the arts have been discovered.

To enhance and mobilise the indigenous knowledge educational/pedagogical model in Phase III, an educator/artist curriculum resource package for teaching rights education through arts education will be created to provide guidance to those working with First Nations children. The overall project will specifically contribute to and disseminate knowledge about arts education, rights education, identity, active citizenship and empowerment as experienced in the Cree community of Attawapiskat.

The educational model and resource package will be of much interest to arts educators, teachers, administrators, parents and elders on reserves across Canada. Indeed, it will almost certainly appeal to indigenous and other educators, curriculum specialists, education theorists, community arts practitioners, children's rights advocates, university students in faculties of education and others. The educational model, resource package, curricular guidelines and sample lesson plans will be distributed electronically and in print. Vehicles for distribution will include education networks for teachers such as the Aboriginal Education Research Network (www.education.gov.sk.ca/AERN) and the Indigenous Education Network (www.oise.utoronto.ca/research), as well as UNICEF and UNESCO.

Documentary film

The film, documenting the process of exploring the rights of the First Nations child through the arts, will be edited in Phase III, and distributed by various First Nations organisations and internationally through UNICEF, the World Alliance of Arts Education, UNESCO and other global organisations. In addition, it will be made available to academic institutions, especially those with First Nations Studies programmes, such as the First Nations University of Canada and Trent University. It is anticipated that the Aboriginal Peoples Television Network Channel will air the film. Not only will the documentary inform arts practitioners, scholars, teachers, administrators and others about First Nations, arts education and children's rights, it will also stimulate further research on rights education through arts education with aboriginal children in Canada and globally.

Impact of the outcomes

It is most unrealistic to think that this research project alone can make all the inequitable situations for First Nations children vanish. Yet surely through the thoughtful, collaborative effort of those involved in this community arts project, change will inevitably follow. Ultimately, it will take everyone involved, including the First Nations educator/artists, teachers, administrators, children, parents and elders, to move the rights agenda forward. As the primary research/creation products, the performance work (*Our dreams matter too: guardians of the Muskeg*), the indigenous knowledge educational/pedagogical model, the educator/artist curriculum resource package and the documentary film will provide new meaning and value for a broad spectrum of society.

However, the project's results and products are particularly significant for First Nations teachers and children regarding arts education, rights education, identity, active citizenship and empowerment. Clearly, the worth and importance of educating First Nations children in the arts by means of indigenous knowledge and pedagogy have been reinforced by the experiential and material outcomes of this project. Moreover, *Exploring the rights of the First Nations child through the arts: Our dreams matter too* has been successful in addressing the overarching UNESCO recommendation of "building creative capacities and cultural awareness for the 21st century" (UNESCO, 2006: 12).

References

Animating Democracy (n.d.). *Participatory action research approach to planning, reflection, and documentation.* PAR handout prepared for the Animating Democracy Initiative. Washington D.C.: Animating Democracy. Retrieved from http://animatingdemocracy.org/sites/default/files/documents/resources/tools/participatory_action_research.pdf [Accessed 7 December 2014].

Auger, A., Lewis, B. and Mould, D. (2011). *Our dreams matter too: First Nations children's rights, lives, and education.* In C. Blackstock, J. King and K. Muscat (Eds.). Ottawa, ON: First Nations Child and Family Caring Society of Canada.

Battiste, M. (2002). *Indigenous knowledge and pedagogy in First Nations education: a literature review with recommendations.* Ottawa, ON: National Working Group on Education and Ministry of Indian Affairs, INAC.

Bennett, M. (2004). A review of the literature on the benefits and drawbacks of participatory action research. *First Peoples Child and Family Review: A Journal on Innovation and Best Practices in Aboriginal Child Welfare Administration, Research, Policy and Practice,* 1(1), 19–32.

Best Start Resource Centre (2010). *Founded in culture: strategies to promote early learning in First Nations children in Ontario.* Toronto, ON: Best Start Resource Centre.

Bouchard, D. and Vickers, R.H. (2003). *The elders are watching*. Vancouver, BC: Raincoast Books.

First Nations Child and Family Caring Society of Canada (Caring Society) and Office of the Provincial Advocate for Children and Youth (Provincial Advocate) (2011). *Our dreams matter too: First Nations children's rights, lives, and education* (An alternate report from the Shannen's Dream Campaign to the United Nations Committee on the Rights of the Child on the occasion of Canada's third and fourth periodic reviews). Toronto: Office of the Provincial Advocate for Children and Youth.

Haldane, S., Lafond, G.E. and Krause, C. (Eds). (2012). *Nurturing the learning spirit of First Nations students*. Ottawa, ON: The National Panel on First Nation Elementary and Secondary Education for Students on Reserve.

Harris, B. (2006). A First Nations' perspective on social justice in social work education: are we there yet? (A post-colonial debate). *The Canadian Journal of Native Studies*, 26(2), 229–63.

Hoare, T., Levy, C. and Robinson, M.P. (1993). Participatory action research in native communities: cultural opportunities and legal implications. *The Canadian Journal of Native Studies*, 13(1), 43–68.

James, S. and Hartwig, K. (2011). *The whole village project: summary of Engusero, Makame, Matui, Ndedo, and Ngipa in Kiteto District*. Minneapolis, MN: University of Minnesota.

Kemmis, S. and McTaggart, R. (2005). Participatory action research: communicative action and the public sphere. In N.K. Denzin and Y.S. Lincoln (Eds.), *The Sage handbook of qualitative research* (3rd ed pp. 559–604). London: Sage.

Lansdown, G. (2001). *Promoting children's participation in democratic decision-making*. Florence, Italy: UNICEF.

Maina, F. (1997). Culturally relevant pedagogy: First Nations education in Canada. *The Canadian Journal of Native Studies*, 17(2), 293–314.

Miles, M. and Huberman, A. (1984). *Qualitative data analysis: a sourcebook of new methods*. Newbury Park, CA: Sage.

Nichol, R. (2009). So, how and what do we teach? Indigenous pedagogy and perspectives in the curriculum. Invited keynote address for the Principals' Australia National Curriculum Perspectives Conference, *Dare to lead – Partnership builds success, so what do we teach?* Canberra, Australia, 14 August 2009.

O'Farell, L. and Meban, M. (2003). *Arts education and instrumental outcomes: an introduction to research, methods and indicators*. A paper commissioned by UNESCO under contract with the Faculty of Education, Queen's University, Kingston, ON.

Save the Children (2006). *Children's rights: a teacher's guide*. London, UK: Save the Children. Retrieved from http://toolkit.ineesite.org [Accessed 7 December 2014].

UNESCO (2006). *Road map for arts education*. Report from the United Nations Educational, Scientific and Cultural Organization on the World Conference on Arts Education: Building Creative Capacities for the 21st Century in Lisbon, 6–9 March 2006.

Wilson, J. (2011). *Shannen and the dream for a school*. Toronto, ON: Second Story Press.

Web resources

www.fncaringsociety.com
www.amazon.com/The-Elders-Watching-David-Bouchard

2.2

DANCING BEYOND THE POST-TRAUMA PARADIGM

Community projects in the Occupied Palestinian Territories

Nicholas Rowe

Introduction

In October 2000 I began facilitating an arts education project entitled *Our Kids*, in response to the escalating political crisis in the Occupied Palestinian Territories. Over the following two years, the *Our Kids* project provided 800 hours of dance, drama and music workshops to more than 12,000 children (aged 5–16) in refugee camps, cities and villages of the West Bank and Gaza Strip. Administered through the Popular Art Centre, a Palestinian non-governmental organisation in the West Bank city of Al-Bireh, the *Our Kids* project was sponsored by various local and international agencies. Seeking to make the activities more sustainable in each location, the project shifted focus in 2002 to become *Our Kids' Teachers*, which provided training in arts workshop methods to 1,100 local teachers and youth leaders over the following four years.

The *Our Kids/Our Kids' Teachers* project was a deeply transformational process for me personally and professionally. As a foreign dance teacher living and working in the West Bank city of Ramallah, the outbreak of the Second Intifada and the resultant shift in the local political landscape in late 2000 prompted me onto a reflexive journey. This journey made me question the ethics and values of engaging in intercultural dance exchanges, particularly within the context of communities undergoing massive political, cultural and economic upheavals. From these anxious queries, I sought to more critically consider how community arts projects might contribute to the sustainability of localities and cultures during challenging times.

To more deeply contextualise this investigation into my praxis, I engaged in historical and ethnographic research into local culture and dance practices (Rowe, 2010). This research highlighted the legacy of cultural imperialism and counter-hegemony within a region that has an extensive history of political colonisation (Said, 1993; Rowe, 2008a). My community dance practice therefore sought to extend post-colonial critiques of education and the hegemony it can exert (Freire, 1972), and post-developmental critiques of international development programmes and the economic and intellectual dependence they can foster (Escobar, 1995).

The application of these theories into practice involved diagnostic dialogues with stakeholders in the communities prior to commencing workshops with children, and critically reflexive discussions with all of the local trainees after they had implemented workshops themselves. These dialogues provoked various ideas and challenges for the goals, design and implementation of the workshops, which subsequently informed the methods and activities documented within the manual *Art, during siege: performing arts workshops in traumatised communities* (Rowe, 2003, 2004). This English/Arabic publication became a resource for workshop leaders in Palestine, visiting artists in the region and other workshop leaders in contexts undergoing similar long-term traumas. They emphasised activities that supported four core goals: cooperation, continuation, communication and creativity.

The task-based activities and educational philosophies that supported these goals within the *Art, during siege* resource manual are not particularly revolutionary, as they extend upon activities and philosophies associated with creating, learning, practising, performing and appreciating dance that have been developed in other educational contexts (e.g. Laban, 1956; Smith-Autard, 1992). My focus within this chapter is not, therefore, to explore the design of these particular dance activities. Instead I seek to rationalise the philosophic relevance of the four core goals of the *Our Kids/Our Kids' Teachers* projects and the *Art, during siege* manual within the localised context of Palestinian communities during the Second Intifada. By juxtaposing these goals with alternate philosophies and practices for community arts education that were more prevalent in the region at the time, I hope to emphasise the significance of this approach and prompt further discourse into the role of arts education for communities in crisis.

My own professional journey has since moved on into different geographic and cultural contexts, but I continue to explore the same central query: *How can community dance activities contribute to the cultural autonomy and sustainability of communities undergoing crisis?* To explore this *how* query further, within this chapter I focus on meanings of trauma and community, specifically querying *when* are the dance activities taking place, and *who* is being served by the activities? These two queries lead to a critical analysis of dominant paradigms associated with arts interventions in traumatised communities, including dance therapy, post-trauma arts, cultural trauma and intercultural arts education.

Cooperation: addressing collective, not personal trauma

"How can we dance when people are dying in the streets?" I heard this refrain repeatedly in the Occupied Palestinian Territories in late 2000, during the first few months of the Second Intifada. It voiced the rationale for a collective process of self-imposed cultural censorship; performances were cancelled, community and after-school activities suspended and even weddings became more subdued. Through such gestures of solidarity for those killed and injured within the political conflict, dance began to disappear from the daily lives of Palestinians. This sense of solidarity might be seen as central to the maintenance of community, and yet at the same time could be seen as undermining it.

So what makes a community? A *community* can be an amorphous idea, as individuals inevitably find themselves within multiple communities, from neighbourhoods to nations, that are sometimes distinct and sometimes overlapping (Lugo, 1997). The sense of meaning and purpose that a community provides to its members can, however, be very tangible. Bound by shared sentiments, the borders of a community encircle a space in which members feel *significant-among* and *solidarity-with* others (Clarke, 1973), as "in the minds of each lives the image of their communion" (Anderson, 1991: 6). This sense of an imagined and socially constructed union suggests that no community is inherent or innate, and that any community is as vulnerable as the shared culture and social cohesion that sustains it. When major political, economic or natural upheavals disrupt this social cohesion, the cultural actions that unite a community might be discontinued and even seemingly stable communities can become disassembled (Erikson, 1976). The various communities within the Occupied Palestinian Territories might therefore be seen as phenomena capable of experiencing trauma: their cultural sustainability and social cohesion can be directly threatened by wider sociopolitical traumas.

To address this concern over the disassembling of community, the dance workshops of the *Our Kids* projects were driven by an inclusive social agenda and emphasised the importance of locality. They were dependent on a consultative, social constructivist relationship with the workshop participants and their wider communities (Freire, 1972). In practice, this meant holding community meetings with local stakeholders before and after workshop programmes to negotiate the parameters of the activities. In doing so, the workshops promoted dance activity

> that is conscious of its role in nurturing creativity and contributing to the cultural life of its locale, aware of its potential for educating and enlivening the imagination and, perhaps most importantly, of opening channels of communication between strangers.
>
> *(Benjamin, 2008: 105)*

As Benjamin suggests, communities are inevitably constructed and sustained by the diverse forums that allow strangers to connect in various ways. Within highly politicised contexts (such as the Occupied Palestinian Territories), community forums can become dominated by the spoken and written word, which in turn can define and polarise values and ideals. This leads to an urgent need for spaces in which moving bodies might allow strangers to commune and share more nuanced understandings of the world. It could be argued that without a diversification of such forums, threatened communities are placed at greater risk of disassembling, as individuals become increasingly alienated by the absence of open 'channels of communication'. Within the Occupied Palestinian Territories, the channel of dance became particularly narrow, as the cancelling of celebratory ceremonies and gatherings suddenly restricted avenues for creative corporeal expression. At the same time, local dance practices that previously had diverse meanings were being appropriated and redefined through slogan-like political re-interpretations (Rowe, 2011). The *Our Kids* project therefore sought to provide a space in which individual moving bodies might commune and diversify this discourse to sustain the bonds of a multi-faceted community.

This idea of using dance to address community lesions contrasts markedly with the idea of using dance to address the physiological and psychological traumas experienced by individual people. In this sense the activities within the *Our Kids* project did not seek to attend to the theories and practices developed within dance movement therapy (e.g. Siegel, 1984), which in turn have been developed from group psychotherapy models (e.g. Yalom, 1970). Such practices, which can involve the revealing of unconscious mental processes and the identification of psychological obstacles, can facilitate healing among individuals. Inevitably, individual and collective suffering are interwoven within a community in crisis, as "individual suffering unveils itself within the parameters of other people's suffering" (Kaniasty and Norris, 1999: 26). Addressing collective trauma and personal trauma may, however, require very different processes.

So how might dance activities address a trauma that is impacting on this sense of collectivisation? How might this contrast with dance activities that address more individual traumas? With its focus on community trauma, within the *Our Kids* project the notion of *cooperation* became a central goal: all the dance activities were expected in some way to foster a sense of shared purpose among a group, to re-invigorate the group's belief that there is a value in remaining collectivised. This required a focus on inter-personal activities that advance a sensitivity towards others, rather than on inward-focused activities that seek personal revelation and regeneration. While this approach does not deny the value of introspection, it maintains an emphasis on celebrating the realisations that emerge through collaborative action.

Continuity: not *post*-traumatised communities

Acknowledging the distinction between past and ongoing trauma can become an important point of departure for arts interventions in a community experiencing traumatic events. This can involve identifying whether a safe environment has been established, and can shift the emphasis of an arts intervention from recovery to survival. If the threat is not past but ongoing, how is dance providing tools that will help a community survive?

Collective trauma in the Occupied Palestinian Territories during the Second Intifada might be understood as current and ongoing, as militant actions and economic deprivation continued to disturb daily activity. Such *actively* traumatised communities present a contrast to much of the academic literature on trauma, which has instead "been dominated by the clinical parameters of post-traumatic stress disorder" (Saunders and Aghaie, 2005). This clinical understanding of trauma as a past event being recovered from has been translated into social theory, through post-trauma recovery tools in psychology such as acting-out and working-through (LaCapra, 2000). Such theories derived from post-trauma recovery have subsequently informed dance intervention models for use among communities that have experienced severe disasters (e.g. Harris, 2007).

While reflecting on past traumas (within a post-trauma recovery process) might assist a community's healing, this approach does not necessarily address the particular concerns of those living within an environment of continual threat. This sense of continual and compounding trauma was particularly evident within the *Our Kids* project. As teachers travelling around the West Bank and Gaza Strip each day, we shared with our workshop participants the experience of ongoing threats, humiliation and violence inflicted by the Israeli military and settlers (Rafeedie, 2008; Rowe, 2008b). We could also see that there were very limited opportunities for children in these communities to engage in arts learning activities. Obsessively focusing on the traumatic events in such a context would seem to compound the impact of such events. Moreover, the process of acting-through these experiences to position them as past (and distinct from the present) would seem delusional. Such attempts at distancing the events through post-trauma methods might even be seen as an insidious method of restraining more appropriate survival-focused responses to the ongoing reality of political oppression.

This notion of survival-through-arts-activities aligns itself politically with the popular Palestinian notion of *sumud*, or steadfast resistance. *Sumud*, and the ability to simply survive, endure and remain as a local community, has been advanced as a revolutionary ideal during successive waves of foreign colonisation and imperial rule within Palestine during the past century (Kimmerling and Migdal, 1993). It could be argued that *sumud* requires a constant cultural responsiveness to a political landscape that is far from stable. To emphasise *continuity* within the

Our Kids project, we therefore had to design activities that considered the ongoing political trauma not as a 'post-' sort of phenomenon, but as a malleable layer within the complexity of the ongoing present. This allowed arts activities to incorporate traumatic events without focusing on a need to recover and move away from them.

Communication: not fostering communities-of-trauma

In designing an arts intervention for a traumatised community, it can be useful to further distinguish a community that is directly impacted by ongoing traumatic events from a larger community that emerges through a process of culturally mediating the trauma to others. This distinction becomes valuable when considering how the process of culturally mediating trauma can sometimes support, but also sometimes challenge, the cultural sustainability of a traumatised community.

In such a process of culturally mediated trauma, the tragic experiences of some are projected onto many others through the cultural mediation of television, music, oral histories and literature. The immediate spread of empathy across the world through live news reports of the September 11 terror attacks, or across generations through literature and films on the Holocaust, illustrates the very tangible sense of shared pain from cultural trauma. Individuals who are distant in time and space and have no direct personal connection with the tragic events can nevertheless experience a sense of associated pain through such culturally mediated trauma. The solidarity invoked by such cultural trauma can contribute to a wider collective identity and result in the construction of a newer, larger community (Alexander *et al.*, 2004). Such a collective identity fostered by cultural trauma might be considered to be a community-of-trauma.

Within the Occupied Palestinian Territories in the Second Intifada, the creation of such a community-of-trauma was commonly being promoted through arts activities with children. In the process of extending the *Our Kids* project, I visited a potential partner institution in Hebron. The organisation displayed a room filled with children's drawings of Muhammad al-Durrah being shot. The death of 12-year-old al-Durrah on 30 September 2000, cowering behind his father as soldiers sprayed a volley of bullets across him, had become iconic within the Second Intifada. The death had been broadcast on satellite television and subsequently adapted into montages of the intifada and repeatedly broadcast. While the children's drawings of al-Durrah's death in Gaza resonated with the experiences of the local community in Hebron, this act might nevertheless be seen as a process of constructing political solidarity through cultural action.

Such expressions of art depicting scenes from the political struggle had become ubiquitous in the public arena at the time (Boullata, 2004), and several of the dance performances that were taking place involved rough physical enactments of the death of a martyr. Within the workshops we gave, such expressions were often the first things children would begin to create, not because that was the only life they knew, but because that was the dominant expectation of the art that they had experienced.

Such an intention to promote a wider community-of-trauma through children's artistic expressions was not limited to local agencies. When we were showing examples of the artwork made by children in the *Our Kids* workshops to representatives of a North American NGO that had funded the workshops, they selected infantile images of battles between soldiers and Palestinians (rather than the more creative and intricate pictures of local culture and nature) for reproduction within their fundraising Christmas card series. While well-meaning in their intention to foster a wider international community-of-trauma in solidarity with Palestinians, this international NGO nevertheless presented a particular expectation regarding the type of art that would be more valued from Palestinian children.

Communities-of-trauma only exist, and have meaning, in relation to the traumatic events. Sustaining the collective identity of a community-of-trauma therefore requires the continual cultural mediation of the tragic events and their ongoing tragic effects (Eyerman, 2001). In contrast, sustaining a traumatised community can require cultural activities that transcend and move beyond the tragedy; cultural expressions that do not allow the community to be defined by the tragedy.

Within the West Bank and Gaza Strip, this tension between whether arts activities were to contribute to the cultural sustainability of a community in crisis or to extend a sense of communion with distant others remained a pertinent and contentious issue. Addressing the query, "How can we dance when people are dying in the streets?" was easier to answer if the dance depicted such deaths in an attempt to foster national and international solidarity. Deciding between the need to sustain a community-of-trauma and to sustain an actual traumatised community became, therefore, a design concern for the *Our Kids* project. Central to this decision was a deliberation over *who* was being communicated to by the dance activities; the actual participants within the workshops, or a group of distant others who may be less familiar with the experiences?

By choosing to direct such artistic expression internally within the community, rather than externally to others outside the community, the *Our Kids* projects advanced arts activities that were less intent on representing the trauma to others and more intent on opening up channels of communication between community members about various facets of local life. This inevitably led to dance interpretations of the sociopolitical environment that were less restricted to slogans of solidarity, and more revealing of diverse experiences of the local culture. By fostering support for the acceptance of such diverse expressions within the group, the *Our Kids* project ultimately promoted an agenda of social inclusivity, which might be argued as central to the sustenance of community within the twenty-first century.

Creation: not emulation and re-creation

There was one other model of community arts education taking place within the Occupied Palestinian Territories during the design of the *Our Kids* project: the teaching of skills in particular artistic styles. This model has a long history within international cultural aid and exchange, and forms the basis for many international arts exchange programmes. As an example of this, the West-Eastern Divan Orchestra, founded by Daniel Barenboim and Edward Said, promoted the teaching of Western classical music to children in the refugee camps of the West Bank and Gaza Strip. As Daniel Barenboim explained at the time:

> An hour of violin lessons in Berlin is an hour where you get the child interested in music. An hour in a violin lesson in Palestine is an hour away from violence, is an hour away from fundamentalism. It suddenly has another dimension. Classical music is not something that one associates with the Palestinians, with the Arabs in general. You give it to them with the understanding it can enrich their lives and get creativity out of it. The optimistic view is that if the proper conditions are created – and it's a big if – then the Middle East could become a bridge between Europe and Asia, between Europe and Africa, East and West in the best sense of the world [sic].
>
> *(Cited in Harding, 2004)*

Such a model for arts education can be particularly appealing to foreign donor agencies seeking to engage within a traumatised community, as it suggests that the current problems of the traumatised community can be resolved using tools and skills already developed within the culture of the donor nation. It can further support the donor nation's future engagement with the region, as a format for future cultural exchange will have been established. The wholesale importation of another culture's art forms can, however, lead to deculturation (Ortiz, 1995): the undermining of local artistic expression, and an increasing dependence on foreign knowledge bases (Fanon, 1986; Freire, 1972; Said, 1993). The overt and insidious hegemony of such an approach has been extensively critiqued within the dance culture of the Occupied Palestinian Territories, with expressed fears that "Western cultural invasion increases day by day in our lives" (Alqam, 1994: 195). Such concerns can establish a polarity within local dance practices, dividing a community between those that seek to embrace and those that seek to reject foreign cultural influences (Rowe, 2008a).

Such hegemony and knowledge dependence is not limited to international exchange, however, but is also reflected in the more localised distinctions between urban and rural Palestine, and the contrasting cultures of land-owning city-dwellers and those dispossessed and in refugee camps. Within the *Our Kids* project, we could see that bringing experienced professional artists from the cities into refugee camps to give children workshops (even local artists teaching how to play local traditional music or perform local traditional dances) was also developing a knowledge dependency. It was clear that such activities could not be sustained within the local community in the absence of such highly trained teachers. Moreover, the increasing isolation of such communities through the actions of the Israeli military made the visits of such knowledge experts increasingly less viable. As the project transformed into the *Our Kids' Teachers* project in 2002, we therefore sought to refine our workshop models so that local people could feel empowered to build upon their own local artistic knowledge, rather than depend on experts from the city.

This therefore emphasised the importance of creativity within the workshop activities: that providing a space for children to generate and appreciate their own ways of moving was more sustainable and enriching for the community than providing skills training in particular dances. While this does not negate the value of technique training in particular dance styles, it suggests that such technique training is not fundamental to dance activities.

The task-based activities within *Art, during siege* therefore sought to foster creative, communicative and collaborative experiences that can be sustainably continued with the community and that leave it less reliant on external cultural intervention. To enable this, the dance activities were structured into the form of games, so that children in particular might feel enabled to initiate and direct dance activity spontaneously and independently, within unstructured and informal social learning contexts. The aim of these workshops was not to simply introduce a new set of artistic or cultural practices, but to stimulate new local forums that might promote the moving body as a location of cooperative, creative action.

A time to dance?

> There is a time to mourn and a time to dance.
>
> *(Ecclesiastes 3:4)*

This binary proposition, from the Old Testament, can make it hard for people in present-day Palestine to value dance during a period of collective tragedy. When a community is besieged by natural, economic or political crises, dancing can appear irrelevant, even offensive. Dancing can, however, provide an important social forum. In a bewildering world, dance can be a collective, kinaesthetic way of both realising and expressing new ideas. Removing it from daily life for a 'time to mourn' can thus compound the traumatic effects of a crisis.

Adapting dance practices to respond to precisely *when* and *for whom* the dance is taking place can open up possibilities for dance to remain a vital part of a community's culture. These queries can also provide valuable realisations regarding the nature of trauma and collective expression.

As a dance teacher, I continue to wrestle with ways of effectively understanding these and other issues surrounding how intercultural education projects might support, rather than hinder, greater cultural dynamism and local autonomy, and help sustain communities during periods of extended crisis. As environmental, political and economic disasters increasingly threaten communities around the world for extended periods, this remains a very salient line of enquiry.

References

Alexander, J.C., Eyerman, R., Giesen, B., Smelser, N.J. and Sztompka, P. (2004). *Cultural trauma and collective identity*. Berkeley: University of California Press.

Alqam, N. (1994). Dealing with our folk heritage. In Kanaana, S. (Ed.), *Folk heritage of Palestine* (pp. 179–210). Ramallah, Palestine: Al-Shark.

Anderson, B. (1991). *Imagined communities: reflections on the origins and spread of nationalism*. New York: Verso.

Bhabha, H. (1994). *The location of culture*. London: Routledge.

Boullata, K. (2004). Art under siege. *Journal of Palestine Studies*, 33(4), 70–84.

Clarke, D.B. (1973). The concept of community: a re-examination. *Sociological Review*, 21(3), 32–7.

Erikson, K. (1976). *Everything in its path*. New York: Simon and Schuster.

Escobar, A. (1995). *Encountering development*. Princeton, NJ: Princeton University Press.

Eyerman, R. (2001). *Slavery and the formation of African American identity*. Cambridge, MA: Cambridge University Press.

Fanon, F. (1986). *The wretched of the Earth*. London: Pluto Press (originally published in 1963).

Freire, P. (1972). *Pedagogy of the oppressed*. Harmondsworth: Penguin.

Harding, L. (2004). Europe has to take the initiative now: transcript of an interview between Daniel Barenboim, musical director of the Berlin Staatskapelle and the Chicago Symphony Orchestra, and Luke Harding of *The Guardian*. *The Guardian*. Retrieved from www.guardian.co.uk/israel/Story/0,2763,1362885,00.html [Accessed 7 December 2014].

Harris, D. (2007). Dance movement therapy approaches for fostering resilience and recovery among African adolescent torture survivors. *Torture*, 17(2), 134–55. Retrieved from www.irct.org/Admin/Public/DWSDownload.aspx?File=/Files/Filer/TortureJournal/17_2_2007/art_09.pdf [Accessed 7 December 2014].

Kaniasty, K. and Norris, F. (1999). The experience of disaster: individuals and communities sharing trauma. In R. Gist and B. Lubin (Eds.), *Response to disaster: psychosocial, community, and ecological approaches* (pp. 25–61). Ann Arbour, MI: Taylor and Francis.

Kimmerling, B. and Migdal, J. (1993). *Palestinians, the making of a people*. New York: Free Press.

Laban, R. (1956). *The principles of dance and movement notation*. London: Macdonald.

LaCapra, D. (2000). *Writing history, writing trauma*. Baltimore, MD: Johns Hopkins University Press.

Lugo, A. (1997). Reflections on border theory, culture, and the nation. In D.E. Johnson and S. Michaelson (Eds.), *Border theory* (pp. 43–67). Minneapolis, MN: University of Minnesota.

Ortiz, F. (1995). *Cuban counterpoint: sugar and tobacco*. Durham, NC: Duke University Press (originally published in 1940).

Rafeedie, M. (2008). Roadblock. In N. Jackson and T. Shapiro Phim (Eds.), *Dance, human rights and social justice: dignity in motion* (pp. 3–4). Lanham, MD: Scarecrow Press.

Rowe, N. (2003). *Art, during siege: performing arts workshops in traumatised communities*. Al-Bireh, Palestine: Popular Art Centre (English edition).

Rowe, N. (2004). *Art, during siege: performing arts workshops in traumatised communities*. Al-Bireh, Palestine: Popular Art Centre (Arabic edition).

Rowe, N. (2008a). Dance education in the Occupied Palestinian Territories: hegemony, counter-hegemony and anti-hegemony. *Research in Dance Education*, 9(1), 3–20.

Rowe, N. (2008b). Exposure and concealment. In N. Jackson and T. Shapiro Phim (Eds.), *Dance, human rights and social justice: dignity in motion* (pp. 291–5). Lanham, MD: Scarecrow Press.

Rowe, N. (2010). *Raising dust: a cultural history of dance in Palestine*. London: IB Tauris.

Rowe, N. (2011). Dance and political credibility: the appropriation of dabkeh by Zionism, Pan-Arabism and Palestinian Nationalism. *Middle East Journal*, 65(3), 363–80.

Said, E. (1993). *Culture and imperialism*. New York: Vintage Books.

Saunders, R. and Aghaie, K. (2005). Mourning and memory. *Comparative Studies of South Asia, Africa and the Middle East*, 25(1), 16–29.

Siegel, E. (1984). *Dance-movement therapy: the mirror of ourselves: a psychoanalytic approach*. New York: Human Sciences Press.

Smith-Autard, J. (1992). *Dance composition*. London: A & C Black.

Yalom, I.D. (1970). *The theory and practice of group psychotherapy*. New York: Basic Books.

2.3

THE POLITICS OF DANCE EDUCATION IN POST-REVOLUTIONARY CAIRO

Rosemary Martin

Hala's story

> I don't know if I will get to take class tomorrow, let alone next week. I would just like to learn, to express and to do the thing that I know I am supposed to do – dance.
>
> *(Hala, an 18-year-old female contemporary dance student)*

I interviewed Hala,[1] an 18-year-old female contemporary dance student, in a crowded café in a back street near Midan Talaat Harb in Downtown Cairo. It was June 2013, and I had previously met Hala as a 15-year-old dance student in a contemporary dance workshop I had taught in Alexandria a couple of years before. We had reconnected as I began to seek the stories and experiences of dancers who were working within the unique political context in Cairo for a new research project that was exploring dance in relation to the Arab Spring uprisings. Hala was eager to talk to me about the recent changes in Cairo and how they had impacted on her dance learning; however, some of her peers were a little more nervous to talk. They were more than happy to discuss dance but often a little apprehensive about speaking of politics, especially if they would be identified by name. Perhaps the prior relationship Hala and I had allowed for the ease of conversation.

As the political situation in Cairo changed, I became curious about how dancers, and particularly dance students, were negotiating these changes. As a researcher whose area of interest has been dance education within the Middle East, the context for conducting fieldwork in this region had also changed. Prior to the 2011 uprisings in Egypt, I found the discussion of political issues within interviews to be somewhat taboo, especially for those who were working within a state-supported dance environment. However, it appeared now that politics was a hot topic, and everyone in Cairo had an opinion, although not everyone was willing to talk about it 'on the record'. Things were changing so rapidly people were sometimes hesitant to put their name to their political opinion, and hangovers from the Mubarak regime still meant there was self-censorship that occurred, almost unconsciously. Nevertheless, when I heard Hala's words, points for discussion were illuminated in relation to the context and politics of dance education within a post-revolutionary Cairo.

I just want to learn how to be a good dancer, how to make my professional life as a dancer a success. It is hard enough, and then you have the revolution. At first it was a really inspiring moment, one that showed us new possibilities, opportunities and freedom we did not know of at that point as artists. But it was almost like it was too good to be true, it of course didn't eventuate in the way that we thought it would when we were in Tahrir Square in January 2011.

(Hala, June 2013)

Dance education possibilities in Cairo

Prior to January 2011, the context for dance education in Cairo could be viewed as not too dissimilar from other locations in the southern Mediterranean region. Hala's own dance background reflects this. She studied in a state-run institution promoting ballet and folkloric dance, and attended performances in state opera houses. She then discovered the small but bubbling contemporary dance scene that offered workshops and performances, which occupied more 'underground' performance venues (sometimes even literally underground). As Hala transitioned from high school to university, studying for a bachelor of theatre, she found that dance education is frequently part of theatre studies within tertiary institutions. However, the uprisings in 2011 resulted in specific shifts and changes in the Cairo dance scene, and within this dance education was in turn affected in various ways.

Since January 2011 Cairo has been experiencing a revolutionary wave. Prior to the uprisings, the main locations offering dance education in Cairo were The Egyptian Folkloric Dance Company, Higher Institute of Ballet and The Cairo Modern Dance School. All three are state-funded institutions engaged in the teaching and performance of ballet, folkloric and contemporary dance. Outside of these state-supported institutions there are independent dance centres such as Studio Emad Eddin, dance studios and formal dance education occurring within private and international schools within the greater Cairo region.

After the 2011 uprisings, a noticeable shift occurred in relation to dance education in Cairo. Prior to the uprisings a clear divide in the Cairo contemporary dance scene existed between those supported by The Egyptian Ministry of Culture (or working within one of their state-funded dance institutions) and those who were engaging with independent or private dance learning institutions. The overthrow of the Mubarak regime brought new possibilities and freedoms for dance education. Censorship regulations imposed under the emergency laws were null and void, and the liberal ideals many of the 2011 protestors carried into Tahrir Square were thought to allow potential for a more open artistic environment where a wide range of practices could occur. This atmosphere appeared to exist for a brief period, when the Cairo Contemporary Dance Center was restructured, the D-CAF Festival emerged and numerous public dance performances, many of which were site-specific responses, were occurring.

Mounir's site-specific performance

A work that perhaps demonstrated this new-found freedom and use of public space that was previously devoid of performance was by Mounir Saeed, who choreographed a short work entitled *Small story* for the D-CAF Festival which took place from 29 March to 14 April 2012. In Borsa, a popular café area near the Egyptian Stock Exchange, Mounir staged his performance. It began in the centre of a pedestrian street and then weaved in and around the cafés and shops in the narrow side streets. With Mounir as the sole dancer commanding the paved pedestrian street with slow movements – rippling through from shoulder to fingertip, top of head to toes, back to front, shoulder to hand, and knee to hip – people who were walking by seemed to stop for a fleeting moment, look, then look again before continuing on their journey.

It was when Mounir's movement became more vigorous with jumps, rolls to the floor and turns that the audience began to gather, clustering together initially until a circle formed around Mounir and he had to break through the crowd to begin his journey to the outside seating area of a café. He sat down in a white plastic chair, resting one heel up on his opposite knee, and began an intricate phrase of gesture. Once again Mounir built his movement up from slow to violently fast, until he slapped his own face, and then slapped it again. He stood up carefully and continued to take his audience down into a small side street where the performance continued.

The sight of someone dancing in the street drew in a number of passers-by. Shopkeepers emerged from doorways, a truck driver stopped and began filming the performance on his mobile phone, something that raises the notion of medialisation of global events, an issue that has been frequently documented within the emerging scholarship of the Arab Spring uprisings across the southern Mediterranean region (Dabashi, 2012; Gelvin, 2012; Noueihed and Warren, 2012). A group of police officers gave the show two thumbs up, a sight that would not have been seen prior to the Arab Spring events. However, the optimism demonstrated in Mounir's performance did not survive long within the dance environment in Cairo. As the uprisings continued and government ministers changed, plans that offered so much potential were placed to one side.

Dancing demands for dance education

In June 2013 artists – dancers, choreographers, actors, musicians, directors, writers, painters – occupied The Ministry of Culture demanding changes. Many of the dancers involved in this occupation were dance students and staff from the Higher Institute of Ballet and the Cairo Contemporary Dance Center. These students and staff were demanding access to dance education in Cairo, an education they had worked hard to re-imagine in the post-2011 revolutionary environment in Cairo.

During the occupation of The Ministry of Culture, numerous dance activities were occurring in response to this demand for change. As a researcher I followed these events closely, even when out of the country. I kept in close contact with those who were participating in these activities, hearing their stories and also reading the media coverage that was documenting this occupation. A group of dance students performed in one of the metro stations of Cairo on 2 July 2013. Since the occupation of the Ministry began, artists have been performing in the streets or on makeshift stages in Cairo, dance students and educators have joined these protests and an uncertainty looms in the future for those wishing to engage with dance both informally and formally.

I feel that dance education in Cairo will continue in a sporadic nature for some time, until the wider sociopolitical context settles, but it will continue. It will continue in part due to the few dedicated dance educators, choreographers and performers who understand the vital importance of maintaining locations and practices for individuals to learn and develop their dance. For dance researchers there is an exciting realm of study in Cairo, one that requires much more scholarly investigation and writings. However, simultaneously such research requires immense sensitivity, patience and awareness of cultural specificities. The words of the young dance student in Cairo perhaps provide a summative conclusion to the transient and fluid nature of dance and dance education in Cairo:

> I want to be a dancer. I have wanted to be a dancer for as long as I can remember. To get to the point where I can study dance, to receive my education in dance, has been extremely difficult. . . . It has become worse, it is hard just to dance now because of the situation here.

Note

1 Hala's name has been changed for ethical reasons.

References

Dabashi, H. (2012). *The Arab Spring: the end of postcolonialism*. London: Zed Books.

Gelvin, J.L. (2012). *The Arab uprisings: what everyone needs to know*. Oxford: Oxford University Press.

Ghonim, W. (2012). *Revolution 2.0: the power of the people is greater than the people in power: a memoir*. New York: Houghton Mifflin Harcourt.

Noueihed, L. and Warren, A. (2012). *The battle for the Arab Spring: revolution, counter-revolution and the making of a new era*. New Haven: Yale University Press.

Ramsis, A. (2011). *Forbidden/Mamnou*. Documentary film, 67 minutes, Egypt/Spain.

2.4

TRADITIONAL DANCE IN GHANAIAN SCHOOLS

Maintaining national identity through the involvement of youth and children

Beatrice Ayi

Introduction

> Vibrating rhythms from Ghanaian traditional drums and gongs break through the silent atmosphere on my school compound. It's Friday afternoon and time to dance. I make my way to the large shed designated for dancing and other cultural activities. Dancers gather around the musicians who are seated at one end of the shed, while observers encircle them. Rhythms intensify, singers clap and sing as loud as their voices permit, the atmosphere is charged and dancing begins! Our little bodies perform a series of isolations, with jerky torso contractions, poking arm movements and feet gently caressing the smooth concrete floor.

Dancing at the age of seven was an anticipated moment for me as a child. A moment to physically interpret rhythms that bubbled in me while observing our dance teacher display her dancing skill. It was a time to connect with other pupils as we shared an experience that knitted us together as children of our motherland. As a Ghanaian who was born and nurtured in Ghana, I think of dance not only as a way of life, but also as our breath. Dance is the life centre of the Ghanaian.[1] It permeates all of our social and ceremonial activities. It forms an integral part of all the vital facets of our life cycles. Dance welcomes the newborn child into his community, and bids him farewell at his departure from this Earth. In sum, dance reflects the culture of the Ghanaian and subsequently serves as a symbol of our identity.

The memories of my dance experience at Services Primary School in Accra described above fill my mind as I reflect on the teaching of traditional dances in Ghanaian schools. I had minimal understanding of what I was engaged in at the time, but enjoyed every bit of the dance sessions. As I progressed through the various stages in my primary education, my enthusiasm for dance increased. Joy bubbled in my being anytime I heard the sound of music from traditional drums, and that was enough to keep me under the shed for the entire duration of the dance class. We were privileged to have some members of the nation's dance ensemble as resource persons who visited our class occasionally.

Construction of national identity

Teaching traditional dance in Ghanaian schools has not only served its primary purpose of providing knowledge of Ghanaian culture, but has also indirectly provided an opportunity for the perpetuation of the nation's dance heritage, and subsequently maintenance of national identity. Liora Bresler emphasises that music and the arts are valuable assets for constructing a nation's identity, and are thus held in high esteem in many parts of the world when there is the need for "ideological changes and national independence" (2000: 3). In Ghana, for instance, our numerous traditional dance forms proved invaluable at the time when we needed a national identity.

When Ghana gained independence in 1957, after several years of British colonial rule, the nation was tribally divided, and tribes were symbols of identity. There was therefore the need to construct a national identity and a symbol that would unite and inspire us to work towards a common goal – the development of the nation. The first president of Ghana, Dr Kwame Nkrumah, acknowledging the fact that dance cuts across linguistic and ethnic barriers, encouraged and supported the establishment of the Institute of African Studies at the University of Ghana[2] and the Institute of Arts and Culture in the heart of the capital city, to publicise traditional dance forms of various ethnic groups. Nkrumah mandated the two institutes to recruit and train dancers to perform, as well as teach a collection of traditional dances created by various ethnic groups in Ghana.

By this act of publicising the collection of dances, which represented our national dance heritage, individuals became aware of the numerous traditional dance forms in Ghana and were able to better appreciate them as a symbol of national identity. Thus, traditional Ghanaian dance forms that once identified individual ethnic groups became a collective identity of an entire nation.

Preservation of national identity and transmission of dance heritage

To ensure that the nation's identity was not short-lived, subsequent governments after Nkrumah paid attention to the perpetuation of the Ghanaian dance heritage. The Provisional National Defense Council administration led by Flight Lieutenant Jerry Rawlings, for example, encouraged the teaching of traditional dance by putting physical education and dance together as one non-examinable subject in the national school curriculum, making it possible for dance to be taught as an extra-curricular activity in many schools. This positioning of dance in an academic institution facilitated the formal transmission of the nation's dance heritage.

Educational reforms in Ghana paved the way for an outburst of traditional dance performances in schools. Gone were the days when children were taught several traditional dances without an avenue for performance of what had been learned. Today, occasions such as annual speech and prize-giving day celebrations, founder's day events, graduation ceremonies and the Ghana Education Services' annual cultural competition offer opportunities for youth and children to put on astounding dance performances in display of what has been taught in schools. It is worth noting that the same celebrations and ceremonies occurred in the past, yet with no traditional dance opportunities for pupils.

Two decades after dancing under a shed and on a concrete floor, I still find myself involved with traditional dance, not as a pupil, but rather as a teacher and resource person. Some observations made while engaging with traditional dance in some basic schools in Ghana illuminate the role of youth and children in the perpetuation of the nation's dance heritage. Participation in and performance of traditional dances in basic schools in urban areas are open to the entire school population, although only a small section of pupils who have a keen interest in dance and do not feel shy about performing before a large group of people are involved.

This notwithstanding, almost all the pupils in one way or the other tend to have knowledge of dances that were taught during a school term, and they might also be able to perform them. How did that happen? How did they learn to perform the dances? In my observation of teaching and performance of dance in basic schools, I noticed that many pupils who participate in the school's organised teaching sessions tend to teach those who do not. This happens most often during the lunch break period and at the close of school when pupils are out of class. During these times, pupils who have been taught various dances take pride in displaying their skills, and in the process other pupils also learn the various dances from their peers.

Furthermore, pupils who do not participate in the teaching sessions, but are usually present as spectators, tend to learn by active observation. Thus, whether learned directly from a dance teacher or indirectly from their peers, pupils engage with traditional dances while in school: either through performing at school functions, participating in cultural competitions or simply dancing for the fun that dances provide. These activities of pupils in basic schools across the nation contribute to the transmission of the nation's dance heritage and the preservation of national identity.

Upholding national dance heritage for posterity

The nation's dance heritage offers an opportunity for youth and children in Ghana to develop a sense of belonging and pride as citizens through knowledge of and participation in dance forms that are grounded in Ghanaian traditions. Thus, there is the need to ensure its continuity and authenticity for posterity. Upholding the Ghanaian dance heritage (a traditional dance heritage which is a symbol of national identity) is crucial in this era of increasing global cultural interactions, which have the potential of impacting performing arts in particular and the field of the arts in general.

Through such interactions there is the possibility of abandoning one's own dance form for what may be considered strikingly different and aesthetically appealing, and in the process forfeiting a symbol that identifies the nation. The involvement of youth and children/pupils in upholding the Ghanaian dance heritage ensures that the future custodians who will be responsible for its transmission and preservation for posterity are adequately equipped for the task.

Additionally, the educational reforms that took place in Ghana after independence that were reinforced by successive governments, resulting in the inclusion of dance in national school curricula, have proved to be valuable; they provided and continue to create an avenue for youth and children/pupils in urban settings to formally learn about and participate in cultural practices that breathe life into our existence as Ghanaians and set us apart as Africans.

Notes

1 Dance is the life centre of Africans in general, but for the purposes of this case narrative, the Ghanaian has been singled out.
2 In addition to its mandate as discussed in the text, the Institute of African Studies also conducts interdisciplinary research on Africa's cultural heritage and disseminates its findings.

Reference

Bresler, L. (2000). The relationships of school arts, national goals, and multilayered cultures. *Arts Education Policy Review*, 101(5), 3–8.

2.5

NEGOTIATING MULTIPLE SPHERES OF IDENTITY

A Filipino dance community in Toronto, Canada

Catherine Limbertie

Introduction

Toronto is one of the most culturally diverse cities in the world and remains consistently in the top ranks of "the ten most liveable cities in the world" as judged by *The Economist* (28 August 2013). Results are based on scoring in stability, healthcare, culture, environment, education and infrastructure. In the global urban inventory, my hometown is one where diversity works to create a successful civic environment. There are many means by which diversity is expressed, but I believe that dance has a particularly important role to play in helping Torontonians embody their diversity. My study highlights the Filipino community in Toronto.

Fiesta Filipina

As director of the Community Folk Art Council of Toronto from 1996–2001, I was able to see the power of dance at work in hundreds of cultural communities across the country first hand. I had a special connection with one group in particular: Fiesta Filipina, a Filipino ensemble based in Mississauga, just west of Toronto. George and Estrellita Aguinaldo founded Fiesta in 1966 with the mission to promote, preserve and propagate Filipino arts and culture in Canada. By training first family members, then friends and ultimately admirers in Filipino dance and music-making, the Aguinaldos created a dance ensemble that today serves as an ambassador of Filipino dance in Canada and internationally. In 2004, Fiesta was able to purchase its own building, the Fiesta Filipina Centre for the Arts, where classes, rehearsals and performances are held in Filipino dance and music.

Some characteristics of Filipino dance

The Philippines is a nation of 7,000 islands at the crossroads of many Pacific trading routes, and many cultural influences may be clearly seen in the dances performed by Fiesta Filipina. The aboriginal repertoire of dances referred to as the *Cordillera Suite* pays homage to the Igorot, tribal ancestors of Filipinos, and exhibits a style of movement and dress that is quite different from dances introduced in the later periods of Filipino culture. European contact in the six-teenth century is reflected in the *Spanish Suite* of dances where costuming is much more modest, featuring long, sweeping skirts and lace-covered bodices for the women while the men wear trousers and barong Tagalogs. The dances of the *Morolandia Suite* find their origin in Mindanao, the second largest island of the Philippines that is highly influenced by Islam. The music is an eclectic mixture of percussive gamelan and drum. Movement is abrupt and explosive, the men wearing loosely fitting trousers and vests while the women preen in their richly embroidered sarongs. Terno-clad women perform the rural dances with a loosely flowing skirt while the men wear trousers and the barong Tagalog. The music is a lilting instrumentation of bandurria and guitar that echoes the sustained circular movement of the dance.

Research into experiences of young Filipino dancers

As part of a research project, in 2009 I attended the 'Christmas around the World' festival at Toronto's City Hall Rotunda to observe the participation of Fiesta Filipina in this community event. In 2010 I visited Fiesta Filipina Centre for the Arts to carry out fieldwork by inviting members of the intermediate dance group, aged 12–14, to complete a survey for this study and I attended the 'Easter around the World' festival at City Hall Rotunda. I interviewed Lito Dizon and Josefina Clemente, former dancers with Fiesta, to discuss the roles played by gender, iden-tity and self when teaching and performing dance.

In the ten-question survey, I began by asking the young people why they wanted to join Fiesta Filipina. They said that dance played a strong role in their decision to participate in the

PHOTO 2.5.1 "Pamaypay Sa Maynila", Fiesta Filipina.
Photographer: Personal collection Fiesta Filipina

ensemble. Although Fiesta is involved in many activities, it is primarily through dance that members developed a link to their Filipino heritage. The cultural information contained in dance served in defining a particular culture and was transferrable to its practitioners. Fiesta Filipina (Photo 2.5.1) facilitated meeting "new friends" and thus permitted the introduction of like-minded persons to one another.

Fiesta's membership requirements entailed significant time and financial commitment; clearly, the attractions of participating in the Fiesta community were sufficient in overcoming barriers created by its somewhat remote location, weekend scheduling and financial considerations. The opportunities for travel and adventure and a willingness to take the risk of creating bridges with outside organisations while preserving their Filipino identity was also important. This reinforced an impressive ability to negotiate multiple spheres of identity while performing with members of a 'second family'. One participant articulated this and this also showed that the bonding capital within Fiesta provided a 'safe haven' for the young dancers. Others shared the importance of performing Filipino culture, citing it as "expressive culture" and stating the desire to "keep it alive," indicating awareness of the importance of dance in cultural transmission as well as its fragility. Some simply appreciated the benefits to their health and body control provided by dance practice.

When asking members to assign a value to their membership in Fiesta Filipina, the positive response was unsurprising as they would not otherwise be in a rehearsal hall on a Sunday afternoon. Did they practise other forms of dance? Most specified participation in a broad variety of dance styles. This was consistent with the Fiesta Filipina practice of including diverse dance genres in their repertoire, mirroring the heterogeneous nature of Filipino culture as well as an accepted practice at international dance festivals accredited by the International Council of Organizations of Folklore Festivals (CIOFF), a UNESCO-affiliated institution. When participating in a CIOFF festival, visitors always prepared dances in the style of the host country, which also demonstrates virtuosity of identity negotiation as noted above.

Is the ensemble open to outsiders? There was an overwhelmingly positive response, again reiterating the strong social function within Fiesta. It also confirmed the powerful force of dance in developing identity along with the virtuosity of Fiesta members in negotiating multiple identities. Outsiders posed no threat to this tightly knit ensemble, although one respondent pointed out that a newcomer might "feel lost in the Filipino community at first." Members were anxious that newcomers learnt the skills of identity negotiation that they themselves had mastered and were willing to teach through example. By enquiring whether membership in Fiesta made them feel more Filipino, I addressed one of the major criticisms of multiculturalism as Canadian social policy that supposedly reinforces feelings of exclusion or otherness. Survey respondents' replies indicated that a feeling of 'Filipino-ness' increased when dancing as a member of Fiesta, but this sentiment was perceived as a positive attribute and a valuable addition to their sense of self.

When asked whether they felt more attachment to Canada or to the Philippines, choosing between various spheres of identity, the replies pointed to a well-developed ability to negotiate multiple selves, showing attachment to both Canadian and Filipino identities. Some did express a marked, but not unexpected, preference for the Philippines; the survey was, after all, conducted in a space marked by Filipino dance, music, food and costume. The virtuosic negotiation of multiple spheres of identity is striking and indeed encouraged by Fiesta staff who supply both Filipino and North American food, dance and music during rehearsals. I asked them about the

PHOTO 2.5.2 "Polka Ball", Fiesta Filipina.
    Photographer: Personal collection Fiesta Filipina

role they felt Fiesta played in the Filipino community and it was deemed important that Fiesta helped members stay in touch with their Filipino heritage and kept the community together – again showing the power of dance as a vehicle of identity. The importance of teaching Filipino culture to outsiders and the importance of dance as an articulator of expressive heritage were also highlighted. Finally, I asked them to reflect on their own position within the context of Fiesta Filipina and the Filipino community. Here they attached great importance to the role played by Fiesta within the Filipino community and stated that membership in the ensemble validated their position as 'ambassadors' for Filipino culture (Photo 2.5.2) through dance practice, adding value to their status as members of the Filipino community.

Conclusion

The young dancer-members of Fiesta Filipina are able to negotiate multiple spheres of identities with virtuosity to both embrace and transcend diversity. Within a cultural community, dance serves both to create and maintain strong community networks. The semiotic vocabulary of dance as practised by members of Fiesta Filipina transmits Filipino culture to an audience. The body as a cultural text acts as a bridge between performer and spectator, facilitating discourse. Otherness is both reinforced and transcended; diversity is celebrated and embraced. Through dance, members of Fiesta Filipina are bringing about change by breaking down barriers of otherness.

PART III

Embodiment and creativity in dance teaching

PHOTO 3.0 Young people communicating through dance.
Photographer: Renato Brandjolica

3.1

DANCE AS EMBODIED DIALOGUE

Insights from a school project in Finland

Eeva Anttila

Introduction

Engagement with art often fuels transformative processes. The catalyst behind many dance educators' deep commitment to their work may lie in their personal experiences of transformation through dance. A desire to share and lead others towards similar processes motivates many of us, including myself. These experiences seem to be fundamental in the sense that they amplify the embodied nature of our existence as human beings. They also appear to expand into many areas of life and be present even when we are not dancing and moving. The sense of movement and interest in the meaning of movement seeps everywhere to those of us who engage deeply with this art form. But can dance be meaningful for all human beings, and if so, how? It is evident that not all human beings enjoy dance, and that all experiences related to dance are not necessarily constructive. Feelings of frustration, pain, boredom and shame are all too common among dance students and professionals alike.

Research in dance education is important in generating deeper understanding of the vulnerable and delicate qualities of dance experience, especially in educational contexts. It may be that the holistic, all-encompassing nature of dance is the origin of these deep experiences, both constructive and destructive. Being increasingly aware of the many shades of feelings and meanings that dance may generate can be considered an element of conscious and socially just dance pedagogy. It is crucial that we, as dance educators, take responsibility for our own actions in facilitating these processes and ask: under what conditions can dance be transformative? Is change always a positive phenomenon? What kinds of ethical issues are connected to embodied, potentially transformative activities like dance?

The topic of this chapter is related to these broad questions. It stems from a five-year-long dance education project and a broad study that accompanied it. The purpose of the study was to document and evaluate the project and to unravel the meaning of dance and embodied learning within the school community. Whereas the study aimed to develop a conception of dance as embodied *learning*, in this chapter the focus is on dance as embodied *dialogue*. These concepts are certainly concurrent, since embodied learning is thoroughly intertwined with social and physical reality.[1] The significance of human community as a learning environment is indispensable (see, for example, Wenger, 2009). This long-standing view seems to often be forgotten when virtual means of communication become more prevalent, even in education. It is noteworthy that recent findings in neuroscience affirm face-to-face human interaction as an essential condition for learning and highlight that social cognition develops largely through attending to others' bodily gestures and movements (see, for example, Gallese *et al.*, 2004; Hari and Kujala, 2009).

Although the focus of the study was on a particular school, the aim was to discuss the educational value of dance and embodiment in any school context and to ignite discussion about the significance of embodied learning and the arts education in all learning. Thus, a wider focus on educational policies and school reforms formed a backdrop for the study. The findings and insights this project has generated for me have reinforced my interest in the significance of embodied interaction in strengthening a sense of community, a question that has been important to me for many years (see, for example, Anttila, 2003, 2007a, 2007b).

"The entire school dances!"

The dance education project, entitled "The entire school dances!", was connected to a national arts education project funded by the Ministry of Education and the City of Vantaa (see www.taikalamppu.fi/eng). It introduced dance to all students at Kartanonkoski public school in an attempt to facilitate accessibility of dance, irrespective of students' age, gender or socioeconomic background. The project aimed to enhance the role of embodiment in all learning and develop democratic, collaborative pedagogical practices that involve individuals and communities in a holistic way.

I have been grappling with the notion of embodied learning for several years (see, for example, Anttila, 2007c; Anttila and Sansom, 2012). My interest in this phenomenon has intensified into a need to understand the meaning of the body in learning. My curiosity has been fuelled by new discoveries in literature from various fields, including the empirical sciences.[2] Also, disturbing indications concerning the effects of physical passivity and social isolation on the development of the cognitive system (see, for example, Goddard Blythe, 2009) have prompted me towards conducting projects like this.

A full-time, professional dance teacher, hired by and for the project, was responsible for dance instruction. Since dance is not an independent subject in the Finnish national curriculum, it was integrated into other subjects and dance instruction was intended to support the learning goals of the particular subject. The dance teacher thus collaborated with classroom teachers and subject teachers, who were invited to suggest topics they would like to explore through dance. The areas that were covered in dance ranged from geometry to language arts, history to biology, and from abstract concepts like symmetry and identity to practical skills such as motor and social skills. The Kartanonkoski school teachers were also encouraged to integrate dance and creative movement activities in their own classrooms. They could develop ideas from the dance classes as they were encouraged to participate. They also had opportunities for their own dance classes and professional development training in dance and embodied learning.

As the researcher and project leader, I was responsible for planning the content of the teachers' professional development. I was also the chair of the project steering group and mentor for the dance teacher in pedagogical planning and individual professional development. My multiple roles gave me an opportunity to engage with the community in various ways and develop pedagogical approaches in collaboration with the school community. Although this particular school was a target of intervention, in many ways the study focused on the educational value of dance from a wider perspective. Specifically, it tackled the question of dance as a special form of embodied learning. As a devoted dance educator myself, I was personally involved in all stages of the project. In the end, the study was also a personal trial where my own presuppositions concerning the transformative power of dance were contested as they faced the diverse reality of school life, students' fluctuating interests and motivational states, and teachers' various levels of commitment to the project.

In this project dance was seen as an inclusive force – not just meant for students with special talent and the economic resources to participate in, for example, after-school studies in the arts. It was vital to me that all students should have an opportunity to experience dance. Previously, I had been involved in dance projects in school contexts with only one or two groups of students. Typically, such projects last for one academic year or less. A four-year project that involved an entire K-9 school with 800 students and 50 teachers was a major intervention and provided a special opportunity to gain a deeper insight into the educational value of dance, and to probe my ideas about embodied learning in practice.

As a pedagogical approach, embodied learning is demanding for many teachers, as it transforms the classroom from a silent, motionless space into a space full of motion and sound. It may appear disordered and even chaotic, and indeed, it is more difficult to manage and control. Often, the first challenge for pupils is related to learning how to work without a chair, desk, pen, paper and books – something to hold on to. Pupils are used to being constantly instructed, to pedagogies where knowledge is structured and embodiment is restrained. Embodied learning generates a very different learning environment: open space to be filled by relatively self-directed movement. At first, this situation tends to create either inhibitions or excess movement and noise. Learning to move in a coherent and integrated manner in relation to others focusing on the task at hand, and with your own movement possibilities, is a huge leap – a practice of freedom.

Embodied learning regards the human body as the foundation, locus and medium for all learning. It entails that embodied activity is a fundamental element in learning. Embodied activity, here, refers both to actual movement and to inner bodily sensations, experiences and physiological changes. The aim is to connect movement and concept in space and time so that reflection takes place simultaneously with action. Reflection continues after action in the form of sharing experiences and ideas, where bodily knowledge becomes translated into language, concepts, meanings and interpretation. This process is a cycle where non-symbolic sensation generated by movement and physicality lead into complex meaning-making processes within the social and cultural world. This is how the living, organic body and the lived, phenomenal body may become interconnected (see Thompson, 2007). Reality and imagination may intertwine in these creative processes, and the borders between science and art may also become blurred.

Research as collaboration

Collaboration and dialogue are important to me not only in education, but also in research. My previous research endeavours have drawn mainly from action research. This study is also based on action research. In addition it is inspired by communicative evaluation research (Niemi, 1999). Participatory or collaborative action research is conducted with people rather than on people, and it is based on the participation of the entire community. It aims to give voice to the school community: all students, teachers, parents and staff, as well as the researcher (Reason, 2002; Reason and Bradbury, 2008). Communicative evaluation research considers the researcher a tutor and a subject in the research process and is interested in developing cultural understandings within different communicative subsystems (Guba and Lincoln, 1989; Niemi, 1999). Egon G. Guba and Yvonna S. Lincoln (1989) introduced the notion of "fourth generation evaluation," which departs from measurement, description and judgement and considers results of evaluation as collaboratively created constructions that are related to phenomena that bear meaning to the members of the community.

A wide variety of data were collected from students, teachers, parents and staff. The methods included interviews, written feedback, journals, observation and videotaping. The data provided a broad and rich base for interpretative analysis. Analysing and interpreting the data was a tremendous but exciting task that I undertook with a certain humbleness, acknowledging that even these data are just a peek into the wide array of experiences that the members of this school community may have in connection to the project. The interpretations that I will soon present do not depict a unified, coherent picture of what took place and what was accomplished. They are a collection of diverse constructions that portray the wide variety of experiences, views and conceptions that selected members of the school community revealed to me.

The notion of embodied dialogue rises from the data as one of the main findings. Embodied dialogue is a crystallisation of various interpretations that I have constructed through a long and deep thematic analysis that has consisted of several cycles of reading, reflecting, negotiating, condensing and finally crystallising the meanings that have risen from both textual data and my embodied experiences and observations in the school. Next, I will elucidate how I have arrived at this interpretation. I will do this by presenting voices from the school community.

Dance as embodied dialogue

In the interviews, I asked the pupils to tell me about their experiences and opinions of the dance classes, and also to express their views about dance as a part of school life, curriculum and learning. They spoke about their need for action and collaboration, about their willingness to face challenges and make their own choices. Boys and girls of all grade levels seemed to appreciate the physicality, challenge and joy that dance may involve. Some students addressed this desire for movement in plain words. A 3rd grade boy said that, "it is just what I need, movement and action." An older boy (7th grade) expressed this by stating that, "in dance you don't have to be quiet and sit and slouch at your desk all the time." The same desire is reflected in a 9th grade girl's account, when she said that, "in dance you get to do things yourself and move. You don't have to sit at your desk." The pupils were also directly asked if dance classes included difficult or boring elements. Some pupils responded that slow, ordinary or simple movements were boring: "Peaceful [movements], they are perhaps boring. Inventing [movements] and fast movements, those are perhaps fun" (girl, 1st grade). In all, they seemed to appreciate physical challenge and action that keeps them engaged. This desire seems to be common for boys and girls, from elementary years onward to the last grade of secondary school. In my interpretation, embodied, physical activity is the first, albeit obvious, element of embodied dialogue.

The second element in embodied dialogue, also self-evidently, is collaboration. The pupils expressed a strong desire for collaboration with their peers. Even talking to others during class was welcomed, as one boy (7th grade) stated in an upfront way: "[In dance] you get to move much more and even talk to your mates." Another 7th grader (boy) appreciated the possibility for decision-making in groups: "[In dance] you get to be with your friends and make decisions." Decision-making was often connected with compositional tasks and creating performances. A girl (4th grade) said that, "I like when we do our own performances with friends, that is nice." Another girl (9th grade) appreciated that in dance "everyone gets to do things together. . . . Group spirit, somehow. Then it is easy to perform together." In these accounts, another element of embodied dialogue appears. This element is related to performing. I will return to this somewhat more unexpected topic shortly.

Before performing, there is the process of creating the performance. This creative process can be seen not only as creating a choreography, but also as practising performing. Practising performing entails not only learning to dance and memorising the choreography, but also practising to take part in collaborative, performative action that involves negotiation, decision-making, opinion-stating and demonstrating one's own ideas not only in words, but also with the entire body. This process is deeply and comprehensively about embodied dialogue and democratic life. As the project proceeded and the pupils expressed their desire for collaboration and their own choices, more emphasis on composing dances and choreographic tasks was given within dance classes. They reflected on their experiences in the following ways:

> [In dance] you get to invent your own things and you don't have to do the same than others all the time.
>
> *(Girl, 4th grade)*

> It was easy, you could make up your own movements . . . it would be fun to be able to suggest the dance things, different dances, street dance and others, and then, to choose, and to perform them.
>
> *(Boy, 5th grade)*

> It is fun when you can decide the movements yourself, that you are not compelled, you do not have to do something and you have influence.
>
> *(Girl, 8th grade)*

Over time, the pupils also developed skills in creating movements and making decisions in groups concerning the composition, music and style of dance. Teachers observed changes in pupils' skills as well. One teacher reflected that:

> The joy of dancing is visible. Inventiveness and the ability to put themselves on the line has developed. The children have developed courage in bringing forth their own ideas and thoughts.

According to the dance teacher, "enthusiasm in creating own dances and especially the skills in making them has developed enormously during the project." She also reflects on the gradual process where courage to perform and be seen develops. It seems that pupils have a desire to become seen, but for many, social pressures are often an obstacle. Thus, self-confidence and being seen may develop through embodied dialogue:

> It is about everyone becoming seen . . . when they create these small group compositions and perform them to each other, it is always a triumph when a pupil who did not agree

to perform at first performs and then it is not a difficult thing anymore, and everyone performs their piece to each other, and then we applaud each other.

One girl (4th grade) expressed this sensation clearly: "First, during one second, you feel something down in your stomach, and then it just makes you smile." This kind of embodied experience is something that does not happen every day. It stands out as something extraordinary. In my interpretation, this kind of extraordinary embodied and communal experience constitute experiences that seem to stand out, where an individual's embodied sensation becomes intertwined and shared within a community. Here, a sense of community is created, and at the same time the individual becomes empowered as a member of this community. The courage to step on stage, to become seen and to become accepted in a shared, communal event may also strengthen self-confidence, which in turn makes the next performing situation maybe even more pleasurable. The dance teacher contemplates that, "maybe self-confidence becomes stronger when you are being seen all the time and produce movement." The last part of her account is highly interesting from the viewpoint of embodiment. Producing movement is a visible and concrete way of becoming seen. A classroom teacher (2nd grade) ponders this multifaceted phenomenon where individual and communal experiences intertwine in the following way:

> When everyone gets to do and explore themselves, it is important that they can do this without an audience but also with an audience. Both are important.

Another teacher said that dance has "a positive collective effect on the atmosphere in the school community and a positive individual effect on body image." Also, parents seem to appreciate this connection between individual and collective effects. They reported that in their view dance "supports self-expression and gives courage to perform" and it "develops body awareness and self-image, and creates the sense of community."

All three principals of the school talked about the positive, lively and communal atmosphere that dance has supported. They also reported that in general, inhibitions towards performing have decreased during the project significantly:

> Our pupils really perform, and they have the joy of performing.
>
> They have a really low threshold to come and perform, they have the readiness to step in front of others and let their body be seen.
>
> The project has encouraged our pupils and they are much more enthusiastic about dancing and performing than I noticed before . . . the pupils are more courageous and daring because everyone does it in school.

Based on this study, it seems that dance may trigger a positive cycle where an individual's bodily experiences become intertwined with the pleasure of collaboration. An essential element in this process seems to be the awareness of everyone's participation in dance instruction. This awareness enhances a communal experience that everyone shares. It seems to reduce embarrassment, prejudices and fears towards bodily expression and performing.

Performing appears to be an important path towards bodily awareness and self-confidence. It becomes possible when self-confidence develops, and strengthens it further. Witnessing each other performing seems to create a sense of being recognised and being seen, and this creates a common experience that builds a sense of community that developed within specific classrooms, and through common events and performances extended and affected the entire school community. Here, in my interpretation, sensing one's own body and sensing others became intertwined, and this is how embodied dialogue becomes manifested. A sense of community, then, can be understood as an embodied phenomenon. Performing, including actual performances as well as everyday performative acts, can be seen as embodied and communal events where communities are in motion, or in the making.

When the project ended in May 2013, it was evident that dance was a part of everyday life of the Kartanonkoski school. Pupils and teachers were used to dance being part of the curriculum, and most of them had also accepted it. Dance was not mere recreation and deviation from routine; it affected the way of being in school, as well as the energy and atmosphere within the school. It is evident that dance generated versatile learning experiences within the school community. These experiences are reflected in a comfortable manner in relating to embodiment, bodily expressivity, interaction and performing. I will close this section with an account from a member of the steering group:

> At best, dance was like connecting glue that united the whole school together.

This sentence contains key elements that elucidate the educational power of dance for me. The beginning, "at best" denotes that not every kind of dance works positively for every individual and for every community. This study illuminates that pupils appreciate the possibility to make choices, work together and create their own dances – to be engaged in embodied dialogue. The phrase "connecting glue" reflects how powerful the impact can be – at best. And finally, "whole school" implies that when dance is introduced as a democratic, inclusive practice, it may bring about change that is not imposed, but created from within the community. I suggest that this may be the crucial component of transformative yet ethical arts education.

Conclusion: becoming political

Embodiment is a neglected topic in teacher training and in the pedagogical practices in the Finnish school system; for instance, one teacher reported to me that she had not learned anything about embodied learning in her recent classroom teacher studies. The national curriculum is subject driven and this caused many obstacles for dance instruction during this project. Lack of time, a packed curriculum and teachers' professional autonomy dictate the everyday life and pedagogical practices. Based on this study, it seems that possibilities for teachers' collaboration should be increased. This way, the teachers could give diverse models for collaboration, interaction and bodily expressivity for their pupils.

In technologically developed societies, the need for physical, embodied action in everyday chores, communication and expression is diminishing. For children the lack of physical daily activity may be critical. Diverse physical activity is the basis for sound development and learning. When embodied action involving the whole body becomes gradually replaced by interaction in a virtual world where buildings can be constructed and wars can be fought without using physical force, understanding physical and social reality may become seriously compromised. When social interaction becomes increasingly virtual, the development of social cognition, compassion and emotional life may take a new track, not yet understood by scholars, let alone parents and teachers.

Neglecting the body as the primary locus and medium of learning may have consequences way beyond what we have seen already. The recent drop in Finland's PISA-results (Program for

International Student Assessment; see OECD, 2013) reflects this alarming trend. To date, there seems to be little research that focuses on the significance of everyday physical activity in early childhood for overall development and learning, let alone their social skills and ability to take part in a democratic society. It may well be that neglecting the body will result in serious problems in learning and development for children. Diminishing bodily activity poses formidable threats to the future of humankind, not only in the form of deteriorating physical health and holistic well-being, but also in learning and the overall development of human potential (see, for example, Goddard Blythe, 2009; Hartley, 2004). The question is, how long will it take for educators to acknowledge that the educational practice has to respond to the change in lifestyle?

The findings of "The entire school dances!" and the accompanying study illuminate students' need for more action, choice, collaboration and fun in school. With increasing physical passivity, active, embodied pedagogies are desperately needed. Findings in neuroscience and in the field of embodied cognition substantiate the significance of embodiment in all development and learning (see, for example, Damasio, 2010; Johnson, 2008; Shapiro, 2011; Thompson, 2007). Based on this study, the skills generated by dance and embodied learning extend beyond subject areas and possibly beyond the school world. These skills are related to being together and living together, to accepting oneself and others, to creativity and collaboration.

Notes

1 Embodied learning departs from the dualistic notion of knowledge and human being, and from conventional learning theories that privilege symbolic, conceptual knowledge. Although philosophical, theoretical and empirical literature supports the notion of embodied learning, publications on embodied learning are still scarce (Anttila, 2013; Katz, 2013). A sociomaterial approach to education and educational research presents related developments in educational sciences (see Fenwick *et al.*, 2011).
2 It is now widely established that embodiment forms the core for consciousness, cognition and learning (see, for example, Damasio, 2010; Johnson, 2008; Shapiro, 2011; Thelen, 2008). The findings in neuroscience, for example, are profound and concern epistemological questions; that is, questions of the nature of knowledge and knowing (Pfeifer and Bongard 2007; Sheets-Johnstone, 2009). These developments point out that the Cartesian notion of the mind–body separation is misguided.

References

Anttila, E. (2003). *A dream journey to the unknown: searching for dialogue in dance education* (Doctoral dissertation). Theatre Academy, Finland: Acta Scenica 14. Retrieved from www.teak.fi/general/Uploads_files/Acta%20Scenica/a_deram_journey_to_the_unknown_AS14.pdf [Accessed 8 December 2014].

Anttila, E. (2007a). Dance as a dialogical praxis: challenging individualism in art and education. In S. Ravn and C. Svendler Nielsen (Eds.), *Tidsskrift for dans i uddannelse* 1(1), 57–74.

Anttila, E. (2007b). Searching for dialogue in dance education: a teacher's story. *Dance Research Journal* 39(2), 43–57.

Anttila, E. (2007c). Mind the body: unearthing the affiliation between the conscious body and the reflective mind. In L. Rouhiainen, E. Anttila, K. Heimonen, S. Hämäläinen, H. Kauppila and P. Salosaari (Eds.), *Ways of knowing in dance and art* (pp. 77–99). Theatre Academy, Finland: Acta Scenica 19. Retrieved from: www.teak.fi/general/Uploads_files/waysofkn.pdf [Accessed 8 December 2014].

Anttila, E. (2013). *Koko koulu tanssii! Kehollisen oppimisen mahdollisuuksia kouluyhteisössä.* [The entire school dances! The possibilities of embodied learning in a school community]. Theatre Academy, Finland: Acta Scenica 37. Retrieved from https://helda.helsinki.fi/handle/10138/42322 [Accessed 8 December 2014].

Anttila, E. and Sansom, A. (2012). Movement, embodiment and creativity. In O. Saracho (Ed.), *Contemporary perspectives in early childhood education* (pp. 179–204). Charlotte, NC: Information Age Publishers.

Damasio, A. (2010). *Self comes to mind: constructing the conscious brain*. New York: Pantheon Books.

Fenwick, T., Edwards, R. and Sawchuk, P. (2011). *Emerging approaches to educational research: tracing the sociomaterial*. New York: Routledge.

Gallese, V., Keysers, C. and Rizzolatti, G. (2004). A unifying view of the basis of social cognition. *Trends in Cognitive Sciences*, 8(9), 396–403.

Goddard Blythe, S. (2009). *Attention, balance and coordination: the A.B.C. of learning success*. Chichester: John Wiley & Sons.

Guba, E. and Lincoln, Y.S. (1989). *Fourth generation evaluation*. Newbury Park, CA: Sage.

Hari, R. and Kujala, M.V. (2009). Brain basis of human social interaction: from concepts to brain imaging. *Physiological Reviews*, 89, 453–79.

Hartley, L. (2004). *Somatic psychology: body, mind and meaning*. London: Whurr Publishers.

Johnson, M. (2008). The meaning of the body. In W.F. Overton, U. Müller and J.L. Newman (Eds.), *Developmental perspectives on embodiment and consciousness* (pp. 19–43). New York: L. Erlbaum.

Katz, M. (Ed.) (2013). *Moving ideas: multimodality and embodied learning in communities and schools*. New York: Peter Lang.

Niemi, H. (1999). Opettajankoulutuksen vaikuttavuus. [The efficacy of teacher training.] In R. Raivola (Ed.), *Vaikuttavuutta koulutukseen* [Towards efficacy of education], (pp. 169–94). Suomen Akatemian Julkaisuja 1/2000. Helsinki: Edita.

OECD (2013). *PISA 2012 Results in focus: what 15-year-olds know and what they can do with what they know*. OECD: Program in International Student Assessment. Retrieved from www.oecd.org/pisa/keyfindings/pisa-2012-results-overview.pdf [Accessed 8 December 2014].

Pfeifer, R. and Bongard, J. (2007). *How the body shapes the way we think: a new view of intelligence*. Cambridge, MA: MIT Press.

Reason, P. (Ed.) (2002). Special issue: the practice of co-operative inquiry. *Systemic Practice and Action Research*, 15(3), 169–270.

Reason, P. and Bradbury, H. (Eds.) (2008). *The Sage handbook of action research: participative inquiry and practice* (2nd ed.). London: Sage.

Shapiro, L. (2011). *Embodied cognition*. New York: Routledge.

Sheets-Johnstone, M. (2009). *The corporeal turn: an interdisciplinary reader*. Exeter: Imprint Academic.

Thelen, E. (2008). Grounded in the world: developmental origins of the embodied mind. In W.F. Overton, U. Müller and J.L. Newman. (Eds.), *Developmental perspectives on embodiment and consciousness* (pp. 99–129). New York: Lawrence Erlbaum.

Thompson, E. (2007). *Mind in life: biology, phenomenology and the sciences of mind*. Cambridge, MA: Belknap Press.

Wenger, E. (2009). A social theory of learning. In K. Illeris (Ed.), *Contemporary theories of learning: learning theorists . . . in their own words* (pp. 209–18). New York: Routledge.

3.2

THE TRANSFORMATIVE IMPACT OF DANCE EXPERIENCES IN BRAZIL[1]

Alba Pedreira Vieira

Introduction

Recalling my first dance classes at the elementary school I attended as a child brings several memories: I used to feel a delightful connection with myself and the universe. Dance was very meaningful to me and I knew from the very beginning dance would change the course of my life. And it did. I recall the times when I felt full of joy when I danced, experiencing many moments of pleasure and excitement. But I also remember being perplexed when learning new dance vocabulary and being disappointed when I could not perform movements to my high standards. Fortunately, the bliss from dancing remains and makes my body still 'virtually' dance and feel *saudade*.[2]

When I was employed at the Federal University of Vicosa in Brazil in 1997, my research on dance was generally related to political and cultural studies. I was influenced by the National Parameters for Arts Education (Secretaria de Educação Fundamental Brasil, 1997), whose dance content is informed by Laban's choreology (Laban, 1980) and Paulo Freire's (2002) ideas on critical thinking. This orientation was enriched after I moved abroad in 2003. For four years, I lived in the United States studying dance in a PhD programme at Temple University, where I found myself surrounded by a diverse group of international dance scholars including Americans, Canadians, Asians, Jamaicans, Argentineans, Cubans and Costa Ricans. Our different points of view about dance as well as productive exchanges and dialogues broadened my perspective, studies, artistic practice and eventually my teaching by including aspects of embodiment theories and methods (e.g. Anderson, 2003; Bond *et al.*, 2007; Damasio, 2003). Later, when I went back to my home country, this experience led me to larger discourses and questions about the relationship between dance and ambience, the dancing body's interaction with the environment and everything within it and the notion of meaning in dance from the point of view of neuroscientists and dancers.

Recently, researchers have made important advances in our understanding of the connections between the body and cognition. They have sought to apply findings from experimental psychology and cognitive neuroscience to dance. Some of the principles guiding my doctoral research included the perspective that dance may enable the creation of an 'embodied knowledge' generative environment. Embodied Dance Education (EDE) implies being sensitive and making connections to one's own self/body, to the other and to the environment. Some of the initial 'bodystorms'[3] that motivated the development of this study were to question how to improve the connections between EDE, research and community projects and to increase the dialogue between dance practices and theories on embodied cognition so that one nurtures the other. It is underpinned by my belief that our role as educators is to enhance students' processes of awareness to promote personal and social transformations.

To explore EDE, I started coordinating a dance project in 2008 that was developed until 2014 with students from 12 public high, elementary and kindergarten schools in Vicosa, Brazil. These students had few opportunities to be involved in quality dance education prior to the experiences provided by this study. Therefore, the aim was to offer them diverse dance possibilities exploring a particular dance education proposal referred to later in the chapter.

One of the empowering and transformative aspects of this project is that we asked students to take seriously what they learned from the lived experiences provided. Therefore, this study illuminates elements of how diverse dance experiences are transforming the lives of over 3,000 students (ages 4–16) from low socioeconomic backgrounds. While the focus is on researching the meaning and experiential knowledge of Brazilian dance students, resulting insights may be useful elsewhere.

Methodology

I adopted Karen Bond's hybrid methodology called "experiential inquiry" (Bond *et al.*, 2007),[4] and Max van Manen's (1997) hermeneutic phenomenology. From these researchers I learned that one can strengthen the relation between knowledge and action by foregrounding lived experience itself as a valid basis for both practical action and theorising.

The multi-modal approach to the research included data collected prior to and after the field work, participants' written answers to questionnaires, oral answers to interviews, videotaped classes and performances, systematic on-site observations, and drawings representing the impact of their dance experiences, with captions of their comments to the researchers.[5] These were the sources for analysis of dance as an agent of transformation for these children and adolescents.

Background

Participants attended 50-minute dance classes twice a week for at least six months. The classes offered possibilities to participants so that they could create, recreate and appreciate a universe of different artistic forms and expressions, and exercise what Antonio Damasio (2010) calls "neural maps." These may be affected in two ways: by concrete processes and entities – that is, by actual information from the environment – and through images from our mental actions, constituted by past memories and plans we make for the future. Our interactions with the environment make us produce images, even when we are not aware of it, which in turn generate emotions (Damasio, 2003).

Diverse activities during the dance classes were planned to stimulate children's ability to create theses neural maps. For example, through somatic education, children massage each other with eyes closed (Photo 3.2.1), exercising tactile images; they build auditory images while listening to the sound of the Brazilian indigenous instrument 'rain stick' played by the dance teacher – with their eyes closed and their entire body engaged in the activity by dancing to the sounds.

PHOTO 3.2.1 Somatic learning – children massaging each other with eyes closed.
Photographer: Alba Pedreira Vieira

The students also learned codified and complex dance steps that challenged their comfort zones. To stimulate the dialogue between the dance content and social matters, the students created choreographies in response to issues such as natural environmental conservation. For example, at the carnival parade at the school (promoted by the project team), children created costumes and drum sticks made out of newspaper; they also assisted with the dance show scenery made out of cardboard boxes.

EDE in action

Freire (2002) points out the importance of connecting any educational proposal to the community's context. Therefore, periodic meetings were held between the project team – coordinator, supervisor and dance students – and students' parents and teachers so that they knew the community context, needs and desires. I considered myself, a university teacher, and the dance undergraduate students, who are also members of the project team, as outsiders of each community in which we worked.

At these meetings the entire project team fitted into the everyday running of the schools: all team members entered into dialogue with parents and teachers and we talked about various educational aspects, including the project actions that had been developed. We also collected their criticisms, comments and suggestions for improving our artistic-pedagogical work. During these moments of interaction between the project team and the school leaders and teachers, we discussed and jointly decided with the school community interdisciplinary themes that would be developed in our dance activities so that teachers could also explore these ideas in their own classes; for instance, literature, biology, history and so forth. One example was a meeting held before classes had begun in 2012, when the project team decided with the school members the next theme to be developed in the dance classes: 'The relationships between environment and ecological issues and the arts'. These meetings were also important moments to share the students' data, including drawings, with the school community, which was collected and analysed by the project team.

By reading our research reports, the school teachers were also introduced to an example of knowledge production in and through dance. In this sense, they realised our approach adopted the act of dancing as a way of developing concepts, by means of which the dance students reinvent their bodies and feel their presence in the world. We took the opportunities provided by the meetings to explain to the school teachers the breadth of the kind of analysis we adopted, in which action and cognition are given in the same timescale, without distinctions between theory and practice. Our EDE proposition was a means of operating that way of knowing, since it considers the mental actions and behavioural acts as emerging and committed to the various contexts in which they are developed.

The project team also took the participants to visit places to expand their knowledge of the reality of where they lived, and then connected this to the artistic reality constructed at their dance classes. One example occurred when students visited and danced in the large and well-equipped dance studio of the dance undergraduate programme at the Federal University of Vicosa. Other trips were to the botanical garden, where they learned more about tropical plants and their conservation and the Museum of Zoology, where some students compared their body size to those of other animals. To stimulate participants' neuroimaging of visual maps, they watched videos at school as well as live performances at the school and the theatre, and in alternative spaces such as streets and squares. On many of the occasions, we observed participants engaging in dance appreciation by reproducing the dances they were contemplating.

Allowing participants to show their dances is an important component of our EDE programme. Our aim was not to train professional dancers or to create artists, but to expose young people to lived experiences in dance that may allow personal and social transformations to occur. They created most of the movements and helped with the props and scenery. They also had chances to share their own choreography with a large public audience creating most of the movements performed. The following is quoted from a conversation with a 13-year-old girl: "Today is the big day: we're going to present our choreography at the theatre! I have been so excited that I couldn't sleep last night!"

These artistic showings occurred during the Arts Weeks at the middle of each semester beginning in 2011, and the Dance Festival entitled 'Tile, tiling and playing', which has been presented since 2008 at the end of every semester.

Meanings unveiled

Participants' drawings and voices collected after the fieldwork had finished were important parts of data analysis. The data was categorised in themes titled dance and freedom, dance and emotional cognition, complexity and play dance. The following are two anecdotes from interviews: "Learning the dance steps the teacher brings is a challenge I like. Creating and copying are the two very good!" (8-year-old boy). "I like to create my own movements, but I also like to follow my dance teacher" (12-year-old girl).

Here are the voices of several children through a poetic depiction (Glesne, 1997):

> Dance classes reminds me of happy moments in my life.
>
> It's fun doing the high level with my knees, then with my legs and I end the sequence with my nose.
>
> Hopping, spinning around [Photo 3.2.1], being the bear.
>
> In doing all this there's much more joy in coming to the school!
>
> While dancing with my classmates I feel the bliss is in the air.
>
> I learned to play dancing!
>
> I like to do other things with my colleagues, but what I like most is to dance with them. When we all are moving, there's no fight, no competition and I feel like it could be a non-ending dance.
>
> When we dance altogether, we move as if we were one only and big body.

Based on the interviews and drawings of the participants, we saw that students who partici-pated in the EDE programme experienced self-development. They expressed significant dancing experiences as transformative. This study also elaborated how transformation in and through dance is expansive, challenging the logic of predictable outcomes and fixed student identity. Transformation might be as subtle as the conscious intention to direct action in dance away from the status quo or to occur in full epiphanies as 'ah-has' or "dance is cool!".

PHOTO 3.2.2 Children enjoying the challenge of being upside down.
Photographer: Alba Pedreira Vieira

EDE may come to life as a transformative experience of doing (Vieira, 2007), or what Deidre Sklar identifies as a "transformation enacted upon oneself through the details [nuances] of work [dancing]" (2001: 184). Transformative dance education is the embodiment of one's conscious inter-subjective intentionality, which embraces inner and outer life. Although Sklar does not speak of dance education but dancing, her discussion of the link between transformation and embodiment is salient to this study: "The potential for transformation lies in a property of *doing*: one does and feels oneself doing at the same time . . . it is an ultimate intimacy, a doing while being with oneself" (2001: 184).

Conclusion

This study generates far more questions than it is able to answer: how do we best mediate EDE? Are the embodied cognition studies orienting us or making us look, once more, for 'good' scientific basis for our practices? What is the relationship between dance and transformations perceived in students? Could music or any other artistic language do the same?

Although these are some questions still to be explored, I have realised from the results of this six-year-long investigation that Freire's *Critical thinking* (2002) is not only processed by our minds, as the author expected, but by our entire being, including emotional and kinaesthetic dimensions. The research findings highlight the centrality of participants' bodies in their ordering of dancing experiences. Therefore, the importance of embodiment in perceiving, knowing and meaning-making poses a challenge to the current focus, in Brazil and maybe elsewhere, on intellectual knowledge in dance education for young people. I suggest we need to practise 'bodystorm', which may allow transformations to occur in dance education.

EDE requires one to find a sensibility to one's inner self. This discussion reinforces my proposal that we would benefit from refining our human art of 'bracketing' in delicate situations of facing the unexpected, such as unpleasant bodily and movement responses from our own and/or others' bodies. How may we enhance body knowledge and transcend body prejudice? Patrick Slatery's (2006) point of view on change in relation to the post-modern curriculum in education could inform EDE: for him, *accumulative* change assumes predictable, controlled and well-defined incremental changes. *Transformative* change, occurring in an open system, is exemplified by quantum physics with its unpredictable, spontaneous leaps. Therefore, EDE's poetic of transformation adopts transformative change by a person's embodiment of a flexible attitude in unpredictable situations, as well as collaboration, openness and generosity to the other.

The poetic component is also related to a sensitive approach in learning from our experiences, which requires reflection on them. An opportunity of reflection to occur is when we talk about our dance experiences. Sharing transformational lived experiences may open our eyes, bodies, hearts, minds and souls to imagine and create new possibilities for EDE. Therefore, poetic transformation includes reasoning with the brain and body connected, and simultaneous connection of oneself to the other and the environment.

As the final words for this chapter, I present a quote from a 14-year-old student who participated in this study:

> We, students who participated in this project, learned that dance may transform lives, and we also discovered that we can change our bodies and gestures in a work of art. We won over the shame, fear, shyness, and prejudice. Thank you [obrigado!].

Notes

1 Research funded by CAPES/PIBID/UFV, CNPq, FUNARBE and FAPEMIG.
2 *Saudade* does not have an English translation and is not a word well known abroad. Linguists say Portuguese is the only language that has this word. Its meaning encompasses strong emotions, melancholy, nostalgia and longing.
3 'Bodystorm' is a term I use to refer to bodily knowledge or mind and body working together in knowledge construction and perception.
4 'Experiential Inquiry' integrates perspectives of phenomenology, autobiography and humanistic sociology with creative processes.
5 All participants (students, their teachers and parents) were initially invited to take part in this study. The students' parents and their teachers who agreed to participate signed a consent form in which I explained to them the research approach and purpose. Teachers and students' parents agreed to have their own and their children's data (oral and written responses, as well as pictures) published for academic purposes.

References

Anderson, M.L. (2003). Embodied cognition: a field guide. *Artificial Intelligence*, 149, 91–130.

Bond, K.E., Frichtel, M.C. and Park, H. (2007). Who am I? Who are we? Children perform identity, difference, and community in an intergenerational dance setting. In L. Overby and B. Lepczyk (Eds.), *Dance: current selected research: vol. 6* (pp. 125–52). New York: AMS.

Damasio, A. (2003). *Looking for Spinoza: joy, sorrow, and the feeling brain*. Orlando: Harcourt.

Damasio, A. (2010). *Self comes to mind: constructing the conscious brain*. New York: Pantheon Books.

Freire, P. (2002). *Pedagogy of hope* (R.R. Barr trans.). New York: Continuum.

Glesne, C. (1997). That rare feeling: re-presenting research through poetic transcription. *Qualitative Inquiry*, 3(2), pp. 202–21.

Laban, R. (1980). *The mastery of movement* (4th ed. revised by L. Ullmann). London: MacDonald and Evans.

Secretaria de Educação Fundamental Brasil (1997). *Parâmetros curriculares nacionais: Arte*. Brasília: MEC/SEF.

Sklar, D. (2001). *Dancing with the virgin, body and faith in the fiesta of Tortuga*. Los Angeles, CA: University of California Press.

Slatery, P. (2006). *Curriculum development in the postmodern era: teaching and learning in an age of accountability*. Abingdon: Routledge/Taylor and Francis.

Van Manen, M. (1997). *Researching lived experience: human science for an action sensitive pedagogy* (2nd ed.). Toronto: Transcontinental Printing Inc.

Vieira, A.P. (2007). *The nature of pedagogical quality in higher dance education*. Unpublished PhD dissertation, Temple University.

3.3

DIALOGUE AND 'PEDAGOGICAL LOVE'

Atmosphere and reflexivity in dance

Isto Turpeinen

A forum of dance

I was in the dance studio in spring 2011. There was a group of young, pre-school-aged boys in the dance class. The boys were in the middle of the studio and their parents were sitting on the side. The space was filled with sounds and physical activities produced by the boys. I saw events taking place at many layers at the same time. Although the boys moved in the space at the same time, the movements and dance were not the same. Personalities were running, jumping and turning. Watching this from the outside, I thought the situation appeared to be chaotic. I saw this as a complex-dynamic happening – as a 'forum' of dance in the meaning 'a dialogical space'.

Through that idea, I started to see structured details in individual actions. These personalities started to create dance between us, and we danced in a common field, in a forum. The process went on, and dancing started to intertwine these bodily actions. The forum, the dance studio as a common field, opened opportunities for the boys to find forms of dance. At the same time the boys' physical activities and dance were seeking social relationships in the forum. These peer relations seemed to be the route for importation and exportation of dance with rhythm, spatial levels, directions and qualities. Some of the boys showed fresh inventions in the moment; some imported something already adopted and taught it to the collective field. I saw this as a horizon of possibilities, construction and growing. We experienced stories in-and-through dance. This applied to all of us: these boys, and I as the facilitator, teacher and human being.

Working style – the raw-board method

Time has passed. I have lived 53 years. I have a mission in dance. I will work with these young boys as a dance teacher as long as my health allows. These boys were 5–6 years old when we started this dance group. Now, there are two groups and the oldest boys will soon be 10 years old.

"Young boys in the dance class" (Turpeinen, 2011) is the practical part of my ongoing arts-based doctoral dissertation at the Theatre Academy Helsinki, Finland. In the opening story of my thesis I describe the dance-related resistance I first faced as a dancing boy, then as a man, and later as a dance teacher. In the late 1980s, I started my work as a dance teacher with boys. Dance instruction started with tacit 'traditions': silence, being still and holding positions. Transferring the traditional style of dance was not enough and student learning suffered under discipline. Classes were (this is a caricature!) balanced by 'terror', where prohibitions and commands contributed to dance training. I needed to make a change and my mission was born. As a dance teacher in the 1990s, I was studying my own work and myself from 'the outside'. The working style was developed by organic and heuristic teaching experiences in the dance studio. The change in my working style was to see the dance studio as a forum. Children had a space for action. It was a kind of chaotic state in which the construction of dance started. Working with this mission in the 1990s, I developed a stance or a style by which I returned to the roots of my working style. I called this the 'raw-board method'.

Working with the raw-board method opens a space for personal action and experience. The complex situations start to construct structures in action. Personal experience constructs dance reflected by the learner. Learners share the constructed dance with each other. There is reflected knowledge of these bodily actions in the process. We have dance dialogue – a dance between us. In Greek, *dia* means 'through' or 'across', and *logos* means 'speech', a 'ground' or 'reason'. This means that my presence as a facilitator seeks active relations between persons – face to face. The raw-board process cycle (action – experience – reflection – sharing) explores dance in intersubjective space. The first cycles are short and quite detailed. Cycle-by-cycle exploration creates space for shared and personal processes of dance and the dancing self.

I have called this raw-board method other names. There are formats like 'searching a dance through my own life' or 'starting with general action, finding motoric details'. The learner is a holistic agent of their actions. Dancing will have structures through each learner's actions and experience. The key for this experience is an atmosphere that supports the learner's process. In this forum and through dialogue, I am also studying and learning myself. The positive atmosphere is part of the cycles. There is dialogue, diversity and a learner's own space.

Complexity

Time has passed and people have changed; kids have changed. There are many channels of media that influence children and young people. Western lifestyles seem to me more and more fragmented. I see the tolerance of the chaos as a part of everyday life. The teaching profession is also facing these challenges in institutes and with students. From my point of view as a dance instructor, I approach this state of 'chaos' as a rich beginning for searching. In the dance studio, complex 'happenings' have lots of individual and personal effort, but through my experience these efforts have their own logic connected to a situation. The complex situation may seem chaotic in the boys' dance class, but internally, they are constructing dance through their experience.

As a teacher, I play with this idea. I link it to my teaching experience with the boys. We started dance actions in raw-board with general motion efforts. This open forum and dialogue had complex dynamics. We faced a lot of information through these motions, which we could partly verbalise, partly not. Balancing with the increasing information, I have seen the exercises or the dance classes for children as dialogic spaces that are able to organise themselves.

I use a search tool with the students, which is "acting to reduce the entropy" (Prigogine and Stengers, 1984: 160–7). When the amount of confusion is reasonably low, the flow of action and dialogic space has a constructive influence. Complex dynamics produce (self-) organisation with this social system of the dance students in the learning process. Dance will be between us. Ilya Prigogine and Isabelle Stengers ask: "How can we bridge the gap between being and becoming?" (1984: 209). I see this bridge built in an experiential learning context inside the raw-board circles (see Kolb, 1984; Räsänen, 1997).

Now I will pursue an understanding of the fact that even though we are gathered in the same dance studio space, doing something together at the same time, we are in a disjunctive situation. In my case, a group of children running in the studio have a complex mode. Through the heuristic study of my working style, I can say that this mode with flowing information is related to construction. Children actively seek solutions and share inventions. These are the moments in the exploration when the search tool contributes to the construction. Raw-board processes are often slow, but the entropy decreases gradually through the action in the process circle. We need time and space for dialogue. The process is a state of becoming.

Complexity arises from our human diversity and uniqueness. The learner's own space will be in danger of being lost if the future and outcomes are already given. Without this own space there will be a lack of learners' inventions. In the complex dynamics, construction is based on the process of the incomplete. As a result, dance can arise between us, evolving into a common understanding of something essential.

Love as the ground

Love is a loaded concept. It is influenced by entertainment, criminal justice, policy, romantic ideas and biology. Love dates back to Plato's division (see *Symposium* or *Phaedrus*). When *eros* is associated with erotic and *philia* as brotherly love, I can approach the teacher's work with *agape*, with unconditional respect (Buber, 2008/1937). *Agape* has a Christian interpretation, but I am also interested in Paulo Freire's ideas (1996). He sets dialogical education in relation to love as a crucial medium facing a genuine human existence. For me, expressed the Buberian way, 'pedagogical love' is open to the altruistic relationship with the other, when I face another as a whole, as a person with his character, aspirations and limitations, in addition to his potentiality and actuality. The awakening of reciprocity in 'pedagogical love' means to decrease my grip with my students (Varto, 2012). In my experience, I have seen the learners' growth to independence and to adulthood. Some of them have continued dancing as part of their daily lives.

Allow children to run and move. Allow time for emerging experience. Allow dance to arise between us. Dance is a part of the child's own being and communication. A child running around in the dance studio: the moment of action includes being a holistic human being. When I consider my working style, I see the interface between 'being and becoming' and 'pedagogical love'.

References

Buber, M. (2008/1937). *I and thou*. London: Hesperides Press.

Freire, P. (1996). *Pedagogy of the oppressed*. Harmondsworth: Penguin.

Kolb, D. (1984). *Experiential learning: experience as the source of learning and development*. Englewood Cliffs, NJ: Prentice Hall.

Prigogine, I. and Stengers, I. (1984). *Order out of chaos: man's new dialogue with nature*. London: Heinemann.

Räsänen, M. (1997). *Building bridges: experiential art understanding. A work of art as a means of understanding and constructing self*. Helsinki: University of Art and Design.

Turpeinen, I. (2011). *Young boys in the dance class*. Practical part of doctoral dissertation. Helsinki: Theatre Academy.

Varto, J. (2012). *A dance with the world: towards an ontology of singularity*. Helsinki: Aalto University School of Arts, Design and Architecture.

3.4

TEACHING FOR BETTER LIVES

The philosophy of a Jamaican dance teacher

Carolyn Russell-Smith

Interactive approach to unearthing students' abilities

My early realisation of the powers of the arts came when as a young school teacher in a relatively volatile community in Kingston, Jamaica, I was assigned to teach a class of students whose ages ranged from 11 to 12 years that other teachers were reluctant to teach because of their unruly behaviour. Most of the students were very disruptive, but by observing their behaviour and attitude towards me, I quickly realised that many of the students were semi-literate. My first thought was how to make the class interactive and relevant to the level of these students. I used the first class as a 'fact-finding mission' to measure their temperament, willingness to accept instructions and general areas of interest. By the end of this first class, I came up with a strategy based on my observations.

At the next class they saw me making interesting, colourful word cards, which I placed on the ground, desk and just about anywhere in the classroom. I then turned on a CD player I had brought to class and informed the students that they were going to have fun playing musical words. They were to move only when the music started and when the music stopped they would have to find at least one word, which they would have to sound out and then spell. I explained to the students that they were all winners but the one who found the most words when the game was over would be the champion. The students enjoyed themselves so much that they kept asking for the game to be played over and over. School was no longer boring but fun, and they looked forward to coming to school. Out of this musical word game class was born a dance club, which the students looked forward to attending and supported wholeheartedly.

Many years later, I was approached by one of my adult dance students, Kereda Bryan, a guidance councillor for a rural high school. She knew of my work using dance as an educational tool to empower individuals and sought my assistance in motivating several of her problem students. She wrote to me about her research into the performing arts being an effective tool that can be used to change unacceptable behaviour in children and adolescents, and referred to my work and her own observations. At the early stage of the programme, she stated that:

The students who were reluctant at first about participating in the programme became very excited and constantly requested extra dance sessions. The students expressed that while participating in the dance programme, they felt 'free' to express themselves. The students had fun whilst showing off their talents.

Empowering lives through dance

Dance can make a difference in engaging children and young people in creative activities, which can make development and learning much more enriching and fulfilling. In Jamaica, dance is a part of the physical education curriculum, but many teachers are afraid to teach this aspect of the curriculum as a subject because of non-interest or lack of training. The few who do attempt to teach the subject do so with a product-orientated approach for social needs and enter students into various local competitions, rather than from a child-centred educational standpoint. As an educator, my emphasis is on the latter, in that concerns should be with the child's creative development and learning process, making available opportunities for self-discovery.

Dance is an excellent form of exercise for any growing child. When taught in a child-centred way by focusing on the creative process, it gives them the opportunity to create their own dance phrases within specific guidelines, which allows them to learn coordination skills and facilitates memory improvement. In my teaching career I have covered a wide range of groups – early childhood to primary, secondary and tertiary level. Classes have always been structured to be age appropriate, meaning that what we do matches students' physical abilities, thus ensuring students do not get frustrated or bored.

In many of my classes, students get the opportunity for movement discovery through improvisation, which they then share with the class. Students are given the opportunity to choose their class music from time to time, which lends itself to stimulating their creativity and artistic skills development. On occasion, group work is given and I find that splitting up the groups every so often gets students in the mindset of working with different individual personalities, sharing ideas and opinions. I find that when I give them ideas and instructions on how to approach the assignment to create their own movements, they get very excited in their experimentation. I emphasise the importance of originality, as this encourages their individualities and creative skills development. They are then given the opportunity to view each other's work and at the end of presentations, criticise the various pieces.

As the teacher, I guide them in avoiding excessive destructive criticism that may result in negative feelings. In this forum the students learn constructive criticism and how to share and show empathy towards others. At the end of each creative piece we praise the students and tell them how they could make their ideas better, and emphasise that in the classroom there are no losers; everyone is a winner. It is such a joy to see the students' faces come alive when they realise that they have accomplished the tasks set, and often the chorus "Miss, can we do more creating at the next class?" is echoed. This approach allows the students to be a part of the teaching process, helping them to understand the complexity of movement creation, thus guiding them in transforming their ideas to the next step of development in understanding the different components.

Dance: movement towards positivity

Dance experiences encourage children to listen and be creative and responsive to various rhythms, which also helps in the thought process. It is generally understood that persons who are involved in structured activities such as dance tend to be more focused, organised, better able to reason and good problem solvers. Group activities give students the opportunity to work with each other in a cooperative way, and life skills learnt in relation to social and empathic issues will serve them well into adulthood. Based on these experiences from teaching in Jamaica, I conducted a conflict resolution workshop during the 2012 Global Dance Summit in Taiwan, in which teenagers from five different countries participated in a brief but lively discussion on common conflicts that affect them in their everyday life.

Examples cited by these teenagers were: (1) People with a bad attitude; (2) Hormonal teenage boys constantly harassing them; (3) Quarrelling and use of abusive language; (4) Bullying; (5) Gossiping; (6) Fighting. Using the examples cited as source material, the students were given the task of selecting one of these issues to brainstorm movement ideas within the individual groups. Here students had the chance to use elements of dance to convey messages. From this exercise, the students expressed negative feelings and attitudes towards confrontation as it makes them feel uncomfortable, and sometimes they feel embarrassed after being involved in a conflict situation. The students realised that socially unacceptable behaviours can be avoided by understanding that their bodies can send messages, whether good or bad, and that better observation of other people's body language is useful to avoid confrontation.

In essence, one can see that dance does have the power to change lives. Over the years I have seen students transformed into responsible adults, many of whom attested to the fact that dance played a pivotal role in their development.

3.5

'THE SUMMER WORKSHOP OF DANCE EDUCATION FOR CHILDREN' AT TAINAN UNIVERSITY OF TECHNOLOGY, TAIWAN

JuanAnn Tai

Introduction

Dance is a popular activity for children in modern-day Taiwan. It is common to find dance being offered in formal or non-formal curricula in state-sector schools as well as at privately owned institutions; however, dance classes are often considered as training for technique and skills development rather than creativity. This is particularly true in the south of Taiwan, where only a few private dance schools concentrate on fostering creativity for children instead of emphasising repetitive technique proficiency and performance practice. This situation probably stems from the instructors themselves not having had much opportunity for creative exploration in dance when they received their training. Creative dance, which allows pupils to take charge of moving their bodies and designing their own dance phrases, may be intimidating to local instructors if they lack relevant knowledge in the practice of creative dance pedagogy. In that light, an in-service workshop was proposed and instituted at Tainan University of Technology (TUT) that would help foster dance creativity in dance education at various institutions in the area.

Connecting local teachers to inspirations from around the world

In 2004, the department of dance at TUT, where I have been one of the faculty members for two decades, began to sponsor 'The Summer Workshop of Dance Education for Children'. Its aim is to promote the development of creative dance approaches for local dance instructors and student teachers, linking the knowledge and experience in dance between the Eastern and the Western world, technique and creativity, the young and the more experienced. Many guest teachers from the international dance education community have been invited to teach the workshops since the launch, thus the workshop has become a medium connecting local dance teachers with developments in children's dance education throughout the world. Over the past decade, the workshop has become a forum for practising and developing more student-centred ways of teaching and learning. It is a two-day event that is usually held on a weekend in July. Most of the participants are dance instructors and university students majoring in dance.

In 2012, the department began to include non-dance specialists, and the feedback from them has also been positive. Because of the large number of participants and scheduling considerations, the workshop expanded to include two different sections in 2013: one for the TUT faculty members and another for dance instructors outside of TUT and university students who are interested in becoming dance instructors for children.

How is creativity stimulated?

In most classes of the workshop, participants form small groups and interact with different partners to explore movement in a creative process in response to tasks given by various instructions. This experience of teamwork gives those who are used to strict technique training a chance to stimulate new ideas or movement patterns during the processes of experimentation. As there are no clearly defined rights and wrongs in creative dance, this stimulates a supportive and encouraging spirit rather than a competitive or discouraging situation.

The experience of communicating in dance collectively enables the participants to recreate similar situations in their own teaching, and most of them acknowledge that such collaborative learning processes are meaningful when exploring movement possibilities. Many transform the idea of this learning process from the workshop to their studios and discover that their pupils have better experiences than when their dance classes are technique orientated or focused on competition and performance. This is one of the many reasons that some of the participants attend the workshop regularly every year.

Most of the participants in the section for the TUT faculty members, especially those who specialise in non-dance disciplines, find it challenging but interesting to work collaboratively for communication, decision-making and problem solving. Presentations of group shapes, movement pathways and collective or individual dynamics within their groups show them the unlimited potential of human creativity through joint efforts. Some of them stated that they did not expect to have this experience from a dance class and most acknowledged that the brainstorming processes in the workshop inspired positive outcomes which they could also use in their own teaching.

Experiences of the teachers and their students

From my observation, as seen in Photo 3.5.1, the participants in these workshops comprise a group that absorb the social space for sharing and learning as they reflect on their knowledge of creative dance. They return to their schools with basic ideas for helping children to strengthen self-identity, establish social space and develop cultural skills and knowledge through child-centred dance experiences.

Chiou, a regular participant who is an art teacher at a primary school in northern Taiwan, states that "he has always been able to incorporate his movement experiences from the workshop in his art classes" and he "can see how the children enjoy the materials and recreate by themselves." In Chiou's opinion, the workshop is "a wonderful journey of inspiration and creativity." He further explained that his teaching emphasis is not about the children's movement and drawing skills but their creative explorations, and it is evident that participating in the workshop empowers him to develop his teaching further in this direction (personal communication, 13 July 2012).

Similar to Chiou's experience, the participants who transform the workshop experience into their teaching find that through moving, the children explore themselves and construct

PHOTO 3.5.1 Tainan University of Technology in Taiwan, faculty members' class.
Photographer: Ken Smith

experiences of who they are while interacting with each other. Also, in the child-centred dance classes, the children improve their ways of moving by moving with a creative purpose, but without a concern about any imposed technical skills. They experience it in their own way, establishing a social space through the collaborative creative processes which give them the courage to express themselves through movement.

Conclusion

The workshop is a motivating experience that helps develop the participants' confidence in creative movement expression and enables them to become teachers who focus on the creative process rather than the product. This happens because the workshop provides the opportunity to build new forms of relationships that are developing between the participants and the discipline, theoretical understanding and practical application.

As one of the organisers of the workshop, I sense the growing interest in learning and teaching creative dance in the south of Taiwan. Part of this is due to the outcomes of the workshops during the past ten years. An exciting future can be anticipated as the workshops continue to draw creative talents together to explore creative pedagogies with the purpose of enhancing children's dance experiences.

PART IV

Exploring and assessing learning in dance as artistic practice

PHOTO 4.0 Tainan University of Technology in Taiwan, teacher training.
     Photographer: Ken Smith

4.1

RETHINKING STANDARDS AND ASSESSMENT IN DANCE EDUCATION

Susan W. Stinson

When I was enrolled in doctoral work in curriculum studies in the 1980s, one of the most compelling questions was "What's worth knowing?" (Postman and Weingartner, 1994). This question, whether explicit or not, still underlies all decisions about what to teach. In dance, sometimes we simply teach what we know. Sometimes we teach whatever the students want. Sometimes external accrediting groups determine content.

Emphasis on what students should learn led to the development of the first USA voluntary National Standards in all subject areas, including dance, during the mid-1990s. Today, however, the concern at all levels of education is not just what standards students should meet, but how we know whether they have done so. Even dance educators are now being required to provide quantifiable data as evidence for whether their students have met given standards. In my state, North Carolina, university students who wish to become licensed for public school teaching must demonstrate that all of their pupils have met selected standards taught within a 3–4-week unit, or the would-be teachers cannot be recommended for licensure. When teachers must have hard evidence that all their students have met a standard within a short instructional period, there is great motivation to focus on the 'small stuff': skills and knowledge that the students do not usually start with but which can be learned within limited time.

Struggling with this reality as a teacher educator in dance led me to write two papers presented at conferences and published in their Proceedings. The first (Stinson, 2009) charted my journey in coming to terms with the value of formal assessment, while the second (Stinson, 2013) suggested possible practical solutions to the challenges raised. In revisiting these papers with a little more distance, I have more clearly identified two primary issues in need of rigorous dialogue:

1. What's worth assessing in dance education?
2. How might assessment better facilitate learning and empower students and teachers, rather than judging and ranking them?

These questions reveal a perspective that goes beyond pragmatic issues of developing and implementing an assessment plan. They suggest that, when deciding what to assess, it is necessary to consider our deepest values while remaining conscious of contemporary educational realities.

Ethical issues

My ethical concerns regarding a strong focus on outcomes-based assessment deserve to be made visible at the outset. They begin with historical knowledge of how often efficiency and effectiveness in accomplishing outcomes have been used as criteria for evaluating far more than educational practices. A most compelling example is the development of the 'Final Solution' in 1942, when 15 men in Nazi Germany determined the most cost-effective way to extinguish the lives of millions of people. Those men sitting around the table were highly educated, with over half holding a doctoral degree (Aktion Reinhard Camps, 2005). Clearly education alone is insufficient as a moral compass; we all are subject to seduction when requested by those in authority to use our rationality and creativity to develop policies, even ones that are harmful. Corporate culture and many legislative decisions throughout the world offer more examples.

While one can reasonably argue that educational assessment does not lead to mass murder, thinking only about outcomes, and not the value of the goals themselves and what is required to reach them, is still problematic. Certainly artists know that the best creative work usually comes from being open to possibilities that emerge, rather than maintaining a single-minded focus on an outcome. What do we miss on any journey when we care only about the destination? What is overlooked that might be equally important when we attend only to accomplishing the objectives we defined when we began? When teachers are judging students as better or worse according to pre-determined criteria, are they overlooking what may be unique to an individual? When young people become completely focused on the goals set by their teachers, are we guiding them away from intrinsic motivation and the capacity to discover what gives their own lives meaning? I suggest that these are ethical questions as well.

Among professionals in arts education, conflicts about assessment go back decades; Malcolm Ross argued in *Against Assessment* that

> Many – perhaps most – arts educators feel an innate abhorrence towards many of the traditional forms of assessment practiced in schools. Rank-ordering children in terms of their paintings, their acting or musical performances seems to strike at the heart of the relationship that nurtured them. Constraining and curtailing personal creativity in the interests of meeting the requirements of external examinations . . . forces a compromise over fundamental principles.
>
> *(1986: 87)*

Yet it is clear that dance can remain at the table of public education in those places where it has obtained a presence only if it adheres to the demands of those in power. Is this just another table that someone should have the courage to upset? In going along, when are we participating in a corrupt enterprise, and when are we swallowing unreasonable concerns so that all children might have access to dance education in schools?

Despite these worries, I began to examine my own resistance to formal, data-based assessment, recording my change of consciousness in a 2009 paper:

I have a lot of qualitative data from my own research and that of others, revealing perceptions from [many] young people . . . [of] powerful experiences in dance classes, making new discoveries about themselves, and finding pleasure in working with others to accomplish common goals (Bond & Stinson, 2000/01, 2007; Stinson, 1993a, 1993b, 1993c, 1997, 2001; Stinson, Blumenfeld-Jones & Van Dyke, 1990). But it is quite tempting to simply look for what we want to find. I now find myself just as intrigued by students who *don't* like dance, who don't participate fully, who don't appear to learn much even from teachers I consider top-rate. I am now fascinated by those among my university students who just want to continue doing what they already know how to do, those who don't find learning about dance education to be worth the effort, and those who don't make breakthroughs even though they seem to be trying. What am I going to do about *those* students? How uncomfortable do I allow myself to be when a demographic analysis of student learning reveals that students of color are disproportionately represented among the low achievers in my courses and in all courses in the Department? What are my own students (the ones who are successful and go on to become teachers) going to do about *their* students who don't dance much better at the end of the semester than at the beginning, or those whose ideas about dance aren't changing from ones they entered with? Is it okay to just dismiss those students as not bright enough, not talented enough, or not interested enough to learn? To what extent does that dehumanize them, just as those with power have so often dehumanized those without it?

(Stinson, 2009: 196)

Despite continuing concerns about how assessment may be used and what can be lost in the process, I concluded that formal and informal assessment should be an important part of the learning process, for the purpose of helping students and teachers understand what young people are learning and facilitating learning for all students.

What's worth assessing?

Obtaining good assessment evidence and analysing it well, however, are challenging and time consuming. Before I left my long-time role as a teacher educator in 2012, I was spending a large portion of instructional time helping prospective dance teachers develop check sheets and rubrics to assess whether their students had met the standards-based learning outcomes, and to analyse the pre-assessment, formative and summative data they collected. This meant far less time dealing with child and adolescent development, philosophical issues, and all the other important topics necessary to educate teachers. Of course, as standardised assessments are developed, dance educators will spend less time designing rubrics but will have even more pressure to focus on what the rubrics are assessing; as in other subject areas, administrators will be able to evaluate dance educators based on their students' examination scores and dismiss those whose students do not score well. While I still object to this use of assessment, it becomes critical to re-examine what we think is most important for students to learn in dance.

With recognition of my own complicity in the development of previous national and state standards for dance, and with respect for colleagues who continue to work on such documents, I admit that I find most of the skills and knowledge included in those standards to be relatively trivial within the whole of human existence. Are there new ways to think about standards if we consider more than just modest changes in what-has-been? For the 2013 paper, I asked myself 'What is important for every student – not just those who hope for a dance career – to learn?' In other words, within the context of contemporary schools in the United States, what is truly worth learning by every single student who experiences dance in education?

I propose that, if we are going to spend so much time figuring out how to assess students and then assessing them, we ought to focus on *what really matters*. While it is relatively easy to assess whether students can make shapes on different levels, identify three characteristics of Graham choreography or demonstrate a correct tendu, focusing on this level of skill and knowledge takes us away from what seems more important. More radically, especially considering my own participation in standards development, I now think that what matters most in dance education for young people is *not* learning to dance in any specific style or genre, make dances or respond to dance; these skills by themselves do not matter much (after all, many people in the world live very satisfying lives without them), although they can be entrances to learning what *does* matter.

For me, what matters most are important life skills that can be learned specifically in dance education, especially when there is a focus on critical thinking and somatic experience. These skills cannot be accomplished in one lesson or one unit of 3–4 weeks, but rather require extended periods of time to develop. When trying to articulate such skills, I initially came up with three areas, what I called *Self-Management*, *Performing and Attending*, and *Creating and Communicating* (Stinson, 2013). I noted that many people assume that such skills are not valued in an era when standardised test scores are so significant. However, I also found many commonalities between my list and a recent one developed by a consortium of educational and business leaders (Partnership, 2009). This group, the Partnership for 21st Century Skills (P21),[1] was formed in 2002 through the efforts of entities that included the U.S. Department of Education and a number of large corporations, including AOL Time Warner, Apple Computer, Cisco Systems, Dell Computer, Microsoft and SAP (a German software company). Many state school systems in the USA are now members of this organisation. In words taken from their website,

> P21 . . . advocates for 21st century readiness for every student. As the United States continues to compete in a global economy that demands innovation, P21 and its members provide tools and resources to help the U.S. education system keep up by fusing the 3Rs[2] and 4Cs (critical thinking and problem solving, communication, collaboration, and creativity and innovation).
>
> *(Partnership, 2009)*

In their publications, P21 further elaborates upon these '4Cs' as well as other basic skills, including Information and Technology Literacy and Media Literacy, and the personal attributes (Life and Career Skills) necessary to achieve them:

- Flexibility and adaptability
- Initiative and self-direction
- Social and cross-cultural skills
- Productivity and accountability
- Leadership and responsibility.

Looking for commonalities between my goals and those of the P21 group, I value the self-discipline that comes with dance, and the corporate world wants self-directed workers.

Creativity and Communication appear on both lists, while other C's and many of the skills the Partnership articulated were embedded under my larger categories. Re-reading the P21 list for this chapter has caused me to reorganise and add to my own list. (See Figure 4.1.1 below for a comparison between some of the Partnership's proposals and my own, listing skills that are important for students to develop by the time they complete high school.)

On the one hand, it was affirming to realise that not only can dance education deliver many of the skills that corporate and business leaders want but, in fact, these skills are inherently part of dance. There was a difference in language (between corporate wording and my own, written from the first-person perspective of the learner), but dance educators have always needed to communicate across boundaries. Although the P21 goals seemed to lack any sense of the significance of somatic awareness as a foundation for other skills, my list short-changes some P21 goals that can be addressed in dance education, including writing and use of media and digital information. Certainly different perspectives are valuable and can help us recognise what we might be missing. Yet I still heed Malcolm Ross' warning from 1986: "Everywhere we are exhorted to follow the lead and adopt the practices of the successful businessman" (1986: 85). Had my own thinking been so corrupted by years of enculturation by the military-industrial complex (Eisenhower, 1961) that I could no longer think outside of such values?

In re-examining the P21 goals, I find the unstated but implied value for efficient and effective production one would expect of the business and corporate world. There is mention of ethical behaviour and responsibility to the larger community, but this is quite modest. Recognising implicit values in the P21 standards emphasised the need for me to further probe the values underlying the standards I had proposed.

In many cases, I recognised that my goals simply reflect some of my most cherished experiences in dance. These include feeling so fully alive while dancing, which is why Maxine Greene's work, such as her chapter 'Towards Wide-Awakeness: An Argument for the Arts and Humanities in Education' (1978), has moved me for so many years. Wide-awakeness, or paying attention to what is around us and within us, is also a means for expanding understanding of self, others and the world, a necessary step towards caring for each. In addition, I love the sense of accomplishment that comes when meeting a challenge in dance, although I know that one can experience such pride even when an accomplishment is relatively trivial. I also value the courage to go 'off balance' both literally and figuratively, as a way to avoid stasis.

Other values implicit in my proposed standards include connection and community. At the same time, I maintain the importance of independent thought and action, while knowing that I am under the influence of many forces not immediately apparent to my consciousness. It is so tempting to justify our own positions as *the* right ones. The only defence against self-righteousness is to be as critical of our own thinking as we are of that of others.

Further, I recognise the existence of multiple realities and the uncertainty this brings. And I cherish a sense of possibility: humans have created the systems and structures under which we live, and can recreate them to make a more beautiful, more just and healthier world for all of us.

From standards to assessment

Despite the challenges of determining what is truly important enough for all students to learn in dance, merely having standards which we continue to problematise does not satisfy the current demand for rigorous assessment to determine whether students have met them. As hard and as long as dance educators have laboured to gain a place in public education, few would advocate

My proposal	P21
A. Self-awareness and Self-management	**Initiative and Self-direction, Flexibility and Adaptability, Productivity and Accountability, Critical Thinking and Problem Solving, Creativity and Innovation**
1. Be my own teacher, telling myself what to do and when. Bodily: Both calm and energise myself when appropriate, so I am not a victim of my impulses. Intellectually: Ask and pursue my own questions, ones that don't have easy answers.	*Initiative and Self-direction:* Monitor, define, prioritise, and complete tasks without direct oversight. *Critical Thinking and Problem Solving:* Identify and ask significant questions that clarify various points of view and lead to better solutions.
2. Push myself beyond what I already know and like to do – to be willing to experience ambiguity and strangeness. Remain engaged even when it gets hard and frustrating.	*Flexibility and Adaptability:* Work effectively in a climate of ambiguity and changing priorities. *Initiative and Self-direction:* * Go beyond basic mastery of skills and/or curriculum to explore and expand one's own learning and opportunities to gain expertise. * Demonstrate commitment to learning as a lifelong process. *Productivity and Accountability:* Set and meet goals, even in the face of obstacles.
3. Be as critical of my own ideas as I am of those of others.	*Initiative and Self-direction:* Reflect critically on learning experiences in order to inform future progress. *Creativity and Innovation:* View failure as an opportunity to learn; understand that creativity and innovation is a long-term, cyclical process of small successes and frequent mistakes.
B. Connecting self and others	**Leadership and Responsibility**
1. Recognise the connectedness of the body and movement to the physical world and to ideas.	*Critical Thinking and Problem Solving:* Analyse how parts of a whole interact with each other to produce outcomes in complex systems.
2. Pay attention – to what is subtle as well as what is obvious, to what I see and what I feel on a somatic (bodily) level, and to the words and movement of others.	*Communication and Collaboration:* Listen effectively to decipher meaning, including knowledge, values, attitudes and intentions.
3. Be conscious of the impact of my choices on my work and on others.	*Leadership and Responsibility:* Act responsibly with the interests of the larger community in mind.

FIGURE 4.1.1 Comparison of proposed Stinson principles to selected P-21 principles

4. Be willing to make decisions and take responsibility for myself while also making conscious decisions regarding when to work collaboratively with others.	*Communication and Collaboration:* * Exercise flexibility and willingness to be helpful in making necessary compromises to accomplish a common goal. * Assume shared responsibility for collaborative work, and value the individual contributions made by each team member.
C. Creating and Communicating	***Creativity and Innovation,*** ***Critical Thinking and Problem Solving,*** ***Communication and Collaboration***
1. Imagine something that doesn't exist and work to create it. Recognise that something can be different than it is and contribute ideas for making it better.	*Creativity and Innovation:* * Use a wide range of idea creation techniques (such as brainstorming). * Create new and worthwhile ideas (both incremental and radical concepts). * Elaborate, refine, analyse and evaluate their own ideas in order to improve and maximise creative efforts. * Develop, implement, and communicate ideas to others. * Act on creative ideas to make a tangible and useful contribution to the domain in which innovation occurs. * Demonstrate originality and inventiveness in work. * Be open and responsive to new and diverse perspectives.
2. Look at the same thing (a piece of choreography, a movement) from multiple perspectives and articulate them.	*Critical Thinking and Problem Solving:* Analyse and evaluate major alternative points of view.
3. Be fully present in my body, moving with clear intention and focus, not just going through the motions.	*Communication and Collaboration:* Articulate thoughts and ideas effectively using (oral, written, and) nonverbal communication skills in a variety of forms and contexts.
4. Have an impact upon others through communicating verbally and nonverbally.	*Leadership and Responsibility:* Use interpersonal and problem solving skills to influence and guide others toward a goal. *Communication and Collaboration:* Communicate effectively in diverse environments. *Media Literacy:* Understand and effectively utilise the most appropriate expressions and interpretations in diverse, multi-cultural environments.
5. Attend respectfully to other people's dances and ideas about dance.	*Media Literacy:* Examine how individuals interpret messages differently, how values and points of view are included or excluded, and how media can influence beliefs and behaviours.

FIGURE 4.1.1 *(continued)*

that the field abandon this effort. But pondering how to assess, especially the kinds of complex life skills I envision, and how to do it in ways that support learning rather than take time away from it, raises even more questions.

In the USA, there is continued emphasis on high stakes standardised tests, evaluating the least sophisticated skills and the lowest levels of knowledge. This is not appropriate for assessing the complex life skills both P21 and I propose. But as schools continue the twenty-first-century reformation, there is hope. In fact, there is an interesting document on the P21 website, mapping 21st Century Skills onto rich content from all arts education disciplines. This 'map' creates sample activities that could facilitate development of the skills and knowledge needed to meet each goal. Here is an example of Critical Thinking and Problem Solving suggested for the 8th grade:

> Dance students investigate, identify, and discuss the key components of a successful dance composition and how that composition might be affected by the technical expertise of the dancers performing it. Students then view dance videos of varying styles and time periods and, working first individually and then together as a class, determine criteria for excellence in performance and composition. Students apply these criteria to future viewings of dance and their own compositions.
>
> *(www.p21.org/documents/p21_arts_map_final.pdf:3)*

This arts map makes clear that rich projects to be carried out over time are the only way to accomplish the kind of learning necessary for the twenty-first century, and most of the examples, including this one, could provide exciting educational experiences. Although the map does not offer tools for actually determining the degree to which the goals have been met, it should not be too difficult to develop rubrics or check sheets for assessing how well students accomplished the tasks called for in the example above. But the more I thought about what a rubric for assessing student work might look like, the more questions I had:

> If the dancers were very skilled, what else might an educated 8th grader say besides 'If they were not such good dancers, it wouldn't look so good'? How much nuance should they be expected to notice?
>
> Should a class of 13–14-year-olds be expected to agree on criteria for excellence in performance and composition? Most critics would argue that such criteria are context-specific, so what is regarded as excellent for a classical Asian dance work would not be the same for a hip-hop piece, and in fact critics do not always agree on the quality of a work even when looking at it in its cultural context.
>
> How many videos of dances that students do not like or find 'just weird' would they need to see to recognise how the lenses they bring affect their viewing and their judgements? Such recognition is not accomplished in one semester even by many students in university-level dance appreciation classes.
>
> Would having a rubric get in the way of continued cognitive development? It could if this task were regarded as something that could be completed, rather than always in progress.

While still holding these questions, I also see that the particular example of an educational activity cited above could facilitate development of quite a few of the skills I proposed in Figure 4.1.1:

1. A2: Push myself beyond what I already know and like to do – to be willing to experience ambiguity and strangeness.
2. A3: Be as critical of my own ideas as I am of those of others.
3. B2: Pay attention – to what is subtle as well as what is obvious, to what I see and what I feel on a somatic level, and to the words and movement of others.
4. C2: Look at the same thing (a piece of choreography, a movement) from multiple perspectives and articulate them.
5. C5: Attend respectfully to other people's dances and ideas about dance.

To determine student progress in reaching these goals, I would want to assess over a period of years:

> How willing are students to continue watching something that does not initially look very interesting to them? (One might measure how long students remain engaged.)
>
> How successfully can students describe the feeling of discomfort or strangeness? Is the feeling any different if they try to imagine doing the movement, what it would feel like somatically? (One might assess the depth of description and the inclusion of somatic language.)
>
> How willing are students to ask themselves why this dance looks weird or stupid, and why it might not look that way to others, and to imagine themselves as someone for whom this dance matters? (One might assess the degree to which different perspectives are included.)

Yet in keeping with my values, I need to be as critical in examining my own ideas as I am in examining the P21 goals, and I find similar challenges with trying to assess them, raising both practical and theoretical questions:

> For how long should young people (or anyone) be expected to engage in an activity they find boring or unpleasant? Where is the line between these states and educationally provocative strangeness?
>
> While we can invite children to engage in experiencing other perspectives as an adventure rather than using authority to require their participation, what about students who resist our best 'invitations'?
>
> How open are we to aesthetic perspectives of young people that are opposed to those in the arts education canon? Who decides which 'other' perspectives are educationally valid? Are we as educators equally open to all perspectives? Whose dances are we showing? Should we be open to all kinds of dance, including examples we find offensive? Are all ideas equally worthy of respect?

Such challenges can seem paralysing if we think we must have all issues resolved before proceeding with teaching and assessing. But in reality, similar questions might be part of classroom discussion with adolescents. It might be helpful to assess student work even in relation to problematic standards, as long as the assessment is used as a way of understanding student learning rather than simply as a judgement of the worth of students and teachers.[3] In other words, teachers could note student responses to dances of others, including resistance, as a point of information rather than as a judgement indicating a student has failed. Surely it is educationally valid to understand and explore one's resistance.

Teachers could even use check sheets and rubrics (completed by students as well as themselves) to facilitate ease of data gathering in a large class, and likely get fairly honest responses, as long as the data were used to help understand student learning and to raise further guiding questions. Teachers might also invite students to identify what else they thought they were learning through the activity, and how they could demonstrate such learning, perhaps through portfolios of their work collected over time and assessed annually. Such an approach to assessment, as a way to understand and enhance learning rather than to sum it up and give prizes to those who are most successful in meeting only pre-determined standards, differs radically from most contemporary educational assessment in the United States.

I note my failure to end this chapter with ready solutions to the assessment challenge. It indeed is tempting to simply supply effective and efficient solutions for dance educators when so much is being demanded of them. I do not begrudge ready-made rubrics and check sheets for assessing student progress in meeting mandated standards, as long as they are not regarded as the 'final solution' to the assessment conundrum. My hope is that this chapter will contribute to continued problematising of solutions and exploring the ethical issues underlying practice in dance education.

Notes

1 Although not cited on the P21 site, one of UNESCO's themes is Education for the 21st Century (see http://en.unesco.org/themes/education-21st-century).
2 The term '3Rs' is commonly used in the US to refer to Reading, wRiting and aRithmetic.
3 As of October 2013, 38 of 50 states in the USA require that teacher evaluations be based on student achievement (Lu, 2013).

References

Aktion Reinhard Camps (2005). *The Wannsee Conference attendees*. Retrieved from www.deathcamps.org/reinhard/wannsee/att.html [Accessed 19 November 2013].

Eisenhower, D.D. (1961). *President Dwight D. Eisenhower's farewell address*. Retrieved from www.ourdocuments.gov/doc.php?flash=true&doc=90 [Accessed 25 July 2013].

Greene, M. (1978). *Landscapes of learning*. New York: Teachers College Press.

Lu, A. (9 October 2013). How states evaluate teachers varies widely. *Stateline: the daily news service of the Pew Charitable Trusts*. Retrieved from www.pewstates.org/projects/stateline/headlines/how-states-evaluate-teachers-varies-widely-85899511032 [Accessed 18 February 2014].

Partnership for 21st Century Skills (2009). *Framework for 21st century learning*. Retrieved from www.p21.org [Accessed 19 November 2013].

Postman, N. and Weingartner, C. (1994). What's worth knowing? In F. Mengert, K. Casey, D. Liston, D. Purpel and S. Shapiro (Eds.), *The institution of education, second edition* (pp. 231–44). New York: Simon & Schuster.

Ross, M. (Ed.) (1986). *Assessment in arts education: a necessary discipline or loss of happiness?* Oxford: Pergamon.

Stinson, S.W. (2009). Music and theory: reflecting on outcomes-based assessment. In T. Randall (Ed.), *Global perspectives on dance pedagogy: research and practice. Proceedings of the Congress on Research in Dance 2009 Special Conference* (pp. 194–8). Leicester: De Montfort University.

Stinson, S.W. (2013). What's worth assessing in K-12 dance education? [8 pp.]. In S.W. Stinson, C. Svendler Nielsen and S.-Y. Liu (Eds.), *Dance, young people and change: proceedings of the daCi and WDA Global Dance Summit*. Taipei National University of the Arts, Taiwan, 14–20 July 2012. Retrieved from www.ausdance.org [Accessed 19 November 2013].

4.2

EXPLORING LEARNING IN DANCE AS ARTISTIC-EDUCATIONAL PRACTICE

Charlotte Svendler Nielsen

The role of the body in education

> [T]here is no 'mind-doing' that is separate from a 'body-doing'. My movement is thus not the result of a mental process that exists prior to, and is distinguishable from, a physical process in which it eventuates, nor does my movement involve no thinking at all.
>
> *(Sheets-Johnstone, 1999: 487)*

When working with children the fact that "we come straightaway moving into the world; we are precisely not stillborn" (Sheets-Johnstone, 1999: 136) becomes ever so clear, especially with the very young ones, but also with the 9-year-old children that are the focus of this chapter. Children move, and they do it all the time, unless they are forced to sit on a chair and even then they move, their small bodies just have to, because they are still very alive and sensually aware to all kinds of impressions. By the time human beings grow up, we start to become more physically 'still' as we are socialised into how one has to behave and what it means to be a student, at least in every place where schooling is organised in classrooms with tables and chairs and children all sitting listening and looking in the same direction most of the day.

But changes are in process. There are politicians who are starting to become aware of issues that educators, teachers and researchers have highlighted for years, and stemming back to early twentieth-century educators like philosopher John Dewey who already in 1916 criticised his society at the time and how bodily activity was seen as an "intruder" to school work (Dewey, 1996/97: 141). In Denmark a school reform which is currently becoming implemented puts emphasis on the importance of exploring new ways of teaching and learning and there is a government decision that children must be involved in physical activity at least 45 minutes during a 6–8-hour-long school day. Anybody who is close to a child in daily life would argue that it is impossible that children will not already be doing that and even much more, but the central point is that teachers now have to work with the awareness that learning does not only happen 'the head way'. Going back to the opening quote which I have taken from philosopher and former dancer Maxine Sheets-Johnstone, it is important to also remember that when we move there is also 'thinking', or reflection going on, even if at pre-conscious levels. So more movement in school is not working against the overall purpose of going to school and becoming educated. It might even turn out that the children learn more.

The new Danish school reform also highlights that schools should collaborate with companies, organisations and professionals. This opens the possibility for artists to become more permanently involved with schools than has been the case until now. This chapter goes close to exploring children's possibilities for learning when a dance artist is their teacher.

Learning from a phenomenological perspective

Meaningful experiences are central in the complex processes of creating new knowledge and developing new skills. To learn something and to be open to develop ourselves as human beings, it is a prerequisite that what we are presented for in, for example, a schooling context in some way resonates with and makes sense to us – it needs to become meaningful for the individual to engage in the activity in some way. This perspective of learning is based on a phenomenological philosophy of the body (Sheets-Johnstone, 1999) and emphasises embodiment and meaning-making as being both personal, social and cultural (Sheets-Johnstone, 2010) and being fundamental parts of learning. If a task is too difficult or too boring, a child will always try to find other ways to solve it than the one the teacher thought of as the right one.

For example, when giving a group of children the task to jump over a row of their classmates lying on the floor, some will run, jump and land ('the teachers' solution'), but some will be running in a big circle around the line of classmates to avoid the actual jump, because it is too challenging for them, and only after a while jump closer and closer to their classmates, while others almost from the beginning will start to jump in other ways like backwards and turning to challenge themselves. These different solutions reveal something about different ways of being bodies with different embodied experiences, but it also reveals that these experiences are closely linked to what is meaningful to whom and that most of the children solve the task using their creativity.

Meaning as a prerequisite for learning

When observing a group of children engaged in a dance class, what are 'signs' of meaning? It is possible to observe how the children are present intentionally by paying attention to what they do, what they are directed towards and what they are trying to avoid. From this perspective it is interesting to look at how the children act, and to look at what in those actions seems to be meaningful or the opposite. Meaning is not the same as learning, but meaning must be 'present' for learning to happen. At the same time it is very hard to say exactly when learning happens.

In most cases learning is a process that both has a history linked to former experiences and is directed towards future experiences. The big 'A-HA' might happen when walking home from school and not in the actual class situation, or some years later when the child meets a situation in which suddenly a number of former experiences are drawn upon in solving a task. Only very concrete skills can be observed as 'learning moments' which can be when a child suddenly masters a new skill, like being able to stand in vertical. When learning is a change of viewpoint, a new way of being involved or a new way of experiencing oneself in a situation, it is very difficult to say when the change happened and what the reason was.

Embodiment as a base for learning

When observing a group of children, it catches my eye and I also sense in my body that some children are physically present in a different and more fully 'embodied' manner than others. This can be explored through focusing on how the children participate 'with their bodies' – what do they express interest in? What are they able to do? What are their bodily repertoires? What do the bodily abilities mean to their experiences? Characteristic of the children that are most physical is that they are able to express what they sense 'in their bodies', they move with good coordination, they are able to be present in the whole space (some will only move around the walls or physical objects and never move in a big open space), they have rhythm and they feel well when touching and being touched by others. In a former study (Svendler Nielsen, 2009) I distinguished different dimensions of being physically involved in a variety of movement exercises:

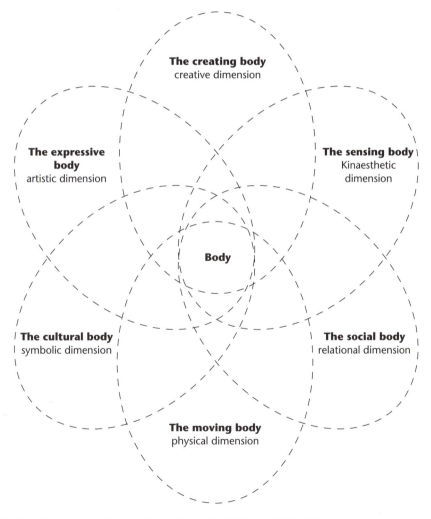

FIGURE 4.2.1 Dimensions of embodiment (Svendler Nielsen, 2009: 192)

Everyone's embodiment holds all dimensions, but some have developed some of the dimensions more than others through their former experiences and thus they are 'bodies' in different ways. In a teaching situation, one dimension can be more in focus than others, for example if the teacher has decided to put focus on relations (which was the case in the dance project I will discuss below). But even though one dimension is in focus, the body can never be not physical, not social, etc. Using this model we can analyse where a teaching activity has its emphasis and what it perhaps lacks if we want to educate children to have a broad variety of bodily skills and knowledge. More of these bodily dimensions come into play as soon as we start doing movement activities. Thus we need to explore what happens in a broader sense than the physical skills if the focus is to understand learning possibilities.

Exploring learning in a dance project

Now let me take the philosophies of learning to a more concrete, empirical level in an exploration of understanding learning in a dance project. In May 2012 I was invited to follow a third-grade class (9-year-olds) while they had dance lessons with a professional dancer who came to their school every day for a week, and while they went to watch a dance performance at a dance theatre. This dance project was part of the SWOP international festival for modern dance focusing on children and young people and organised by the company 'Åben Dans' ('Open Dance') in Roskilde, Denmark. My task was to study the children's learning possibilities while dancing and co-creating a dance piece themselves, and while being spectators watching the professional performance. But this was not an easy task. How is it possible to get close to children's experiences? Which research methods can 'capture' experiences that can hardly be verbalised?

This was a true methodological challenge. To solve this challenge I used a phenomenologically inspired way of interviewing and filming the processes which I call "multi-modal interviewing" (Svendler Nielsen, 2009) and "videographic participation" (Svendler Nielsen, 2012; Degerbøl and Svendler Nielsen, 2014). As part of the interviews the children participated in an exercise in which they were asked to make a drawing of their favourite movement from the dance classes. The exercise had two parts: one in which they drew themselves doing the movement that they chose, and another in which they drew their experience of doing the movement. It is not easy for all children at this age to understand this distinction, which is why I decided to ask them to make two drawings. A couple of examples follow on the next page (Figures 4.2.2, 4.2.3 and 4.2.4).

This method helped to clarify what was at play for the children with regards to their learning. Teachers can often express what they think their students have learned, but the children are mostly not aware of this and thus not able to express by words in a conventional interview what they think they have learned. This exercise helped to bridge this gap as it came close to the 'in between'. But it was a time-consuming method, as to work well it was necessary for me as the researcher to also have time with the whole class to introduce some somatic exercises that could help them pay attention to their bodily sensations and "the felt sense" (Gendlin, 1997) of an experience and to introduce the drawing exercise. In combination, the two methods helped me to explore and to some extent understand the children's learning processes, but in a chapter like this only the words and the images can be communicated.

FIGURE 4.2.2 "To jump over my classmates" was difficult in the beginning (my heart beats heavily) but in the end it was like flying.

FIGURE 4.2.3 "To jump and fly" was like to do two movements at the same time.

FIGURE 4.2.4 "To turn around" was a new and fascinating sensation (felt the legs and the feet in a different way).

What do the children experience while watching a dance piece?

As part of this dance project, the class went to watch a modern dance performance at a theatre. The piece was 'Ritual' by the Danish company Next Zone/Lene Boel. The choreographer describes that it is a visual journey inspired by Inuit culture, urban breakdance battles, arctic nature and global warming. The following narrative is one outcome of the analysis of a video I recorded during the performance, and an interview I did with two boys[1] sitting on the stage just after:

> Rhythmic music [da-da-dam, da-da-dam] and voices used as instruments [ya - ya, ya, ya] are filling the space of the theatre. Two dancing men are rolling their shoulders and bending their knees rhythmically in front of each other. They are dressed in baggy white clothes. Victor is staring at them while his neck is moving silently in the rhythm of the drums: da-da-dam, da-da-dam, da-da dam. Suddenly, he turns to a boy sitting beside him, smiling, and with his blue eyes wide open, as if saying, "did you see that?!" The sound changes to the loud noise of breaking ice flakes [hhrrrrrrr]. I turn the camera towards Mehmet who sits beside Victor. He sits on his knees staring and smiling at the dancers. When the dancers move to a certain place on the stage, he moves his whole body in that direction. When they point to the ceiling, he gets higher up on his knees and bends his neck all the way back in his efforts to see what they are pointing at. The light is all blue and gives an impression of a cold and icy landscape. Victor and Mehmet do not seem to pay attention to anything else other than the two dancing men on the stage. They move closer to each other and start talking about what they see: "Hey, look there! Wow, what a jump!" "Yes! And see there!" The lights go out and all of the children start clapping. The performance is over.
>
> I grab Victor and Mehmet and we sit in a corner of the stage to talk about their experience. I first ask them what they think the piece was about. Mehmet answers, "it is a story that they tell in a dancing way." And I ask what the story was about. He says, "there were many stories," and Victor adds, "there were many places where they were. They were in Egypt and then they were in the jungle." Mehmet continues, "and they were looking for a treasure. And they were in the woods where there was a wolf." I ask why they thought they were in the jungle and those places. Mehmet says that he "could see that they were digging and found a coffin with a treasure." Victor says, "the music also told that. And they were moving stones." I go on asking if they saw anything which was like what they did with the dancer who taught them for some days at their school two weeks earlier. Victor recognises "that what we did with the arms." While Victor talks, Mehmet is rolling his head toward the floor, sitting up, and then says, "there was something from the warm-up," and then he does the movement, rolling forwards again. I ask, "and they also did that in the piece?" "Yes! They did," he says while nodding. I finally ask if they would like to try to do what the dancers did. "Yes!" they say at the same time. And Mehmet continues, "I would really like to be able to do . . . what they do when I grow up! Somersaults and all that." And Victor says, "me too!" Mehmet then spontaneously says, "I think everybody enjoyed this because it was . . . it was really cool."

When looking into what the boys are saying, I can highlight the following as being what they have learned in the process:

- it is possible to tell a story in a "dancing way";
- they both use their imagination and creativity to 'see'/make meaning of what is going on;
- they relate to music in a new way (explain that music can help to tell a story and make meaning of a dance);
- they both recognise special, new ways of moving, which they have tried themselves;
- mehmet sees new possibilities for his own life (he wants to dance when he grows up).

Mehmet is a boy who is having difficulties in school in different ways – both with the subjects and socially. He is sometimes isolated. In dance, he has obviously had an experience of being someone different and with other relations to his peers. His example shows that being involved in dance gives possibilities for developing personally, which might also have an influence on what it is possible for him to learn in the other subjects.

What do the children experience while dancing?

In one of the lessons I am observing the children are practising a phrase inspired by jazz dance in which every movement has an image linked to it (a plastic bag, a snake, a strict teacher, etc). Afterwards they work on some duets which they have created themselves inspired by the themes: friends, enemies and love. Three couples do their duets at the same time as part of the choreographic piece which they are creating all together. After the lesson has finished, I sit down on the floor together with three boys and a girl. Two of the boys were a couple when they did the duets. I ask them all what they liked to do most in the lesson. One boy says, "the jazz dance." The rest are nodding and saying, "yes." It seems that they all agree about this, but then another boy says, "also the one where we had to walk forwards with the feet like this" (he shows the movement while still sitting) "and from side to side" (a snake-like isolated movement of the torso which goes in the frontal plane from one side to the other and back again).

I ask why he liked that. He says that it was "a little strange to do this movement quickly from side to side." I ask if it had to do with a certain rhythm in the body and the girl says, "yes," and also the boy who mentioned the movement nods while he says, "it has actually all been fun." Another boy takes over: "I think it was fun when we stood like this" (he shows while sitting how they were standing with the arms in diagonal in the frontal plane looking towards the hand closest to the floor). He repeats the movement and does it in the exact same well-coordinated manner with perfect tension and relaxation of the different parts of the movement so that he not only repeats the movement, but also its dynamics while he says: "you look down, you look up and then you do like this" (he sweeps his arm in a big circle movement in front of his body). "This was the best movement of them all."

Later in the day I interview two girls from the class. They have brought a drawing that I have asked them to do as part of the preparation for the interview. I start by saying that, "in the last class you had to invent the movements of friends, enemies and love [both of the girls are nodding] in some groups and then today you had to try the movements of another group. How was that?" One girl says: "they were three and we were five so we had to do it all together and invent a totally new one, but it still included some of the other ones we made." I go on asking if there is anything about dance which is different from other things they do in school. The same girl smiles and says, "yes, you do not have to do homework."

The other girl adds, "yes, and it is totally different and also more fun. And then in the night I could not stop talking about it. I said to my dad: tomorrow we have arts and then we have dance and then we have math. I said it more than ten times. I was looking so much forward to it. It is something new and it is fun." "But what was it apart from not having to do homework that made you look forward to it?" I ask. The first girl replies, "it is more fun than being in the classroom, because we get out and move." The other girl adds, "and then we are more together as a class. It is more fun with the class. When you sit in the class you are not allowed to talk to each other. You are not really allowed to do anything. We also have to work together in class, but here we kind of work more together, are more together."

Through the interviews with the two groups of children, it comes forth that what makes meaning to them in the dance lessons are experiences of moving in new ways (which feels either good, 'fun' and/or a little 'strange'). I also see that they develop an ability to move with certain qualities which they grasp, they are able to repeat them over and over and they are able to articulate this both verbally and by showing the movements. In those movements that they highlight, they move very intensely and focused. When observing them it is obvious that those moments seem especially meaningful to do. The two girls highlight how they in dance are together in a different way, they "are more together," which shows that the relational dimension is very important to their meaningful experiences.

Learning opportunities in dance as artistic practice

Analyses of what the children's learning processes seem to hold through working with dance as an artistic practice are summarised below. The analyses include their experiences as articulated in words during interviews and their visual expressions in drawings. They also include what I was able to see through my camera when filming, both when they were dancing themselves and when they were watching dance.

The children seemed to develop an expanded bodily repertoire which includes new movement abilities and new sensuous experiences. Some tasks were difficult in the beginning, but were overcome and developed into good experiences. Some movements were difficult, felt different, but were also "fun." There were new embodied experiences like a sense of doing two movements at the same time, and fascinating sensations of moving in new ways and feeling body parts in special ways. They also developed:

- an expanded consciousness of a new way of working with movement (the creative, expressive and sensuous dimensions are in focus);
- new ways of solving tasks (with a creative focus);
- consciousness about who they are themselves and development of new relations to some classmates.

Making meaning and learning involves reflection which can be both at a verbal level and at a pre-conscious level like when knowledge cannot be verbalised, but perhaps shown through the body. Both philosophers like Sheets-Johnstone (1999) and neuroscientists agree on this. Neurophysiologist Jens Bo Nielsen explains the connection like this:

A separation of movement and cognitive functions is problematic. The brain is developed through interaction between the body and the surroundings, and all of our cognitive functions are founded in our understanding of ourselves in the world . . . a separation of motor skills and cognition is artificial and does not reflect the way a brain works.

(Nielsen, 2011: 12)

The feeling of having control of one's own body and the movements that are performed are termed "the sense of agency" by neuroscientists (Ritterband-Rosenbaum, 2013). Sheets-Johnstone (1999) refers to the same concept, but from a phenomenological perspective, putting emphasis on how this sense is connected to meaning and experiences of being able. It is documented through neurological methods that through physical activities children develop their "sense of agency." This is not documented in the area of dance specifically, but Sheets-Johnstone's descriptions of processes of movement and experiences of the moving body in dance make it clear that in dance, when the sensuous/somatic dimension is in focus, human beings' consciousness of sensing their own bodies and understanding and relating to each other at an embodied level are developed, which is what I saw happening to the children in this dance project.

Conclusion

Learning can be seen as an individual process, especially when the learning is about physical skills, but learning in a school dance project has a very strong relational dimension as the children are always engaged in social processes with others in the room – social processes they experience as being different from when they have group work in the classroom. This difference probably has to do with both the feelings that come into play that are experienced and expressed more openly in their collaborative choreographic work, and the issue of being together physically, often touching each other and in that way coming much closer to each other as human beings.

The elements that I have drawn out from the interviews and observations point to a phenomenological concept of learning in dance as artistic practice to be characteristic of developing consciousness in/or about dance. This is connected to new abilities and knowledge, a new sense of agency, ways of participating, and expressing and experiencing in relation to oneself, others and/or the subject. This learning is important because it can give children more tools to have a good life through more varied experiences and an ability to be conscious of those experiences and the experiences of others.

In some countries the body is 'moving' more into broad areas of education, and dance is an area that can contribute to learning generally as a way of working with body consciousness and relations through creative processes – skills and knowledge that are useful to anyone, anywhere.

Note

1 The children's names have been changed for ethical reasons.

References

Degerbøl, S. and Svendler Nielsen, C. (2014). Researching embodied learning by using videographic participation for data collection and audiovisual narratives for dissemination. *Ethnography and Education*, 9(3), 60–76.

Dewey, J. (1916/1997). *Democracy and education*. New York: The Free Press.

Gendlin, E.T. (1997). *Experiencing and the creation of meaning. A philosophical and psychological approach to the subjective*. Evanston: Northwestern University Press.

Nielsen, J.B. (2011). Ændringer i hjernen [Changes in the brain]. *Fysisk aktivitet og læring-en konsensuskonference [Physical activity and learning – a consensus conference]* (pp. 10–13). Copenhagen: The Cultural Ministry's Committee on Research in Sports, the Arts Council.

Ritterband-Rosenbaum, A. (2013). *The sense of agency: movement perception and behaviour in healthy individuals and individuals diagnosed with cerebral palsy*. Copenhagen: Department of Nutrition, Exercise and Sports, University of Copenhagen.

Sheets-Johnstone, M. (1999). *The primacy of movement*. Amsterdam: John Benjamins Publishing Company.

Sheets-Johnstone, M. (2010). Kinaesthetic experience: understanding movement inside out. *Body, Movement and Dance in Psychotherapy*, 5(2), 111–27.

Svendler Nielsen, C. (2009). Children's embodied voices: approaching children's experiences through multi-modal interviewing. *Phenomenology & Practice*, 3(1), 80–93.

Svendler Nielsen, C. (2012). Looking for children's experiences in movement: the role of the body in 'Videographic Participation' [31 paragraphs]. *Forum Qualitative Sozialforschung/Forum: Qualitative Social Research*, 13(3), Art. Retrieved from: http://nbn-resolving.de/urn:nbn:de:0114-fqs1203185 [Accessed 14 December 2014].

4.3

STEPPING INTO SKIN

Expanding empathy through dance

Kristen Jeppsen Groves and Marin Leggat Roper

Introduction

As dance educators at home or abroad, we enter the classroom as vessels of our own cultural knowledge, including experiences shaped by race, nationality, religion, gender, sexuality and economics. In our desire to become more culturally sensitive educators, we reflect on experiences, as educators, where empathic learning occurred across 'borders' of cultural, political or religious difference, and seek to expand our understanding of empathic pedagogy as applied in dance education around the world.

Empathic pedagogy

Empathic pedagogy, those teaching practices and philosophies cultivating empathy within the classroom, has developed through the work of scholars and practitioners in the fields of arts and education over the past century. The English term 'empathy' was translated in 1908 from the German 'Einfühlung', used in 1873 by aesthetician Robert Vischer (as cited by Foster, 2011) to describe the process of viewing a painting or sculpture. This process, Vischer claimed, involved a distinctly physical experience whereby the viewer, through imagination and kinaesthetic sensation, would "enter into and inhabit" a work of art and respond emotionally to the physical sensations the body felt within the work (Foster, 2011: 10–11). As a student of art and architecture, Rudolf Laban also sought to codify the relationship between the inner world of feeling and emotion, and outward physical form.

In twenty-first-century education, empathy is often understood as the "ability to understand the thoughts and feelings of self and others" (Arnold, 2003: 13) or "being able to imagine, often intuitively and instinctively, how the other feels" (2003: 20). Beyond the realm of thought and feeling, however, empathy, as articulated by early twentieth-century visual and performing artists, must also be understood as a *kinaesthetic experience*, a kinship mediated in and through the lived experience of the body.

Students learn about themselves, and their relationship to the world around them, through moving their lived experiences. As a "site for critical reflection on one's life" (Shapiro,

1998: 11), the lived experiences transcribed in the body shape the way we view the relationship between the many parts of ourselves, our relationship with others and our relationship with our environment, as fully integrated beings. This ability to connect 'self to self' and 'self to other' lies at the heart of empathic pedagogy.

Self to self

'Self to self' connection is facilitated through teaching practices guiding students towards deeper meaning-making through the medium of their body. Physical sensations are experienced within the body, then identified, articulated and interpreted within the context of a student's lived experience. These sensations, often overlooked in methodologies focusing primarily on stylistic perfection, might include:

- muscular tensile forces of binding and freeing;
- aerobic cycles of exertion and recuperation;
- weight sensing and groundedness;
- breath phrasing;
- opening and closing of core and limbs;
- gravitational forces;
- dimensionality within the body and in surrounding space;
- spirillic and linear movement;
- personal and social kinaesphere.

In a recent choreographic project, Marin directed a group of six female university students in creating a dance exploring female identity through Rudolf Laban's light and strong weight efforts (Laban, 1971: 81). The choreographic process involved the following elements:

1. *Guided improvisation* with principles of light and strong weight effort.
2. *Journaling* that included describing felt sensations, identifying supporting imagery and claiming personal movement preferences.
3. *Group discussion* connecting individual experience to a larger cultural context. Where is weight effort revealed in my life? What purposes do light weight or strong weight effort serve in my life? What cultural forces are at work as we consider our individual and collective experiences of weight effort?
4. *Individual movement generation* capturing the most salient aspects of weight effort as related to the students' experience of female identity.

Individual movement statements were developed and woven throughout the dance. One commonly occurring theme about dancers' mothers translated into a repeated motif involving dancers carrying and being carried by one another.

The experience was transforming for all involved. One cast member, Sarah,[1] described the process as "unlike anything I've experienced before," and Elisabeth described a "special feeling" and connection felt among the cast members. When students experience and identify these basic yet subtle kinaesthetic sensations, then contextualise such sensations within their own cultural framework, they recognise their bodies as meaning-making agents, the sites of embodied knowledge.

Self to other

Self to other connection can occur as heightened kinaesthetic experiences facilitate deeper emotional connection with others. Shapiro says the "recognition of how one's personal experiences shape one's critical thinking is directly linked to issues of cultural diversity" (1998: 10) In dance classrooms abroad, shared movement experiences can help overcome barriers of language, culture and traditions.

In Mumbai, India, movement improvisation, writing exercises, partner interviews and group discussion were used with a group of 26 dancers of diverse spiritual and religious traditions. Using general prompts such as, "Dance is a reflection of my values, which include . . . " and "When I dance, I . . . ", dancers created, revised and developed individual movement phrases reflecting identity and culture. Partner and group feedback facilitated reflection about movement and meaning within a cultural context. Solos, duets and small group phrases were incorporated into a final dance. Afterwards, dancers described having a transformative experience, experiencing their body as a powerful reflection of personal identity, and deeper empathic connection to their peers than before. One dancer shared, "I actually *felt* the dance for the first time. I was very happy." Another reported, "It was a culmination of everything. I honestly felt like I've not felt before. It was a *new* feeling, which I really liked."

Simple movement activities like mirroring allow one student or group to validate others' experience and can lead to deeper empathic connections between participants. In El-Funoun, a dance company preserving and promoting Palestinian culture, outreach sessions held with youth in the West Bank generally begin with a dabkeh-inspired improvisational warm-up, where participants take turns leading the group in improvised variations of traditional dabkeh steps. Group members watch and model, with little speaking taking place, validating the choices of each student. One El-Funoun trainer describes using this improvisational structure to create a fluid, equitable relationship between dancer and choreographer, in his words, "to cross boundaries with each other and give (them) a chance to feel, learn and share with each other" (A. Abuoun, personal communication, 7 June 2012). El-Funoun uses these types of activities to bridge difference to fulfil its stated mission of "present[ing] the long-suppressed Palestinian culture before other nations."

Beyond student to student connection, educators connect with students when they recognise the cultural underpinnings of their own empathic teaching practices and expand those practices to validate student experience within their own cultural context. Viewing traditional Cambodian dance performance in Phnom Penh gave Marin insight into the moment-to-moment performance quality of Khmer dance as a reflection of Hindu-Buddhist thought. She recognised how Western aesthetic values, including the use of a large kinaesphere and outpouring focus, informed her assumptions about empathic connection between performer and audience. As a result, she expanded classroom experiences to include more reflective, somatic activities, honouring the performance values described by her students.

To facilitate an empathic group experience with a hip-hop class in Wuhan, China, Kristen introduced students to dance concepts such as weight sensing and energy qualities and invited them to explore and develop individual ideas through improvisations and solo work. However, Kristen discovered this focus on individual expression as a portal to empathy was problematic for students, who preferred more unison movement and group work. She recognised students felt greater connection to their peers by working together towards a group goal. They felt individual validation through preparing and presenting a group performance. Kristen compromised by clarifying improvisational activities that could be practised and replicated so students felt prepared for a final showing.

Conclusion

In dance education, as well as in larger conversations about diversity and conflict, we assert the need to consider empathy as not only laying within realms of cognitive and emotional under-standing, but also as an aspect of kinaesthetic experience. The examples included above illustrate specific teaching practices transcending cultural boundaries and facilitating increased connection, self to self and self to other. Questions to consider when assessing empathic practices in one's classrooms abroad might include:

- How is this experience validating an individual's movement choices, opinions or life experiences?
- Does acknowledgement occur publicly, in a small group or privately? What is the most appropriate way to express and share acknowledgement?
- What methods of feedback and assessment confirm empathic understanding is occurring?
- What are the observed indications of physical or emotional transfer?
- Does the group seem more cohesive, better connected?
- Does it feel safe for more individual or collective sharing?
- What transformations are seen? What student feedback indicates a transformative empathetic experience has occurred?

Movement and dance are key in expanding the ability to 'feel into' another's lived experience. We make meaning of the physical sensations associated with living, exploring such felt sensations through empathic teaching practices rooted in acknowledgement of the body as a culturally constructed subject. Such bodies are diverse, the life experiences unique, and, we assert, they create the foundation from which knowledge, wisdom and ultimately empathy can grow.

Note

1 Names of participants have been changed for ethical reasons.

References

Arnold, R. (2003). *Empathic intelligence: the phenomenon of intersubjective engagement*. Paper presented at the First International Conference on Pedagogies and Learning, University of Southern Queensland.
Foster, S.L. (2011). *Choreographing empathy: kinesthesia in performance*. New York: Routledge.
Laban, R. (1971). *The mastery of movement* (3rd ed.) L. Ullman (Ed.). Boston: Plays, Inc.
Shapiro, S. (1998). *Dance, power and difference: critical and feminist perspectives on dance education*. Champaign, IL: Human Kinetics.

4.4

MAKING THE LEARNING VISIBLE IN CREATIVE DANCE EDUCATION

Marc Richard

Documentation as a research methodology

To make the learning visible within dance education, both teachers and researchers need to find a means to document the *processes* of creation and the rich layers of learning embedded within it. This will allow both teachers and students to become more conscious of their own learning and engagement with the creative process in dance education.

On a study group trip to Reggio Emilia, Italy[1] in 2011, I witnessed first-hand the power of documentation to provoke and engage the public in dialogue around learning. I had a chance to visit three Reggio Schools including the Choreia School, which places an emphasis on learning through the body. This visit made me interested in exploring how pedagogical documentation can be used as a form of teacher research that teachers could bring to their classrooms and it made me believe that used in conjunction with creative dance education, pedagogical documentation can begin to "unmask – identify and visualize – the dominant discursive regimes which exercise power on and through us" (Dahlberg *et al.*, 1999: 152). In the domain of creative dance education I believe these dominant discourses involve the bodies of teachers and students, as well as discourses around creativity and what it means to learn.

As an example of the process of pedagogical documentation, I offer you a glimpse into a grade six class creating dances in groups from lines of poetry. Through pedagogical documentation I observed that students were learning to discover their own personal movement voices but at the same time had many pre-conceived notions about dance that were tied to gender.

Rinaldo is a very shy boy who seems to come to life through dance. His teacher, Eva, says, "He has just progressed so much in wanting to express himself in movement. He is able to get what he feels inside to be on the outside." Eva also believes it is because he has had no previous dance training "that he is able to use his body like a paint brush." When Rinaldo commented on his group work, he explained: "I am good, especially in this group because other members of my group take dance." This comment, along with a picture of his group, is placed on a documentation panel to provoke a discussion about the underlying assumptions and gender biases in dance, i.e. that the girls who take dance after school are more creative and more capable than those who do not (in this class the boys). The richness and authenticity of the dialogue that resulted from this provocation was profound. One girl stated, "It's hard sometimes because the boys seem like they don't care." Greg, who had many creative ideas, interrupted, "I really care about dance." One girl, whose mother runs a dance studio, clarified her theory about the primacy of girls who take dance after school:

> I think that for some people it can be easier if you take dance outside of school, but in other cases it's harder . . . because you might get stuck on a script, like what you've done in ballet class or whatever and if you don't, you have more of a free mind so you can think and let your mind go and do whatever.
>
> *(Margie)*

Later in a small group interview we watched some video documentation from their first day in this project. Rinaldo's two female group members were really upset at what they saw on the video footage because they recognised they had been completely ignoring Rinaldo. Bertha observed, "We were so mean." Rinaldo reflected, "I wasn't saying much, I was the only guy there and the girls were getting along so well, so I felt like an outsider. I was just waiting to see what the girls were going to come up with." Eva, their teacher, recognised: "The girls have pre-conceived notions of the boys and the boys know it, so they function that way." (Photo 4.4.1.)

The comments, pictures and video footage from this one moment of learning provoked cycles of reflections and discussions around creativity, personal voice and pre-conceived notions

PHOTO 4.4.1 Rinaldo[2] and two girls from his group (grade six).
Photographer: Marc Richard

in dance education. Through pedagogical documentation, we are able to unearth many of the deeply rooted perceptions of dance as gendered. Boys such as Rinaldo, whom Eva perceived as excellent creative dancers with unique movement voices, saw themselves as 'less than'. As Eva recognised, documentation allowed us to see what they were *really* thinking. Many teachers and parents assume that boys will dislike dance: the opposite is true. Based on this, it is an interesting perspective to consider whether it is possible that creative dance education in public schools could change some of our cultural myths about gender and provoke the general public to see dance as a gender-neutral form of art.

Pedagogical documentation

The cornerstone of the Reggio approach is their image of the child as a protagonist in their own learning, "rich in resources, strong, and competent" (Rinaldi, 1998: 114). Pedagogical documentation, for Reggio educators, is the practice of attentively studying and actively recording the process of a student's learning – which involves their knowledge, understanding, thinking, communication and application in a given social context. Documentation places emphasis on how each person's values and culture have significance in meaning-making processes and animating this process of learning for others (Rinaldi, 2001).

These others might include the students themselves, other educators, parents, siblings and the community at large. Documentation might take place in a variety of formats including note taking, photography, audio recording, video recording, samples of student works and written reflections on the learning experience encountered. Because documentation is a tangible form, it allows for constant revisiting and reconstruction of the original learning event; it is a spiral process (Dahlberg *et al.*, 1999: 154). Pedagogical documentation offers a chance to make visible the children's theories but documenters recognise that these are provisional theories that are constantly re-worked and re-visited by the teachers and students, as well as by those who read and interact with the documentation.

I use Reggio-inspired pedagogical documentation as a research methodology in an attempt to animate the intersubjective space between teachers and their students, and uncover the learning that is happening for both teachers and their students, as teachers facilitate creative dance classes. Pedagogical documentation as a methodology can animate the many layers of embodied learning available in creative dance education. Based on this methodology, I have created an exhibit of double-sided pedagogical documentation panels titled *Traces of motion: making the learning visible in creative dance education* which I can use to provoke, teach and advocate for dance education in our Ontario elementary schools. The traces of learning are present in the panels which include pictures and transcriptions of actual conversations as well as interpretive text from the pedagogue.

Notes

1 In Reggio Emilia, education is a communal and constructivist activity based on the traditions of progressive education (Dewey and Bruner), the constructivist psychologists (Piaget and Vygotsky), systems theory (Bateson) and Italian left-reform politics and intellectual traditions (Ciari and Rodari).
2 Names have been changed throughout the case narrative for ethical reasons.

References

Dahlberg, G., Moss, P. and Pence, A. (1999). *Beyond quality in early childhood education and care: postmodern perspectives*. London: Falmer Press.

Rinaldi, C. (1998). Projected curriculum construction through documentation – progettazione: an interview with Lella Gandini. In C.P. Edwards, L. Gandini and G. Forman (Eds.), *The hundred languages of children: the Reggio Emilia approach – advanced reflections* (2nd ed.) (pp. 113–25). Greenwich, CT: Ablex.

Rinaldi, C. (2001). Infant-toddler centers and preschools as places of culture. In C. Giudici, C. Rinaldi and M. Krechevsky (Eds.), *Making learning visible: children as individual and group learners* (pp. 38–46). Reggio Emilia, Italy: Reggio Children.

4.5

WATCHING DANCE TO DISCOVER 'NEW WORLDS'

Liesbeth Wildschut

Discovering 'new worlds'

In a dance performance the audience may enter into new and strange situations in which the ordinary may take unexpected turns. Sometimes this changes our expectations, and may even lead to a change in the way we perceive the world or ourselves. To give free rein to the experience and the imagination, the audience has to approach the work with an open mind. To stimulate an open-minded view, teachers and dance makers should not explain the content of the performance in advance, because that will guide expectations in a specific direction. If we want children to have an open-minded approach to dance, we have to stimulate their curiosity.

The aim of the Dutch choreographer Jack Timmermans, who creates performances for children, is to challenge them not just to see what is actually happening on the stage, but to discover other 'new worlds' by association and interpretation. He is passionately triggering the young audience to engage their imagination. Experiencing one of his performances made me curious to find out how he prepares children before they attend his performances, and whether this preparation enlarges their ability to make associations and interpretations.

Timmermans invited me to observe differences between children without preparation and children who attended several dance workshops, organised by the dance company. The goal of these workshops was to make them curious about the performance, but also to make them aware of various possibilities to express ideas in dance and options for interpretations. During the first workshop they were made aware of the potential of various body parts. In the second and third workshops they discovered how to translate an idea into dance and realised that there are myriad ways to do so. They also watched each other and were taught that there is room for many interpretations of the dance movements.

Exploration of children's experiences as spectators

Seventy children, 9 and 10 years old from several schools, watched *Alice* together in Theater *De Stilte* in Breda, the Netherlands. I selected three episodes of the performance to ask questions about. I used open questions because I wanted to give the children freedom to express their associations and interpretations of what they had seen on stage. For each episode I formulated questions evoking an image in such a way that the child could finish the sentence, like: "At the moment the hand appeared, I had to think of . . . ." After the performance the children stayed seated. Before answering the questions, a research assistant gave instructions that the children could finish the sentence and write down even more. She stressed that there were no right or wrong answers. She then introduced the first scene in a few sentences and asked the children to recall this episode. Then one by one she read out the questions, while the children wrote down their thoughts.

In cooperation with two research assistants we coded all the remarks of the children and decided whether an answer was an interpretation: yes or no. No interpretation included: A. I don't know; B. A description; or C. A judgement. A judgement is an evaluation, for example "how beautiful it was." A description means that what is described is perceivable for everybody. Interpretations can be different for each individual. The given answer is subjective. I also looked at differences in the marks the children gave for each episode and to the performance as a whole. The lowest mark was 0 and the highest 10.

How can the impact of a dance performance be enlarged?

Many children showed their ability to see not just what was 'really' there. We noticed that for many of them what was visible on the stage opened a new world, but significantly more interpretations were given by the prepared group. The children's interpretations were mostly labelled as thoughts about objects, animals, characters, activities or situations. Only a few utterances were categorised as related to something outside the possible world of the performance. In these utterances a connection was made between their own interpretation of what was on stage and something that happened or will happen in society, in their own life, in the past or the future. Both groups were very enthusiastic about the performance. The children without preparation were even more impressed by *Alice* than the prepared children. Almost all the children who did not attend the workshops gave the highest possible mark on a 10-point scale. A plausible explanation is that these children were less critical than the prepared group.

Usually, back at school after such an experience, the teacher (in the Netherlands) will give the children the opportunity to talk about their experiences. In many cases this is a mode of 'testing' the children's memories of the performance. Of course a performance can be entertainment for 45 or 60 minutes, but it can also be a starting point for reflection. Teachers in this project could profit from the enthusiasm and positive feelings expressed by the children. The reflective approach could be nurtured with inspiration; for instance from Matthew Reason (2008a) who in a project conducted in three primary schools in Scotland discovered that there are possibilities to allow children to engage more deeply on critical and creative levels in such a way that the theatrical encounter has a beneficial impact beyond the immediate experience itself. To achieve this, teachers need to provide an active structure through which children can explore and extend their experience. Structured investigation through drawing and talking about their drawings was used in this project and is one possible approach; philosophical enquiry is another possibility (Reason, 2008b).

Conclusions of the study showed that ways to enlarge the impact of a dance performance could include:

1. To prepare the children with a clear aim in mind. The aim can vary and needs a translation in the design of the preparation. (In this study the aim of the preparation was to challenge children not just to see what was 'actually' there on stage.)
2. To intensify and extend their experiences after the performance by giving them possibilities for further exploration of these experiences in a structured way.

References

Reason, M. (2008a). Drawing the theatrical experience: how children watch theatre. Retrieved from: www.yorksj.ac.uk/pdf/Drawing%20the%20Theatrical%20Experience%20Final%20version.pdf [Accessed 15 December 2014].

Reason, M. (2008b). Thinking theatre. Enhancing children's theatrical experiences through philosophical enquiry. *Childhood & Philosophy*, 4(7), 115–45.

PART V
Imagined futures for dance education

PHOTO 5.0 Showcase performance. Dance and the Child International and the World Dance Alliance 2012.
Photographer: Lai Chih-Sheng from 'On-Works'

5.1

DANCE EDUCATION

Embodied knowing in the digitalised world

Ann Kipling Brown

Vision for education

Today many educators are concerned with the development and implementation of curricula that provide quality lifelong education for all. They are struggling with the influence of PISA (Programme for International Student Assessment) and the implementation of standardised testing. The attempt to balance the required testing with the demands of core curriculum places a strain on the activities that can be scheduled in a school day. Many are concerned that such testing narrows the scope of what is learned. Some Canadian school districts have removed what they deem as less relevant knowledge areas. The addition of new subjects and the demand for inserting specific skills, character development and interdisciplinarity have placed further stress on an already burdened curriculum. Additionally, there seems to be very little latitude for the exploration of non-formal and local curricula. The challenges of new technologies that have changed the way we communicate and express ourselves socially and artistically place further demands on what can be achieved in the school context.

The need to identify what is required to prepare students for lifelong learning has been addressed from many perspectives; for instance, in the report *Better skills, better jobs, better lives: a strategic approach to skills policies* of the Organisation for Economic Co-operation and Development (OECD), it is reported that, "Skills affect people's lives and the well-being of nations in ways that go far beyond what can be measured by labour-market earnings and economic growth. For example, the benefits of skills to an individual's health are potentially great" (2012: 10). The organisation, involving many countries, in addressing economic issues and the high levels of unemployment seen today helps to identify "how to invest in skills in a way that will transform lives and drive economies" (2012: foreword).

The report classifies policy for relevant skills: changing skills for the present demands, work with partners to design and deliver curricula and education and training programmes of high quality, promote equity in access to and success in quality education for all, ensure that costs and tax systems do not discourage investment in learning; and maintain a long-term perspective on skills development (2012: 18). The relevance and impact of these policies can be seen in the work of other organisations. For instance, in support of quality education UNESCO has focused on education to achieve the aims of building peace, eliminating poverty and the development of intercultural dialogue. As such UNESCO, in the statement "Education for the 21st Century," has committed "to a holistic and humanistic vision of quality education worldwide, the realisation of everyone's right to education, and the belief that education plays a fundamental role in human, social and economic development" (2014). Further the Education for All movement identified six goals to be met by 2015 that focus on ensuring that there is quality education for all.

Scholars, educational institutions and researchers have responded to these challenges through plenary sessions, papers and investigations into how we prepare students for the twenty-first century and the skills that learners will need to lead a creative and sustaining life. The International Bureau of Education (IBE) in *Learning in the post-2015 education and development agenda* identified the concern about the poor levels of basic learning in numeracy and literacy and encouraged the international community "to improve the quality of education and, more specifically, student learning" (2013: 1). The IBE further emphasised "the promotion and value of learning" and reiterated that "the idea of lifelong learning, for instance, was first introduced as early as 1972" (2013: 1).

Further concerns were expressed by the IBE regarding "the rather narrowly defined conceptions of and approaches to learning in many post-2015 documents" (2013: 2). They identified that "learning outside the formal school system is largely ignored" and that "learning outcomes are generally only those measurable in standardized tests" (2013: 2). Finally, IBE outlined how "insufficient attention is given to learning processes and pedagogical approaches, and to the diverse expectations, needs and experiences of learners in classrooms and educational programmers" (2013: 2).

Educational psychologists, sociologists and economists have critically analysed what is happening in the formal and non-formal learning settings and have outlined various models and ideas for preparing students for the twenty-first-century global scene. Sistla Venkata Krishna (2008) reports "that existing test-based education systems will not be able to produce the innovative, skilled workforce required for the twenty-first century, unless it changes course by incorporating Project Learning using technology as part of the formal curriculum."

Additionally, Richard Halkett, Director of Strategy, Research and Global Education for Cisco Systems, draws on the work of Howard Gardner (1993) who has had a profound impact on thinking and practice in education and believes that students who develop the identified intelligences[1] become more engaged and able to lead constructive lives. Halkett also considers the work of Daniel Pink (2009) who recognises three elements of true motivation – autonomy, mastery and purpose. Pink believes that human motivation is largely intrinsic and external rewards and fear of punishment do not encourage good work or behaviour.

Drawing from the work of Gardner, Pink and others, Halkett (2010) acknowledges the pressures on schools and suggests eight themes that are needed to develop twenty-first-century skills: gathering, synthesising and analysing information, working autonomously with motivation and self-discipline, influencing others with consideration, working with creativity and innovation leading to action, thinking critically and asking the right questions, understanding others' perspectives both culturally and globally, communicating effectively with technology, and working ethically. The eight themes suggest change in the way we develop curricula and present learning environments for students.

Similarly, Ronghuai Huang *et al.* identify that "learning is no longer confined to the knowledge maze in traditional textbooks or of matching questions and answers but rests on understanding and defining the problem, how to ask questions and how to find the solutions to the problem" (2013: 7). In defining knowledge-connected learning and knowledge transferability, Huang *et al.* (2013) identify the importance of learning with the use of technology, collaboration, problem-solving and using information in context, thus fostering good study habits and leading to lifelong learning.

Arts education

In this chapter the focus is on how arts education, and in particular dance education, can meet the demands of the scholars and organisations cited above while dealing with the challenges of setting standards that do not allow for individuality, creativity, imagination and curiosity. One of the challenges for arts education, an area that is often viewed as one of those less relevant knowledge areas, is that it may be removed from the school day and placed as an extracurricular programme. It seems as if any budgetary cuts need to be made, the arts are the first to go! In spite of the lack of respect and understanding of the value of an arts education, many countries, states and provinces have managed to establish the arts in the core curriculum and to provide arts education programmes within the K-12 school system.

These countries have recognised that arts education is as important literacy, and in fact offers other literacies, such as expression in movement, visual art, music and digital technologies. The noted educationalist Ken Robinson champions "a radical rethink of our school systems, to cultivate creativity and acknowledge multiple types of intelligence" (TED, 2006).[2] Connecting with the work cited above, one of the best ways to nurture creativity, to find the best way to express oneself, to work collaboratively, to think critically, to understand oneself and others and to communicate effectively with technology can be achieved through arts education, something that should be available to every child.

Arts educators have responded to UNESCO's suggested approaches: *Learning through the arts/culture* and *Learning in the arts/culture*. Both approaches promote drawing on the rich heritage of arts and culture to develop the student's knowledge and understanding, to develop and understand the processes inherent in the arts and to value the expressions of the individual and community. Integral to the two emphases that promote learning about and in the arts is to engender cultural sensitivity and social cohesion. For instance, in Saskatchewan, Canada, the Arts Education curriculum aims "to enable students to understand and value arts expressions throughout life" (*Aims and goals*, 2014) and requires that all students receive instruction each week in dance, drama, music and visual arts.

Students are engaged in investigating the content and aesthetics of the arts within cultural, historical and contemporary contexts and understanding the connection between the arts and human experience; responding to artistic expressions of Saskatchewan, Canadian and international artists using critical thinking, research, creativity and collaborative inquiry; and inquiring, creating and communicating through dance, drama, music and visual art. In 2010 the Saskatchewan Ministry of Education introduced the cross-curricular competencies to be addressed through all areas of study. As a result of these curricular developments and implementation, the Saskatchewan Arts Education curriculum covers broad areas of learning that focus on a sense of self, community and place, lifelong learning and becoming engaged citizens (*Broad areas of learning*, 2010).

The defined competencies have three goals: to develop thinking contextually, creatively and critically; to develop identity and interdependence through understanding and valuing oneself and others; and to develop various literacies to express understanding and communicate meaning (p. 1).

Accordingly, in Saskatchewan and in many other provinces, states and countries, dance educators are concerned with more than learning a routine of dance steps that can be performed with technical proficiency or finding the perfect body for dance, thus excluding the majority of students in our classes. We find that the dance curriculum is not only designed to provide knowledge about dance elements, dance forms, performance and choreographic skills, dance notation, human anatomy and cultural and historical features of dance, but also about how dance can assist in the student's development of self, community and relationship to others.

As Gayle Kassing and Danielle Jay purport, "dance education can be defined as educating the learner through the media of dance, dance making, and dance appreciation" (2003: 4). The learner is central to the learning and dance is the means by which the student is educated physically, socially, emotionally and intellectually. The movement foundation of most dance programmes is creative dance that through structured improvisation assists each student to develop his or her own movement creativity.

Thus, dance educators are concerned with the notions of embodied knowing and embodied enquiry where the student comes to understand dance at a deeper and more personal level. This embodied knowledge is a type of knowledge where the body knows how to act, reflecting one of Gardner's multiple intelligences: "the core elements of the bodily-kinaesthetic intelligence are control of one's bodily motions and the capacity to handle objects skilful" (1993: 6). The concept of embodied knowledge is derived from the phenomenology of the French philosopher, Maurice Merleau-Ponty (2005), who questioned the Cartesian dualism of mind and body.

We perceive the world through our bodies and thus lead embodied existences. Merleau-Ponty's philosophy has underpinned the work of many dance scholars, such as Sondra Fraleigh, who accepts his account of perception as the centrality that the lived body plays in our understanding of ourselves and our expression through dance. As Fraleigh points out, "Dance is a creative and aesthetic extension of our embodiment. The body and the dance are inseparable" (2004: 31). Our aim as dance educators is to empower students to move with aesthetic intent, exploring and expressing personal ideas and additionally coming to understand other's perspectives through dance.

The digital world

UNESCO leads the way in setting policy for technology.

> The UNESCO ICT Competency Framework for Teachers (ICT-CFT) is intended to inform educational policy makers, teacher-educators, providers of professional learning and working teachers on the role of ICT in educational reform, as well as to assist Member States in developing national ICT competency standards for teachers with an ICT in Education Master Plan approach.
>
> *(ICT in Education)*

The integration of telecommunication and computers, and the development of software and audio-visual systems that enable users to access, store, transmit and manipulate information, is significant to the discussion of relevant skills for the twenty-first century. Krisha, while talking about developments in Asia and India, identifies facts relevant to this discussion.

> Transformative changes have taken place in the world during the last decade due to the explosion of inter-connectivity linking people from all walks of life across the globe. Low-cost Information and Communication Technology (ICT) tools, especially internet and mobile technologies, are powering this wave of change. As a result, new skills and innovative abilities are required of students and workers in their learning, livelihood and life.
>
> *(ICT in Education)*

Young people today are no longer consumers of new digital technologies, but are multimedia literate and able to use the new digital technologies for self-development and to express themselves. At one time, touchscreen laptops, desktops, tablets and mobile phones were both unavailable to many and often banned from the classroom. However, we have come to see how these devices are changing the way we live and how we learn. More people, in both rural and urban settings, have access to the internet and are able to communicate and access information quickly and efficiently. In matching the skills outlined above, the use of digital technology is noticeably significant and relevant in generating and realising curriculum in all areas.

The use of digital technology in arts education and in particular dance education opens up new perspectives for arts education and requests new roles for educators in the twenty-first century. In the world of dance, where the body/ies interact with the chosen spatial environment, it would seem that there would be no interest in working with digital technology. However, this is not the case. Dance educators have found use for the camera to record and review students' performance and choreography, the availability of dance works via the internet has provided access to works that would never be seen in some towns and cities, and the use of software like DanceForms and Labanwriter have offered a means to both choreograph and notate movement and dance. And, of course, dance artists have enhanced their choreography through technological elements in both media-created works and live performance. Technology has transformed the way they express themselves.

For instance, Merce Cunningham was a leader in applying new technologies in dance from his early work in film, his choreography with the computer programme DanceForms, and later motion capture technology with digital artists Paul Kaiser and Shelley Eshkar. Thecla Schiphorst (2006), a computer media artist, computer systems designer, choreographer and dancer, presented *Bodymaps: artifacts of touch*, which constructs a space inhabited by the body as mediated by technology. Lisa Naugle's work centres on computer-based applications for dance including motion capture, internet-based performance and interactive technology.

There are some exciting choreographies that have merged dance and technology, but there are critics who have asked how the fusion of dance and technology will affect the future of dance as an art form. Alyssa Schoeneman (2010) asks this question in her *Technology and dance essay*, and suggests: "Technological effects walk a fine line between enhancing or overpowering dance choreography when they exist in such close quarters; it is easy for audience members to get lost in the 'eye candy', or special effects, of a piece and to ultimately disregard the choreography altogether" (*The Future*). She provides several examples of successful works and draws on a personal interview with graphic designer Andrew Moffat (4 April 2010) as well as others, concluding that "shared kinaesthetic and intellectual constructs from the field of dance and the field of technology will reinforce and enhance one another, resulting in an ultimately deepened experience for both viewer and performer" (*The Future*).

This discussion leads me to a re-evaluation of dance curricula. Our students should be introduced to digital technology, including digital music and sound design, video editing and camera techniques, DanceForms, motion capture technology and dance production technology, as well as the use of information and communication technologies. It is important to understand and engage with such technologies and practices and include them in learning practices to stimulate creativity. However, some critics find that while the use of digital technology may produce a more eager engagement in arts/dance education, such an approach may result in a devaluing of both the process and product of creation.

Integrating digital technology in dance education

Although technologies have been implemented by many dance artists to create, present and record their work, I would suggest that dance educators in formal education, both for school-aged and university students, have used technology incidentally in their courses. Some of us have supplemented our face-to-face classes and created websites that contain course information and suggested readings and YouTube performances that students can view and study in their own time. Additionally, many of us have been charged with delivering online courses that provide access for distance learning. Most students have responded positively to these enhancements, responding that they appreciate having additional materials that they can view in their own time.

Zihao Li, while recognising the paucity of integrating technology within the dance curriculum, offers a successful example of how technology can enhance dance learning. Li used podcasts with undergraduate BFA students. He describes the process thus: "While dancing in class, [students] were randomly featured on recordings, which were then transferred to a Mac Pro computer to produce YouTube-like podcasts" (2011: 5). Li explains that a podcast was usually posted online a few hours after the first class and that in the beginning only a few students accessed the podcast. However, this changed as students saw how important "it was to review class material online prior to the next class." The students provided feedback on the experience, many noting how they "enjoyed having the freedom and flexibility to choose when and where to engage with class material" (2011: 7). One significant outcome was that students felt "they better connected body and mind after examining their dancing in virtual space" and were able to scrutinise "how they actually executed the steps, moves, jumps, or how they used their breath, rather than the perceived version in their heads" (2011: 8).

In creating online courses for senior students in a dance education programme, I was challenged with providing an experience that considered the importance of embodied knowing and the requirement to make a course accessible for distance learning. In a dance history course, covering ballet and modern dance, the ten modules contained written content, visual images and video and podcast links. Some of the video and podcast links were created specifically for the course and others were acquired through the internet and dance resources. The course required that students keep a written and video journal of the information covered. Additionally, students were obliged to submit six video assignments that asked them to perform specific movements, create in the style of a choreographer or attempt a selected dance. Students enjoyed the chance to dance and commented that they were challenged by those dance forms with which they were not familiar; for instance, many of the students had studied ballet extensively and had minimal experience in contemporary dance.

The responsibility and benefits of creating an effective and worthwhile dance education programme require that educators consider the focus of education for the twenty-first century as outlined by such organisations as UNESCO. In particular, UNESCO offers insight into arts education through the approaches, *Learning through the arts/culture* and *Learning in the arts/culture*. The question of whether our arts education curriculum today reflects the suggested focus and assists in the development of those twenty-first-century skills needs to be considered. It is not suggested that we relinquish the practical work of the dance class, or only use computers to create and record our dances.

Technology can be embedded to enrich the experiences of dance performing, making and appreciating, and dance educators need to explore how technology can enhance learning. Students can gather information about dance forms, choreographers and performers from sources provided by the internet, come to understand the cultural and historical significance of the information and learn to synthesise and analyse the information critically. The dance class offers opportunities to work independently and in groups using technology to assess the performance of a set sequence or dance creation. Students can experiment with technology to find how they might enhance their work or create for the digital world. The goals of education for the twenty-first century and the focus of an embodied understanding of dance using technology to enhance learning are the aims of a good dance curriculum.

Notes

1 Howard Gardner, a developmental psychologist, identified distinct intelligences that enable people to learn, remember, perform and understand in different ways: Visual-spatial, bodily kinaesthetic, musical, interpersonal, intrapersonal, verbal-linguistic, logical-mathematical, naturalistic and existential.
2 TED (Technology, Entertainment, Design), founded in 1984, is a global set of conferences owned by the private non-profit Sapling Foundation, providing talks for free viewing online through TED.com.

References

Cunningham, M. (2014). Merce Cunningham Trust. Retrieved from www.mercecunningham.org/merce-cunningham [Accessed 15 December 2014].

Fraleigh, S. (2004). *Dancing identity: metaphysics in motion*. Pittsburgh: University of Pittsburgh Press.

Gardner, H. (1993). *Frames of mind: the theory of multiple intelligences*. New York: Basis Books.

Halkett, R. (2010). Building 21st century skills. Cisco podcast. Retrieved from www.youtube.com/watch?v=Wcv8NVR0VEA [Accessed 15 December 2014].

Huang, R., Chen, G., Junfeng Yang, J. and Loewen, J. (2013). The new shape of learning: adapting to social changes in the information society. In R. Huang, J. Kinshuk and M. Spector (Eds.). *Reshaping learning. frontiers of learning technology in a global context* (pp. 3–42). Berlin: Springer-Verlag.

Kassing, G. and Jay, D.M. (2003). *Dance teaching methods and curriculum design. Comprehensive K-12 dance education*. Champaign, IL: Human Kinetics.

Krishna, S.V. (2008). *The use of technology to build 21st century skills in formal education*. Retrieved from http://linc.mit.edu/linc2010/proceedings/session9KRISHNA.pdf [Accessed 15 December 2014].

Li, Z. (2011). *How technology shapes the way we teach dance*. Retrieved from www.twu.edu/downloads/dance/Zihao_How_Technology_Shapes_our_Way_of_Teaching_Dance_-_Zihao_Li_%282%29.pdf [Accessed 15 December 2014].

Merleau-Ponty, M. (2005). *Phenomenology of perception*. Trans. C. Smith. New York: The Humanities Press.

Naugle, L. *Research and performance*. Retrieved from http://dance.arts.uci.edu/lnaugle [Accessed 15 December 2014].

Pink, D.H. (2009). *Drive: the surprising truth about what motivates us*. New York: Riverhead Books.

Robinson, K. (2006). *How schools kill creativity*. TED talk. Retrieved from www.ted.com/speakers/sir_ken_robinson.html [Accessed 15 December 2014].

Saskatchewan Curriculum Education (2014). *Arts Education K Aims and Goals*. Retrieved from www.edonline.sk.ca/webapps/moe-curriculum-BBLEARN/index.jsp?view=goals&lang=en&subj=arts_education&level=k [Accessed 15 December 2014].

Saskatchewan Ministry of Education (2010). *Broad areas of learning*. Retrieved from www.edonline.sk.ca/bbcswebdav/library/curricula/English/Broad_Areas_of_Learning_2010.pdf [Accessed 15 December 2014].

Schiphorst, T. (2006). Affectionate computing: can we fall in love with a machine? Institute of Electrical and Electronics Engineers. *Multimedia*, 13(1), 20–3.

Schiphorst, T. (2014). *Bodymaps: artifacts of touch. The sensuality and anarchy of touch*. Dance & Technology Zone. Retrieved from www.art.net/~dtz/schipo1.html [Accessed 15 December 2014].

Schoeneman, A. (2010). *Technology and dance essay*. Retrieved from www.hastac.org/blogs/aschoen2/technology-and-dance-essay-written-spring-2010 [Accessed 15 December 2014].

The Organisation for Economic Co-operation and Development (OECD) (2012). skills.oecd. Retrieved from http://skills.oecd.org [Accessed 15 December 2014].

UNESCO (2010). *ICT in Education*. Retrieved from www.unesco.org/new/en/unesco/themes/icts/teacher-education/unesco-ict-competency-framework-for-teachers [Accessed 15 December 2014].

UNESCO (2013). *Learning in the post-2015 education and development agenda*. Retrieved from www.ibe.unesco.org/fileadmin/user_upload/Publications/UNESCO-IBE_Statement_on_Learning_Post-2015_eng.pdf [Accessed 15 December 2014].

UNESCO (2014). *Education for all goals*. Retrieved from www.unesco.org/new/en/education/themes/leading-the-international-agenda/education-for-all/efa-goals [Accessed 15 December 2014].

5.2

PARTNERSHIPS FOR CREATIVITY

Expanding teaching possibilities

Kerry Chappell and Veronica Jobbins

Introduction

In the current UK political educational climate, dominated by the drive for core skills and subjects, with a diminishing arts education offer, we find ourselves searching afresh for evidence and rationales for the dance discipline within education. We not only have rationales at our fingertips (e.g. National Dance Teachers Association, 2004; Eisner, 2004; Abbs, 2003), but also evidence from recent empirical research. These investigations demonstrate the empowering capacity of dance education pedagogies and young people's creative learning shifts and personal journeys of becoming that can ensue (Chappell *et al.*, 2011).

The roots of this research lie in conversations begun in 2007 by the group[1] who formed the university team for the Arts and Humanities Research Council-funded Dance Partners for Creativity (DPC) project. We came together with shared concerns regarding an increasing prevalence of teaching methodologies and assessment agendas stifling creativity within schools. Our professional backgrounds spanned dance teaching in schools, initial teacher training, dance education research, dance education policy and advocacy and broader research in creativity in education. Through both theoretical and practical discussions about dance education and beyond, we formulated the premise for the research that dance education in secondary schools was suffering as a result of the performativity agenda and pressure from testing and attainment agendas (Chappell *et al.*, 2009).

We surmised that despite having found a relatively secure place within the national curriculum, albeit as part of physical education, dance in schools was not fulfilling its creative potential within the school curriculum. Rather individual pupils' creativity was frequently sacrificed in favour of prescribed teaching that could result in formulaic choreographic outcomes meeting externally prescribed targets from examination boards and schools' assessment policies, rather than encouraging risk-taking and imagination. This reflects Stephen Ball's (2003) concern as an educational policy analyst regarding 'performativity' that students' achievements are used as measures not only of students' worth but also of schools' success, and that this outcomes focus dominates the students' individual learning journeys.

Some years later writing this chapter, the educational climate where performativity flourishes has become even further embedded within school settings. Recent UK government policies have sought to emphasise so-called core skills, harking back to traditional values with the apparent aim of providing an education system for children that keeps pace with accelerating "economic and technological change" (Gove, 2011). Far-reaching structural changes to the organisation of schools and accountability systems that prioritise the teaching of a narrowly defined set of subjects have increasingly pushed arts subjects further down a hierarchical curriculum structure.

More and more, the cluster of subjects valued by the prevailing government, termed the English Baccalaureate (EBacc) – Mathematics, English, Sciences, Humanities and Languages – are being favoured through teaching time, funding and a host of direct and indirect measures that discourage young people from pursuing creative and artistic subjects as part of their school curriculum. The Cultural Learning Alliance[2] has shown that the number of children studying arts GCSEs has fallen since the introduction of the English Baccalaureate performance measure, with 14 per cent fewer arts GCSEs being taken in 2013 than in 2010, and a 12 per cent decline in those taking dance. This is happening within a UK landscape of reduced funding for the arts which is being echoed across Europe. As schools prioritise other subjects, the funding needed to support the creative partnerships that DPC sought to highlight is becoming less available.

In this climate the DPC working approach and evidence from the original study become all the more important. We aim to demonstrate how dance education strongly connected to the professional dance community can contribute to positive and meaningful changes in learning for young people in a way that also values the professionalism of the adults around them. In this chapter we show what is special about creative partnership and its pedagogies, and how it alters practice for the school and external partners and changes learning in dance for the young people involved. We also consider how the DPC approach and outcomes might provide "a lifeline to individuals and initiatives which would otherwise tread water in wait for the next wave of supportive policy" (Chappell *et al.*, 2011: 159).

DPC approach and methods

DPC involved four university-based researchers supported by six consultant research assistants and ten school-focused researchers.[3] This team was spread across four English dance initiatives.[4] Mostly, collaboration took place between a school partner (an experienced teacher – most with a dance specialism), external partner (with professional dance practitioner expertise) and university researcher (Kerry Chappell, Linda Rolfe, Anna Craft at Exeter University or Veronica Jobbins at Trinity Laban) guiding the progress. All researchers were focused on answering one shared research question: what kinds of creative partnerships are manifested between dance artists and teachers in co-developing the creativity of 11–14-year-olds in dance education, and how do they develop? Each site also had a 'site-specific' research question. As an example, in the London site, the school partner (a teacher), Caroline Watkins and external partner Bim Malcomson (a professional dance artist) collaborated in DPC with Linda Rolfe and Veronica Jobbins (university researchers). As well as contributing data to answer the main shared research question, they also queried: how do the external partner and school partner work together; what are their roles and relationships? (See Malcomson *et al.*, 2011 for findings.) This question was specifically asked in this school context, where dance begins in the first year with 11–12-year-olds having weekly hour-long practical lessons. Later, students are offered various courses, from pure dance to combined performing arts. Many of those pursuing dance at 16+ progress to university to study dance. The school also offers a variety of enrichment and extra-curricular opportunities.

In the London site and the project as a whole, the university team were committed to acknowledging the social construction of reality and multiple lived perspectives. This meant gathering data using a qualitative methodology. In addition, we sought to develop theory oriented toward critiquing and changing, as opposed to theory oriented only toward understanding or explaining (e.g. McCarthy, 1991). It was distinct from purely social constructivist research, stretching beyond researching 'on' participants to researching 'with' participants. Perhaps most significantly, this project was designed to nurture open dialogue. Influenced by philosophers Mikhail Bakhtin (1984) and Henri Lefebvre (1991), the DPC methodology evolved into what we came to refer to as 'living dialogic spaces' characterised by creative learning conversations. These are highly reflective conversations based on evidence, with a focus on stimulating action.

Data was generated through a range of provocation mechanisms designed to re-frame research space for powerful learning conversations. Examples include conceptual and journey mapping using visual media such as post-its, phrase completion exercises (e.g. "Teacher is . . . Artist is . . . Partnership is . . . "), and graffiti work around student body outlines. Mapping work generated visual media resources as a source and focus of discussion for researchers in each site. Mechanisms used later for analysing and representing ideas within learning conversations included shape-puzzles and photographic montage. DPC also made use of traditional qualitative methods such as interviews, field notes, observations and audio-recorded, photographed or video-recorded data.

What we found

Current government education policies in the UK have been criticised, particularly in the media,[5] for seeing children as empty vessels to be filled. This attitude connects to the perspective that young people should be viewed as passive, at risk and in need of protection. As Anna Craft (2011) argues, in the continuum of western worldviews on the nature of youth, at one extreme is policy and accompanying practice which sees young people as at risk in this way, a view increasingly dominant in England. At the other end of the continuum young people are treated as empowered, capable, active individuals who can be independent of adults. Whilst acknowledging the need to safeguard children from risk, it is this other end of the continuum that the DPC evidence fits within. In so doing, the research demonstrates possibilities for empowering creative partnerships, their pedagogies and how these can change learning in dance for young people, and perhaps how they apply to their learning more widely. This is rooted in seven core principles: ownership, difference and dialogue, quality, embodiment, professional wisdom, communal cohesion, and generative possibility (Chappell et al., 2011). These are represented in Figure 5.2.1 below.

These principles were derived from all the research strands led by both university and partner researchers. Here we will highlight those strands that help us to understand partnership structures and their pedagogies. Four key characteristics of partnership particularly helped to define the principles of ownership, difference and dialogue, and community cohesion (Chappell, 2011). First, in all four research sites, in one way or another, students were viewed as partners in their own right. Adults talked about 'learning from them' as much as vice versa. Second, young

FIGURE 5.2.1 Principles of creative partnership practice.
Photographer: DPC research collection

people and adults engaged in identity shifting, e.g. teacher, choreographer, manager, learner, surrogate family member. This shifting meant that students especially took on identities that went beyond what was usually expected and in turn empowered them to create new dance ideas.

Third, all partners engaged in different kinds of leadership roles, e.g. a co-leader role meant two or more individuals collaboratively guiding activity and an inclusive leader adopted a flattened hierarchy that incorporated different voices in a small group. These different role structures shifted how adults and students were positioned in relation to dance ideas and took them in new and unexpected directions. Last, all of these partnership characteristics took place within a temporary shared creative group identity, much like a dance company, and provided a safe, empathetic place to create.

Together, these partnership characteristics contributed to flattening hierarchies in dance classrooms, forming the bedrock of the partnership pedagogies that ensued, and working to nurture creativity. Other strands of the research considered the kind of creativity that was nurtured within DPC (Chappell *et al.*, 2012). In brief, it was defined as wise, humanising creativity at the heart of which is an embodied dialogic generation of ideas. Through the creative process young people were making and being made; they were 'becoming'. Wise, humanising creativity is therefore an active process of change guided by compassion and reference to shared values. Change comes from people engaging in collaborative thinking and shared action to imaginatively develop new ideas, which are valuable to them and their community.

Craft (2011) was able to tease out an overarching way of thinking about being a teacher or facilitator of this kind of creativity within DPC, drawing on educational researcher Erica McWilliam's (2008) work to articulate the teacher role as meddling in the middle. This means that teachers acknowledge that they do not 'know' it all but can work alongside their students to learn together, they allow for risk rather than 'risk-minimisation', they design, assemble and edit ideas with their students and they become a 'collaborative critic and authentic evaluator'. This shifts us away from the dichotomised idea that teachers/facilitators are either 'sage on the stage' (experts filling students with knowledge) or 'guide on the side' (coaching students, recognising their existing knowledge and experience).

When viewed as a lens to understand the DPC approach and evidence, 'meddling in the middle' helped to define the principles of difference and dialogue, professional wisdom, communal cohesion and generative possibility. What was special about the partnership structures within DPC sites was that partnerships emerged as respecting adults and students alike, allowing for different identity and leadership roles within a shared creative group identity. The traditional adult role of 'teacher' could be seen reconceptualised as 'meddling in the middle'. So what of the actual pedagogies that ensued – what were they and how were they creative and empowering? The DPC data showed that in the research sites, with these structures as a foundation, external and school partners were able to extend their teaching approaches and come up with new possibilities for teaching.

Extending teaching approaches into a mutual journey of discovery

Data analysis showed five key features of partnership pedagogies were important regarding teaching approaches: understanding that the partnership was a joint journey of discovery; partnerships creating new emergent possibilities through giving and sharing knowledge; partners co-constructing choreography; partners complementing each other's teaching; and partners exploiting their shared repertoire of chorographic practice to go in new directions. As these themes emerged, it became apparent that there was a strong resonance with educational theorist Etienne Wenger's notion of "communities of practice" in which he identifies three dimensions that form the basis "by which practice is the source of coherence of a community" (1998: 72). These are the mutual engagement of participants; a joint enterprise defined as a process that pushes practice forwards and invites new ideas; and a shared repertoire whereby shared histories of engagement can become resources for negotiating meaning. Wenger's turns of phrase are therefore used in the findings where appropriate.

All partners were mutually engaged in their project activities and viewed them as a joint enterprise. They often, however, began with differently motivated starting points. The external partners' driving force tended to be an artistic vision, as Bim, the dance artist from the London site, explained:

> I don't think about their learning . . . My starting point is an artistic vision.
>
> *(London site, beginning of project)*

Caroline, her school partner, was motivated by the need to prepare students for dance examinations and a wider school agenda. Bim, having less responsibility for the students' wider learning, could focus on what needed to be done to stimulate imaginations and create new choreography, as reflected in the following conversation:

Caroline: I would still be honed into can these children talk about it? Can they express it? Have they developed it? To what level have they developed it? . . . What about their performance, what about . . . all the skills that they're meant to have?

Linda: Can I ask Bim then, are you thinking about those things?

Bim: No, I'm thinking about are they fully engaged with the task in the class, really important. Are they being careful of people around them? And are they making work that's interesting? And if they're not, what tools do I need to give them to make their work interesting?

(London site, beginning of project)

Another external partner (a dance artist) commented on the importance of venturing into new and challenging areas of dance experience:

Where's this going to go . . . and that sense of surprise and mystery and the cliff-hanger of next week we'll carry on. I think all that's really important to this sort of work to keep them engaged and interested and not tell them what's going to happen . . . you haven't said by the end of the lesson you will all be able to do X, Y and Z.

(external partner, East of England site, middle of project)

Despite external partners' differences, these comments show a sense of the importance of the creative process and choreography voyaging into the unknown and a recognition of how the teaching approaches engage pupils and capture their interest in learning.

Creating new teaching possibilities

The shared understanding that working with young people was a voyage of discovery allowed the partners to make the most of new teaching possibilities. Two sets of partners talked about keeping the content and teaching strategies used in a session relatively open and of prioritising the interaction with each other and the pupils. They did not delineate teaching approaches between themselves as they reflected in action and responded to situations as they emerged. This resonates closely with Wenger's ideas:

Teaching must be opportunistic because it cannot control its own effects. Opportunism does not mean laissez-faire . . . what matters is . . . the ability for teaching and learning to interact so as to become structuring resources for each other.

(Wenger, 1998: 267)

This implies that while there might be a map for the journey, different routes were possible. It was often the external partners' different kinds of knowledge about the learners that helped provide an open-ended structure to lesson planning between them.

The mutual engagement of partners allowed for complementary approaches to emerge. These drew on what partners did and knew as well as connecting with what they did not do or know. The new ideas that emerged through the joint enterprise of teaching in partnership reflect what Graham Jeffery (2005) refers to as the artistry of teaching. This artistically exchanged knowledge became a teaching resource which was further fuelled by the partners' overlapping dance competences.

Co-constructing choreography

Within the partnerships, dance-making involved establishing teaching methods that valued collaborative choreography, with not only adults but also pupils who became actively engaged in, for example, exploring ideas, using their imagination to solve problems and structuring movement material. The following comment from an external partner explains the processes and their connection to school practice:

> The making process is . . . through the students composing their own movement material, or at the very least developing material that Lîla Dance teach to them . . . much of their material is created in response to tasks, feedback, images . . . the process becomes entirely applicable to their own practices at school.
>
> *(South-East of England site, middle of project)*

This often involved the external partner teaching little pre-choreographed dance material for students to learn, and instead using more risk-taking approaches perhaps because their presence allowed for the exploration of teaching approaches with the potential to develop more creativity. As one external partner commented:

> The bravery to work in absolute partnership, you absolutely trust [the students] to create movement material, even when it doesn't look quite right.
>
> *(South-East of England site, middle of project)*

Part of the external partners' teaching approaches was to share skills and expertise with the students as they worked alongside them to co-construct the choreography. Studio sessions were often structured with open tasks to encourage pupils to explore physical responses and generate their own vocabulary. In the image below, pairs of pupils from the South-East of England site are working to create a phrase based on imagery.

Using complementary teaching approaches

The shared understanding of choreographic practice strengthened the common ground between the partners as they worked together using a common spoken and physical language of dance. There were, however, some subtle differences between how the partners expressed the movement tasks. In the London site, for example, Bim, the external partner, described her way of working:

> I think the way I encourage students to learn is through asking them open-ended questions like how could you do that differently or what could make that more exciting.
>
> *(London site, middle of project)*

This approach differed from that used by the school partner, evidenced in one of the university researcher's reflections:

> Caroline explains why they are doing the task, use of space and body parts, asks questions of pupils, breaks task down and layers how they might answer the task.
>
> *(London site, middle of project)*

PHOTO 5.2.1 Pairs of pupils working to create an imagery-based phrase.
Photographer: DPC research collection

In another lesson her reflection notes that:

> Bim insists that they try using different body parts, calls out "carve a road through your kinaesphere", asks for ideas for pathways through space, a pupil calls out "a square" and they all try that idea. Caroline suggests how to connect the movements, the only time that she takes a lead role.
>
> *(London site, middle of project)*

These examples evidence differing teaching approaches seen across the three sites where external partners (dance artists and dance companies) more often left the students more space, physically and mentally, to explore and solve choreographic problems (Photo 5.2.1). The artists' language encouraged pupils to push for originality, particularly through imagery. School partners tended to suggest potential ways to answer the task, for example by the use of action, space or dynamics. Although they also used imagery and encouraged pupils to answer questions, their focus seemed to be more on students' learning processes than artistic outcomes. As the projects developed, partners began to reflect and share approaches.

Dancing together

The partnerships opened up possibilities to teach in different ways. By dancing together, the partners were able to physically demonstrate choreographic ideas, for example using lifts and contact, which pupils could observe, discuss and try for themselves. Physical demonstration generated great interest and enthusiasm in pupils as the activities connected personally with them and demonstrated how ideas could be explored through taking physical risks. The learning power of live demonstration in dance provided a model of what might be possible and how to work collaboratively with another person in dance as well as more widely. The demonstrations provided a compelling example of working relationships in dance which are a key element in current ways of working choreographically. Pupils in the London site supported this by saying:

> Bim and Miss Watkins worked together very well and when they were demonstrating they improvised very well.
>
> I thought that they were best friends.
>
> They help us feel more comfortable and confident.
>
> They work together well. They discuss and make it happen. They are equal.
>
> *(London site, middle of project)*

Collaborating as learners

Dance requires personal exploration and collaboration as integral parts of the choreographic process. The DPC sites provided abundant evidence of pupils working collaboratively as choreographers. More unusually, the partners became role models in co-creation, as both external and school partners moved away from teacher-centred instruction towards a shared understanding of working as dancers alongside the pupils. In the London site the external partner continually pushed Caroline, the school partner, to work as a choreographer with an artistic vision for the project. Letting go of familiar ways of working meant that Caroline allowed the artistic process to be in the foreground. It also involved Bim letting go of some artistic responsibility, which she found a challenge but rewarding. They shared a collaborative approach to choreography with the pupils which involved them re-thinking and refining their pedagogy.

An equally strong element in this site was the partners learning from each other. Bim felt that previously she had not entered a partnership expecting to use the teacher's expertise or consider what she might learn. In this project it was different and she clearly learnt from Caroline as shown in their discussion:

> Bim: I don't think artists use the teacher's expertise . . . because of how artists are defined and how teachers are defined, particularly in this relationship, that is just not in the equation usually.
>
> Linda: Is it not also about sharing and developing one's expertise between two professionals?
>
> Caroline: Your creativity and the way that maybe . . . I work with the kids might be different in the way that you do, and you might learn new skills.
>
> Bim: Right.
>
> *(London site, end of project)*

Being exposed to new ideas encouraged all the school partners to take a fresh look at their teaching and the following extract is typical:

> I'm exposed to new ideas, and it's sparking off my creativity and making me want to go away and think about things that I am doing in lessons and perhaps revisiting them in a new light.
>
> *(Helen, school partner, East of England site, beginning of project)*

Conclusion

In the introduction, we outlined our concerns and rationale for undertaking the DPC research as being the premise of performativity resulting in formulaic teaching and artistic outcomes that lacked imagination and creativity. While not surprised, we were saddened to find that consistently across all sites there was evidence that teachers were constrained by assessment agendas that did not encourage more open-ended and risk-taking teaching approaches. Caroline, a school partner, commented:

> As teachers, we are governed by assessment frameworks and . . . in our school we've just adopted a new lesson planning format . . . to a certain extent, [it] lend[s] itself to what we do in dance, because it is about setting aims and objectives. It is about a creative task that they will explore . . . but it is very much in [an] order. And sometimes it's nice just to be able to start with something and let it just drift in the manner that you want.

Evidence from all sites showed that despite these constraints, partnership approaches were able to challenge and influence teaching as shown above, leading to greater engagement in learning from the young people and demonstrably more creative outcomes. One of the South-East England students commented:

> It's good because [the external partner] pushes us, and you never know obviously where you're going to finish . . . I want to do it for myself and everybody else, but you . . . also want to push yourself for [the external partners] as well.
>
> *(South-East England site, end of project)*

As seen above, such approaches as co-construction of choreography, the way in which young people benefited from the learning power of live demonstration and gained greater ownership as they worked alongside both school and external partners to explore new creative territories, provided many ways in which performative agendas in schools could be mitigated by creative dance pedagogies, to the benefit of young people's learning in dance and potentially beyond.

As we draw this chapter to a close, it is easy to bemoan the state of our education system where an entitlement to arts education and especially dance is being eroded. It is much harder to find lessons in our research that can be meaningful within such an arid educational landscape. But we recognise that it is vital for those of us who believe that creativity and the arts should be at the heart of any high-quality education for young people to keep alive the DPC findings and principles. Even if funding is now scarce for ongoing partnership projects, we can still find small incremental ways to keep extending teaching approaches and come up with new possibilities for teaching towards the future by focusing on the core principles of ownership, difference and dialogue, quality, embodiment, professional wisdom, communal cohesion, and generative possibility.

It would be unrealistic to expect that current government policies that prioritise performativity can be confronted and changed in the near future. However, our understanding of creativity and learned qualities of adaptability and flexibility can equip us, as Ben Okri so eloquently puts it, "to become adaptive mariners" (1999: 48). We need to work to support each other from our complementary positions within the larger systems to navigate beyond performativity rather than be stifled by it. We can draw support from alternative educational futures analysts such as Michael Fielding and Peter Moss, who advocate what they call "education in its broadest sense" (2010: 46), a concept with which we find much resonance. They argue against the limited 'official' future offered by the policymakers, who articulate closed, prescribed educational models rather than diverse alternatives that acknowledge the fast pace of change outside education and the wider needs of the individual.

As well as this, we know that the educational landscape in UK schools does at least still include the arts and dance in the national curriculum. There are many at both primary and secondary levels who support and encourage creativity in our schools. We can work with them to practically explore how partnership is a relevant pedagogical model for the future. Creative headteachers can be encouraged to understand that the borders between subjects can be more fluid because real life does not reflect the false subject divisions of our education system. Themes can and must be explored via partnerships across traditional subject borders involving more professionals. It is time not to complain but to continue to research together and encourage evidence-based pedagogical change to keep incrementally, cumulatively, proactively fuelling the quiet revolution.

Acknowledgements

Thanks to the Arts and Humanities Research Council for the research grant (Grant number: AH/F010168/1), which made the DPC project possible, and to Trinity Laban for in-kind support. We are also very grateful to all our partner researchers for their contributions, and to our colleagues Anna Craft and Linda Rolfe for their inspiring collaborative conversations during the project (both of whom are sadly no longer here to co-author this chapter with us). Thanks also to Scott Walker (www.mildlyartistic.co.uk) for the digitised visual representation in Figure 5.2.1 and Trentham Books, publisher of *Close encounters: dance partners for creativity* (Chappell *et al.*, 2011), who has given us permission to use the figure and the photo included in this chapter.

Notes

1 Kerry Chappell, Anna Craft, Veronica Jobbins and Linda Rolfe.
2 The Cultural Learning Alliance is a collective voice in the UK working to ensure that all children and young people have meaningful access to culture by bringing the cultural sector to work together with the education and youth sector, with parents and with young people (www.culturallearningalliance.org.uk).
3 University researchers: Anna Craft, Kerry Chappell, Linda Rolfe, Veronica Jobbins. Research assistants: Margo Greenwood, Chu-Yun Wang, Linda McConnon, David McCormick, Debbie Watson, Maria Gregoriou. Partner researchers: Helen Angove, Sian Goss, Abi Mortimer, Jackie Mortimer, Carrie Whitaker, Rachelle Green, Bim Malcomson, Michael Platt, Caroline Watkins, Helen Wright.
4 London site initiative, SW site initiative, SE site initiative, East site initiative.
5 www.theguardian.com/books/2013/jul/13/michael-gove-teaching-history-wars.

References

Abbs, P. (2003). *Against the flow: education, the arts and postmodern culture*. London: RoutledgeFalmer.

Bakhtin, M.M. (1984). *Problems of Dostoevsky's poetics*. Ed. and trans. by Caryl Emerson. Minneapolis: University of Michigan Press.

Ball, S.J. (2003). The teacher's soul and the terrors of performativity. *Journal of Education Policy*, 18(2), 215–28.

Bannerman, C., Sofaer, J. and Watt, J. (2006). *Navigating the unknown: the creative process in contemporary performing arts*. Middlesex: Middlesex University Press.

Chappell, K. (2011). Journeys of becoming: humanising creativity. In K. Chappell, L. Rolfe, A. Craft and V. Jobbins. *Close encounters: dance partners for creativity* (pp. 89–100). Stoke on Trent: Trentham Books.

Chappell, K. and Craft, A. (2011). Creative learning conversations: producing living dialogic spaces. *Educational Research*, 53(3), 363–85.

Chappell, K. and Craft, A. with Rolfe, L. and Jobbins, V. (2011). Not just surviving but thriving. In K. Chappell, L. Rolfe, A. Craft and V. Jobbins, *Close encounters: dance partners for creativity* (pp. 143–59). Stoke on Trent: Trentham Books.

Chappell, K., Craft, A., Rolfe, L. and Jobbins, V. (2009). Dance partners for creativity: choreographing space for co-participative research into creativity and partnership in dance education. *Research in Dance Education Creativity Special Issue*, 10(3), 177–97.

Chappell, K., Rolfe, L., Craft, A. and Jobbins, V. (2011). *Close encounters: dance partners for creativity*. Stoke on Trent: Trentham Books.

Chappell, K. with Craft, A.R., Rolfe, L. and Jobbins, V. (2012). Humanizing creativity: valuing our journeys of becoming. *International Journal of Education & the Arts*, 13(8). Retrieved from www.ijea.org/v13n8 [Accessed 28 November 2013].

Craft, A. (2011). Becoming meddlers in the middle: stretch, leap and challenge? In K. Chappell, L. Rolfe, A. Craft and V. Jobbins, *Close encounters: dance partners for creativity* (pp. 113–27). Stoke on Trent: Trentham Books.

Craft, A. with Chappell, K., Rolfe, L. and Jobbins, V. (2011). Creating fruitful research spaces: methodology. In K. Chappell, L. Rolfe, A. Craft and V. Jobbins, *Close encounters: dance partners for creativity* (pp. 11–27). Stoke on Trent: Trentham Books.

Eisner, E. (2004). What can education learn from the arts about the practice of education? *International Journal of Education and the Arts*, 5(4), 1–13.

Fielding, M. and Moss, P. (2010). *Radical education and the common school: a democratic alternative*. London: Routledge.

Gove, M. (2011). *Commentary on the announcement of the National Curriculum Review in England*. Cited on Department of Education website, January 2011. Retrieved from www.education.gov.uk [Accessed 15 December 2014].

Jeffery, G. (Ed.) (2005). *The creative college: building a successful learning culture in the arts*. Stoke on Trent: Trentham Books.

Lefebvre, H. (1991). *The production of space*. London: Wiley-Blackwell.

Malcomson, B., Watkins, C., Rolfe, L. and Jobbins, V. (2011). The double act of partnership, breaking the rules to explore new possibilities for dance pedagogy. In K. Chappell, L. Rolfe, A. Craft and V. Jobbins, *Close encounters: dance partners for creativity* (pp. 31–44). Stoke on Trent: Trentham Books.

McCarthy, T. (1991). *Ideals and illusions*. Cambridge, MA: MIT Press.

McWilliam, E. (2008). Unlearning how to teach. *Innovations in Education and Teaching International*, 45(3), 263–9.

National Dance Teachers Association (2004). *Maximising opportunity. Policy paper 2004*. Burntwood: NDTA.

Okri, B (1999). *Anti-spell for the 21st century: mental fight*. London: Phoenix House.

Rolfe, L. (2011) The development of partnership based pedagogies. In K. Chappell, L. Rolfe, A. Craft and V. Jobbins, *Close encounters: dance partners for creativity* (pp. 101–11). Stoke on Trent: Trentham Books.

Wenger, E. (1998). *Communities of practice: learning, meaning and identity*. Cambridge: Cambridge University Press.

5.3

STEPPING BACK TO STEP FORWARD

Reflections on future directions for dance education

Ralph Buck

A time to reflect

Taking a step back can so often help you see forward. My sabbatical year in 2013 gave me the opportunity to step back, to reflect on achievements, issues and dreams. This chapter outlines a personal perspective on what I see in the dance education community, what I see in the work I do, and what I would like to see more of in the future. This report blends a chronological travel digest with my musings on emerging persistent themes or issues and future directions for dance education. As a personal account, my thoughts pick up on ideas, images and discussions found when gazing at Rangitoto Island from my local café in Kohimarama Beach, New Zealand; waiting in a taxi queue at Buenos Aires; meeting friends at conferences/meetings in Munich, Beijing and Paris; and visiting my aging mother and her senior citizen friends in Sydney.

My musings ranged across philosophical and pragmatic issues; however, I found myself returning to key points concerning values, leadership, alliances and community. As an educator I firmly believe that dance teachers need to identify and articulate the values that drive their practice; being a leader and developing leadership skills requires time, trusting relationships and work; and alliances and networks amongst individuals and organisations are vital and require constant nurturing, as do the communities of learners in our classrooms.

Behind the above statements are volumes of obvious and difficult truths, but really it is the why and how questions that come to the fore and will be discussed in the following.

What drives your teaching?

I am a teacher. Behind nearly everything I do, and everything I learn, is my love of teaching. I think about how I teach, what causes me to return to the classroom (when my dean tells me to cut back) and what drives me. My simplistic answer is that I want to make the world a better place and I believe that dance holds huge scope in achieving and maintaining change. And so I teach dance; but even this short statement needs explanation.

In November 2013 I was preparing to travel to Maraba in Brazil, visiting a colleague in Cabello Seco, a small urban community known for its poverty, violence and historical value at the confluence of two rivers flowing into the Amazon. Before leaving Auckland, New Zealand I was having an ever vital coffee conversation with Nick Rowe, a colleague in the University of Auckland Dance Studies Department. He asked me, "What are you going to teach in Brazil?" which then led to a discussion about bigger philosophical questions regarding transformation and change.

As a tertiary educator I tend to focus on teaching future teachers how to teach. My role is getting the next generation of educators excited about education and excited by their role in changing the world. So Nick and I began discussing how I/we do this: how and what we teach when we teach dance.

With Nick's prompting and a second coffee I listed 'big value' questions that drive my teaching. These included statements like:

- Everyone can dance.
- There is no one right way to dance.
- Dance is about sharing ideas and creating.
- Dance should feel good and be fun.
- We engage in dance in different ways.

These statements, however, present considerable hurdles or thresholds for students to cross. Too often perceptions of dance are constrained and limited. Students tend to only see what they have experienced, be that the practice and performance of classical and contemporary dance on proscenium stages, or ethnic/cultural performances or hip hop. Educating students to see dance and dancers in their diversity and also to see dance's diverse roles, past and future, is in my mind essential. Nick and I have gone on to write more about these statements in terms of threshold concept theory (Land *et al.*, 2008). Threshold concept theory focuses on understanding curriculum and teaching and learning by transforming mindsets rather than accumulating knowledge. Asking learners and teachers to problematise the learning hurdles that are crossed invites critique of personal challenges and preconceptions. When reflecting upon my teaching with Nick, I found myself pondering what I valued. I valued participation, access, diversity and doing. While none of this is new, I do feel that as educators we need to be upfront and honest about what we value and how this contributes to a student's/teacher's education.

Too many teachers can dance, but not teach

Returning to the question, "What are you going to teach in Maraba, Brazil?", I found myself returning to my usual ideas about what any schoolteacher needs to know that enables their teaching of dance. The key idea is that when the teacher works with the students to build meanings of dance together, then the educational value of dance resonates in the classroom. When children and teachers collaborate, they see dance for what it is, a physical and intellectual amalgam of ideas, thinking and laughing together. That is what I taught teachers in Brazil, and yes, once we were on the floor, purposefully tangling our arms with rhythms and legs, they felt like a community, they felt safe to 'play and say', to be individuals, to accept each other in that moment. Outcomes not to be taken for granted in Brazil. The same tangles, laughter and learning happened a week later in Buenos Aires when I taught seven-year-old girls in Crear Vale la Pena, a community youth arts centre.

While in Buenos Aires I attended different tango classes each day. I have been tangoing for several years, though still a beginner. I enjoy tango and I enjoy being a learner. As always I had good and not so good lessons, and as always I found myself thinking why one lesson works for me and the next doesn't. Over too many coffees I ponder, what makes a good dance lesson? Who are my favourite teachers – why? Why do I act like a naughty kid in so many lessons and then in others, never?

At Buenos Aires Cultural Centre my first lesson included six students (four absolute beginners and two at intermediate level). The young male teacher swooped in late (all my teachers were late in Buenos Aires) and yet quickly and efficiently had us all doing basic exercises. We all danced with each other, learning and practising a basic move. He prompted all of us at our appropriate level and constructed the partnering delicately. The hour came around quickly and he was off, I dare say to his next teaching gig. I quickly realised that the teaching circuit is very competitive for the 'tourist dance dollar'.

My next lesson was an even smaller class, me and three beginners. This teacher, a young woman, focused firmly on the most basic skills, walking and holding your partner. I loved this lesson, simple with quiet attention to detail in a beautiful room. I danced with a woman from Switzerland and we enjoyed our one hour together tangoing in Buenos Aires. But it went downhill from there. I had too many teachers who could dance, but not teach. They could not break down their own expertise into bite-sized portions that made sense to the class; they did not see the mismatch between their lesson and the learners in that room on that day; they did not hear the absence of happy chatter that learners make when comfortable in a community of learners. I could go on.

What I found in Buenos Aires is what I find around the world: too many dance teachers who can dance but cannot teach, and yet it is clear that their main income is coming from teaching. I did not have to go on sabbatical to realise this ongoing dilemma, but my sabbatical offered me time to reflect on my own leadership of a suite of tertiary degrees wherein learning to teach dance holds a central role. It remains my firm belief that *all* tertiary dance programmes should include courses that attend to the art of teaching dance. Yes, that includes conservatoire-orientated dance degrees. Dancing is a career and requires skills and so does teaching dance. The past and emerging roles and functions of dance will not be fully realised if future dance teachers are not more literate and practised in the art of teaching. Dance's future relies on better dance educators.

The art of teaching

Increasingly I am aware that for me the most important characteristic of a healthy dance education classroom is the presence of community. The classroom community is a space created by the teacher, a space where individuals have agency and the group has coherency. A space where peers support and teach each other through discussion, action, critique, observation and laughter. I believe that future educators' major challenge is to learn how to make 'community', how to make communities of learners irrespective of age, culture, ability, gender and location, be it in a school, professional dance studio, hospital, forest or retirement village. The skill of learning how to transform a group of people into a 'community of dancers' is vital for the future of dance education.

During my travels I saw diverse people exercise this skill. But no-one created a community out of a group of disparate people better than the manager at my local café in Auckland.

Beginning with warm welcomes by name, insightful conversation with humour, and recognition of individual taste/preferences, he worked the room, balancing the need to manage crowds with personal interactions. He made a community where you wanted to be. With a glance around the room, around the complete street corner I found a hum, a collective, a vibe that has now gone since he has gone. I asked him before he left – why? "Exhaustion" was his reply, working with people, making and re-making 'this work' in a café community (staff and patrons) all day was exhausting and for very little financial reward (how many times have I heard the same comment from teachers?). He moved on and has since set up his own café in a new city. But he had it, he knew how to make and re-make community and he knew why it was important.

Alliances and advocacy

Teachers do not work in vacuums. Teachers in Brazil, NZ, Argentina and so on operate to various degrees in local, national and international communities. Government and non-government organisations (NGOs) have considerable interest in advocating for quality teaching in these communities. They focus on supporting teachers in their provision of 'good education'. Of interest to me is how arts education NGOs can support teachers; especially in countries and communities where government support is minimal at best. Over the last ten years I have been keenly involved with the World Dance Alliance (WDA) and more recently with the World Alliance for Arts Education (WAAE) which is inclusive of the WDA.

The WAAE is about making community. It is an alliance between international peak arts education organisations that aim to foster diverse and sustainable arts education. The WAAE includes the International Association for Drama/Theatre Education, International Society for Arts Education, International Society for Music Education and WDA. Emerging from and formed at the first UNESCO World Conference on Arts Education in 2006, the WAAE has consistently met for over seven years. We have forged an alliance with an overall aim to champion arts education in its diversity. We have achieved a great deal. We have successfully influenced the tone, structure and content of the UNESCO *Seoul Agenda: goals for the development of arts education*; initiated and then advocated for the establishment of International Arts Education Week; hosted four world arts education summits; developed an international awareness of the role of arts education in partnership with key agencies such as Korean Arts Culture Education Service, UNESCO, International Network for Research in Arts Education and multiple universities; and raised awareness of each other's arts discipline organisations including governance structures, membership needs and visions.

Making an alliance that advocates for arts education is vitally important. It takes time, energy, insight, trust and so much more. Having worked with and within the WAAE, I deeply believe that it is becoming a resource that has huge potential in shaping global policy agenda. The WAAE Executive Forum works slowly but surely in establishing common concerns and directions, knowing that our strength is in our unity. As we look to the future, the unified role of WAAE will be increasingly important in advocating for arts education in terms of social, economic and cultural development and prosperity.

The last sentence is such an easy thing to write, but in reality, maintaining, working and driving such alliances is very difficult. As a member of the WAAE Executive Forum since 2008, I can attest to the work that is required. As always, the Executive meets when we find natural and coordinated travel intersections. In May 2013 we met in Paris, and as with many of our executive meetings our meeting was about setting aims and agendas for our larger gatherings, the next being at the Arts Education World Summit, Wildbad Kreuth, Germany, the following week. We often meet in Paris as we also keep an alliance with UNESCO, keeping our eyes on big and bigger pictures.

What strikes me about these international meetings is the ongoing need to negotiate relationships between individuals and the organisations. Also what is clear is that these meetings about meanings and relationships only effectively work face to face.

Re-visiting common goals, differences between organisations' structures and foci requires listening and clarity in communicating key ideas. With limited time and money informing our meetings, precise critical analysis is required to find and solve key issues. The WAAE relies on four persons' abilities to hold conversations together, delicately balancing the greater alliance's needs with the needs of the constituency one represents: in my case the WDA. Over time, common understandings are made, trust is established, voices valued and community made. We did this in Paris and then re-made our community in Wildbad Kreuth a week later. Irrespective of my jet-lag I found that week in May 2013 extremely tiring. Again, it is not until one steps back from the fray that you realise how much energy is required in keeping an alliance not only together, but also active and relevant.

Is it relevant? Is the WAAE needed? This is a question that arises often, and it is answered at the end of every summit with a resounding "Yes!", even when the summits are expensive, frustrating and full of limitations (pedagogically, ideologically and pragmatically). Bringing diverse arts educators together is valuable; it is our unity that provides scope, and dare I say, power. Not for one moment do I think that the WAAE is an ideal alliance, but it is a beginning; most importantly it is providing a model for national arts educators and a conduit of communication (and alliance) with other large organisations such as UNESCO and OECD.

Creating a better world

Arts educators (or in my case dance educators) have a valuable role to play in setting future political, social and cultural agendas. Yes, it is a 'soft power' as the Singapore Ministry of Education states, but arts educators are connected to the heartbeat of society. We deal with people's core values, ideals and dreams. We teach children how to pursue ideas using diverse mediums for articulating thinking. Arts education is very close to the heartbeat of what matters to people and we need to be alert to arguments that tend to subsume the value of arts and culture as subsets of economic value.

As mentioned, the WAAE liaises with UNESCO. I am increasingly comfortable operating with UNESCO and also being critical of UNESCO. However, again when one steps back and sees the bigger global social and political landscapes, it is easy to see UNESCO's challenges in respect to security, education and health.

As I enter into international planning meetings, I am ever conscious of grass roots needs and struggles. Teaching in communities like Cabelo Seco, and teaching in my university, which is full of diverse students, reminds me of the myriad of reality issues. As I traverse boardrooms and dance studios that are implicitly connected, I am increasingly aware of the vital necessity of having skills that allow you to work in the boardroom and the classroom. I firmly believe students need to begin to develop an insight into the relevance of the boardroom advocacy skills as much as the classroom teaching skills.

I ask my students at the University of Auckland, NZ what future they imagine for their own children. I then ask, how will their love of and expertise in dance help create that future? My dance education lessons are less about 'how to teach dance' and more about 'how to create a better world'. The task is to figure out how dance can attend to issues around security, health, ecology, politics, economy, education and humanity. I ask my students to read UNESCO policy, to reflect on personal values and foundational policies and principles that inform NZ society. I ask my students to make dance relevant. I am driven by enquiries into how dance might provide unique pathways for people and communities to take greater control of societal and personal issues. Repositioning dance as a socially relevant academic discipline is not always easy within a society that has historically marginalised the moving body as a way of knowing. We live, however, in an era defined by both great technological advances and urgent political and environmental problems. We may find some responses to these challenges and opportunities within the creative, communicative, cooperative and ever-dynamic practices of dance.

Letting go is never easy

Stepping back during my sabbatical in 2013 required that I step back from multiple university leadership positions. This step was probably my most difficult. Letting go of projects, students, curriculum and budgets (yes budgets, who would have thought) is not easy when you have invested many years into building, protecting and advocating for them. Moreover, it is also not easy for someone else to step in and take on leadership in a caretaker's role.

Providing leadership is a key part of my professional life in university and in professional organisations. Irrespective of the quality of this leadership, stepping back and watching others has revealed my style to myself and where I put my energy as a leader. I am not a facilitator; I am more a 'maker' or transformer. I see myself making opportunities and working with staff to realise those opportunities. Such an approach requires considerable communication and patience. I have found that I can improve both my communication and patience. I can also improve my ability to delegate, and certainly improve my ability to let go, letting others hold responsibility and consequences. I think I tend to over care about students, staff and projects, taking on worries not necessarily mine.

This reflection afforded by my backward step causes me to see that for dance education to step forward, we need to better educate ourselves to lead complex projects and courageously step up to leadership positions. Most importantly, we need leaders who can create, educate and mentor future leaders. I firmly believe that the dance community has many skilled people, but they need to be valued and we need tertiary dance programmes that consciously educate for new leadership. I asked my staff: are we educating our tertiary graduates to be leaders; are we mentoring them into leadership positions within professional organisations; are we developing leadership skills alongside our colleagues; and are enough people volunteering to step up into leadership positions? I firmly believe that developing new leaders and supporting present leaders require specific attention as we look to the future directions of dance education.

Ever onwards

As stated at the outset, this chapter is a personal report. I have profiled my experience and shared my adventures while reflecting on stepping back. In sum, in stepping forward my thoughts on future directions for dance education globally include:

- Build communities of learners in the classroom, the studio, the retirement village, the hospital.
- Build alliances with other arts educators and work on making them strong.
- Build more tertiary degrees that educate for more and better dance educators.
- Build more leaders with more support and mentoring.

We have the tools and the resources; with some sensible designing we can build the above and step forward.

Reference

Land, R., Meyer, J.H.F. and Smith, J. (2008). *Threshold concepts within the disciplines*. Rotterdam: Sense Publishers.

5.4

TWINNING

An intercultural approach to dance education

Maria Speth

Introduction

> Thirty young dancers from eight different nationalities move around in the studio. They are asked to recall their cell phone number and picture themselves inside an invisible three-dimensional cube, with each corner representing the numbers one to eight, the middle of the top the nine, and zero in the bottom of the cube. They have to reach to the corners to 'dial' their number using a different body part each time. After that, they find a partner. They open up the space to a bigger cube, and perform their dances with each other while exploring the open space in between. Although most of the young people do not speak a language other than their own, the space is filled with vibrant communication.
>
> *(Dance workshop, Taiwan, July 2012)*

The example above stems from a pilot Twinning project called 'Creative Meeting Points' (CMP) that was realised during the 2012 Global Dance Summit organised in a mutual collaboration between Dance and the Child International (daCi), the World Dance Alliance (WDA) and Taipei National University of the Arts. This project was built on the concept of Twinning.

Twinning is about interweaving skills and knowledge between people from different cultures and different places to create dialogue and new knowledge. The concept of Twinning was originally introduced after the Second World War between French and German cities and villages with the intention of promoting friendship, sharing and understanding. It is known as the 'Town Twinning Movement'. In these projects Twinning dealt with a wide range of issues on the level of economical, social and cultural development. Twinning later evolved because it connects to needs in many different corners of the world. On the one hand there is a growing desire for intercultural exchange, and on the other the value of using the arts as a means of developing creative skills and possibilities of experiencing empowerment in one's own life is receiving growing attention.[1]

The Twinning concept in a dance context was first put forward during the 2006 daCi Conference in the Hague (the Netherlands). The British community art researcher François

Matarasso suggested employing the Twinning concept to promote mutual exchange between present daCi members and other possible participants.

In a Twinning project, all participants are equally involved in a creative process of mutual learning and sharing, in this case with a shared interest in dance as the main medium in the exchanges. Seen from this angle, Twinning partners can share and exchange their ideas and views on dance and dance education. This can take place at various levels: between dance groups with different dance backgrounds, between children and adults, from interactions between researchers and young dancers to meetings of dance teachers and choreographers; on national and international levels and with involvement of art or policy levels. It is important, though, that the partners have a common subject to work from. They will be in a constant learning process by communicating with each other. Tasks and results can be shared and ideas exchanged in many different ways. This artistic Twinning concept stretches boundaries, resulting in new mutual relationships blending, both consciously and unintentionally, colours, scents and tastes of the diverse cultures. Curiosity for each other's cultural backgrounds also makes a strong connection towards respect and understanding.

Description of a Twinning process through dance

The focus of the CMP was on the cultural, social and emotional development of the more than 300 participating young people. During CMP sessions, young dancers were working collaboratively, divided in age groups consisting of mixed nationalities; this under the guidance of expert facilitators. These adults were involved in the young people's creative processes, listening to their ideas and offering feedback. Each facilitator also twinned with an assistant, mostly an undergraduate dance student. Twinning thus occurred on different levels: between the young dancers, between facilitators and their groups, between facilitators and their assistants. The three-hour daily workshops gave all participants the opportunity to meet and share in a creative process encompassing different themes and ideas. The fact that we worked from a philosophy of respect for who they were, for what they thought and where they came from, created a unique situation in which the young people felt they were seen and treated as equal partners. This process was, as much as possible, in the hands of the young dancers as their own ideas and initiatives were the main course of input. Below are some impressions from the young delegates:

> We worked in pairs and then we gathered into a circle to show the others what we had achieved. At first this was quite scary, but afterwards a very opening experience. It was great to receive feedback from such different and skilful dancers.
>
> *(Finnish girl, age 17)*

> It was amazing to meet people from all over the world and learn about other cultures. And I am so glad I got to make such strong friendships through dancing.
>
> *(American boy, age 13)*

> By experiencing Creative Meeting Points I thought that dance is able to put people together. Even if I don't understand English it is possible to express feelings with gestures to people from anywhere.
>
> *(Japanese girl, age 15)*

PHOTO 5.4.1 Young dancers in their creative process.
            Photographer: Noortje van Gestel

Alongside the lively communication about the shared dance tasks during their meetings, we noticed other issues that arose: some groups even got together after the workshops to spend more time with each other. Several of the young dancers expressed the need to learn the English language as they experienced the value of exchange, not only when it came to dance. And a number of young participants invited their new friends for a visit to their home country, wanting to show them their life and cultural heritage.

For the young people this was a process of acquiring knowledge and understanding through experience, which resulted in new perceptions. They exchanged information and new ideas as well as experienced the means of connections between people, places and social interactions. They shared feelings as well as facts. It is the sharing that is even more important than the content of that sharing. Dance was their mutual base of interest and in dance they met (Photo 5.4.1). But from there new insights were shared, also outside the dance. They wanted to know more about each other's lives.

The fostering of a creative approach in a Twinning project

In line with the Twinning concept of close cooperation between partners, a democratic approach is essential. This emphasises the focus on the young people and their own initiatives. Based on the concept of empowerment, the adults' main role was to facilitate the young people in such a way that they not only found pleasure in the dance activities, but also became enriched in different ways throughout the creative process of dance. That required three points of view: sometimes they were teachers, offering new possibilities; in other moments they had a coaching role whereby they encouraged the development of skills and ideas; and their primary role of the facilitator, supporting the creative process of the young dancers. This process of guidance went through diverse pathways, varying from playful warm-ups to step-by-step discoveries in dance, investigating and analysing, exploring, collaborating, observing, discussing and sharing new knowledge. Asking questions rather than giving solutions helped to set the group in motion, both verbally and non-verbally. Fostering curiosity activated the desire to know or do more and led to new discoveries.

Below are some comments from a facilitator and an assistant:

> It is a humbling process. You have to let go of your concepts of norm and find creative solutions for communication. I learned (again) about the great possibilities of dance dialogue.
>
> *(Danish facilitator)*

> We shared our dance experiences and the type of work that we aimed to achieve. We achieved this with very little dialogue. Rather, we performed activities as a group. This sharing and exploration was wonderful! The facilitators and assistants bonded immensely and I began to feel like I belonged with this group of passionate people.
>
> *(Canadian assistant)*

Twinning – a meaningful approach in future creative and empowering pedagogies

Globalisation increases the possibility for contact between people of different cultures, which both requires us to develop broader capacities for understanding each other and also gives possibilities for communicating through social networks. This development gives rise to new demands from students and can inspire new ways of teaching. In a creative process, ideas are born and nurtured and boundaries are crossed, knowing that new experience will be exchanged leading to new possibilities. Creativity is a problem-solving process, whereby imagination or original ideas generate the production/process of artistic work (Photo 5.4.2) and can also provide solutions to our everyday living.

The core challenge for all participants in a Twinning project becomes the creative process itself. Exploring any engaging endeavour together naturally provides a context for constructive learning experiences that inspire the development of mutual trust, tolerance and talent. Such educational values can be found when interweaving the constructive skills and knowledge that connect people creatively.

Twinning as presented here can thus make a significant contribution to future dance education.

PHOTO 5.4.2 Young dancers performing.
Photographer: Noortje van Gestel

Note

1 See for example the Twinning page of the European Commission: http://ec.europa.eu/enlargement/
tenders/twinning/index_en.htm.

5.5

THE POST *NATYAM* COLLECTIVE

Building a grassroots artistic community online

Cynthia Ling Lee

The Post *Natyam* Collective is a transnational, web-based coalition of women dance artists who critically and creatively engage in South Asian dance. Our members include Sandra Chatterjee (Munich/Salzburg/New Delhi), Shyamala Moorty (Los Angeles), Cynthia Ling Lee (Los Angeles/ Greensboro) and Anjali Tata (Kansas City).[1] Founded in 2004, the Post *Natyam* Collective largely shifted to virtual, web-based collaboration in 2008. Unique to our networked nature, we use collaborative processes online to produce innovative dance and media work that rigorously tackles South Asian traditions and theory, creating feminist-of-colour,[2] postcolonial, border-crossing artistic works shared with audiences on the web, in theatres, in universities and with communities.

We collaborate transnationally because there are very few contemporary South Asian choreographers in central Europe and the United States, let alone ones who engage critically with postcolonial, queer and feminist-of-colour issues. The internet enables us to bridge geographical isolation, "disaggregat[ing] 'culture' from specific territorial boundaries" to build a grassroots online community around our specialised interest of contemporary South Asian dance (Chatterjea, 2011: 85). Collaborating in cyberspace, we mobilise "the 'we' potential in Internet technologies," "build[ing] our knowledge commons" through "idiosyncratic, alternative, or 'off-label' uses that serve the particular needs of our community" (Carl and Mathew, 2011: 10). Our web-based collaboration does not emerge from artistic interest in cutting-edge technology and globalised avant-garde intercultural networks, but out of a lack of resources. Self-taught, we use free internet tools such as blogging, video posting, Skype, email and Google Documents to stay connected across the distance despite being chronically underfunded. Our work, while carefully crafted, espouses a raw, do-it-yourself, lo-fi aesthetic, reflecting how internet technologies can be used "as a grass-roots medium connecting people of lesser means and political agendas on a global level" (Wulff, 2003: 190).

The Post *Natyam* Collective's online creative process

Our creative process is centralised on our blog (www.postnatyam.blogspot.com): our online workspace. While our methodology varies slightly from project to project, generally our creative process is as follows: each month, we rotate giving choreographic assignments. After posting our responses, we provide feedback to each other through blog comments. In addition to our

PHOTO 5.5.1 Cyber chat series: The Post *Natyam* Collective's dance-for-video series depiciting a long distance creative process.

creative assignment process, the blog has proved useful for sharing research notes, references and links; giving reports on exhibits or talks that we attend; and sharing and archiving lecture-demonstrations, performances and workshops that we present live in different contexts. All this is available to the public online (Photo 5.5.1).

Several key aspects characterise our online choreographic exchange:

1. Horizontal, peer-to-peer learning exchange.
2. Public nature of our creative process.
3. Open-source collaboration.
4. Mediatisation of artistic product.

Democratic dialogue and peer-to-peer learning

Post *Natyam*'s online learning community positions participants in a peer-to-peer exchange that emphasises multiple voices, supportive feedback and rotating leadership. As such, our horizontal structure differs from the vertical power hierarchy that suffuses more 'traditional' forms of dance pedagogy and dance-making. Rather than having an expert teacher who exerts artistic author-ity over his or her students, we are positioned as equal collaborators learning from each other. Moreover, we honour multiple politico-aesthetic perspectives, embracing democratic disagreement rather than trying to smooth over difference.

For example, when working on translating Shyamala Moorty's *My silent cry*, a performance based on Uma Singh's story of surviving domestic violence, from a community-based context to the concert stage, we ran into disagreements about the importance of communicating a message of empowerment vs. privileging complex emotional nuances. Our energetic, sometimes conflicting comments on each other's studies create critical dialogue in the public sphere, demystifying and democratising artistic process while inviting the public to take part in our critical discourse on dance-making. Because our assignments are archived publicly online, this also has the effect of creating an informal, ad-hoc South Asian contemporary choreographic curriculum available to anyone with internet access.

Creative recycling and open-source choreography

In addition to grounding our working process in horizontal models of dialogical, peer-to-peer learning, the Post *Natyam* Collective has an open-source policy that troubles conventional choreography's emphasis on single authorship and fixed choreography. Repurposing the hacker ethic of open-source software for online dance-making, we embrace "collaboration instead of competition; openness instead of proprietary rights and trade secrets; quality code [or choreography] instead of profitability" (Bergquist, 2003: 223). In essence, within the collective we encourage each other to steal, translate and remix each other's material. This 'creative recycling' may take the form of layering other members' videos, movement vocabulary, text or sound design into one's own work (Chatterjee *et al.*, 2011).

For example, during our 2008–11 project, *SUNOH! Tell me, sister*, Cynthia Ling Lee wrote a poem, *]wrist[*, that inspired a dance-for-camera video by Anjali Tata that used close-ups of her hands engaged in a visceral, tactile deconstruction of Indian classical mudras. This video was integrated into a mixed-media work as part of an art installation, *Trace*, and later choreography from Anjali's video was performed live, projected onto Shyamala Moorty's back via video feed as part of an evening-length performance. This example of creative recycling in different media and contexts illustrates how we have come to embrace choreographic process as an ongoing series of transformations rather than linear progress towards a finished choreographic product.

Mediatised futures for online dance

We have found that the digitally mediated nature of working online has resulted in increasingly mediatised products, such as dance-for-camera videos, sound scores, poems, scripts, art books, scholarly papers and art installations. Indeed, many of the multiple choreographic products we create during a process do not resemble conventional live 'dance'. We have become interested in alternative ways of presenting work, developing transmedia artistic manifestations and using web-streaming and Web 2.0 tools to supplement live performance. As we continue collaborating across distance, our process continues to adapt to our members' changing interests, geographical locations and life circumstances.

Thus far, we have used different versions of our online process for a variety of projects, including *SUNOH! Tell me, sister*, a multi-year project that brought to life women's stories of being silenced, finding voice and the power of sisterly community; the *Cyber chat series*, a series of dance-for-camera videos modelled on Skype call aesthetics; *Un(epic) wonder women*, inspired by Indian and American comic books; *Subversive gestures feedback loop*, choreo-theoretical explorations of gender fluidity in Indian dance, and *Cabaret travels*, which explores the translations of cabaret across South Asia, the United States and Europe with New Delhi-based guest director, Aditee Biswas.

We have found that the internet provides invaluable tools for bridging geographical isolation, allowing us to build much-needed artistic community around our specialised interest in critical, contemporary approaches to South Asian dance. As a grassroots alternative to institutionalised dance education, we hope that our methodology of online, peer-to-peer, open-source choreographic collaboration will inspire other groups of people with niche interests to deploy internet tools to create border-defying networks of exchange, artistic affinity groups and vibrant grassroots communities for dance.

Note

1 The Post *Natyam* Collective's membership is now including Meena Murugesan (Los Angeles/ Montreal) and Anjali Tata is not currently a member.
2 Feminism-of-colour or third-world feminism critiques second-wave feminism for privileging the experiences of white, Western, middle-class and heterosexual women as 'universal'. Feminism-of-colour demands that feminist issues be looked at intersectionally, taking into account other identity components such as race, class and sexuality.

References

Bergquist, M. (2003). Open source software development as gift culture: work and identity formation in an internet community. In C. Garsten and H. Wulff (Eds.), *New technologies at work: people, screens, and social virtuality* (pp. 223–41). New York: Berg.

Carl, P. and Mathew, V. (2011). Building a new American theater of the commons. *Shareable: sharing by design community*. Retrieved from www.shareable.net/blog/building-a-new-american-theater-of-the-commons [Accessed 15 December 2014].

Chatterjea, A. (2011). Why I am committed to a contemporary South Asian aesthetic: arguments about the value of 'difference' from the perspective of practice. In U. Munsi and S. Burridge (Eds.), *Traversing tradition: celebrating dance in India* (pp. 83–103). New Delhi: Routledge.

Chatterjee, S. and Lee, C.L. (2012). Choreographing coalition in cyber-space: Post *Natyam*'s politico-aesthetic negotiations. In E. Zobl and R. Drüeke (Eds.), *Feminist media: participatory spaces, networks and cultural citizenship* (pp. 146–58). Bielefeld, Germany: Transcript Verlag.

Chatterjee, S., Lee, C.L., Moorty, S. and Tata, A. (2011). *Post* Natyam *Collective manifesto 2.2*. Retrieved from www.postnatyam.blogspot.com/2011/10/post-natyam-collective-manifesto.html [Accessed 15 December 2014].

Wulff, H. (2003). Steps on screen: technoscapes, visualization, and globalization in dance. In C. Garsten and H. Wulff (Eds.), *New technologies at work: people, screens, and social virtuality* (pp. 187–204). New York: Berg.

INDEX

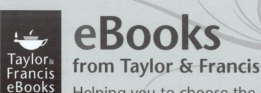